dog's day

also by matthew j. prigge

Damn the Old Tinderbox: Milwaukee's Palace of the West and the Fire That Defined an Era

Milwaukee Mayhem: Murder and Mystery in the Cream City's First Century

dog's day

The True Story of a Bank Robbery, Gay Liberation, and Toxic Love That Inspired a Hollywood Classic

matthew j. prigge

COUNTERPOINT
CALIFORNIA

dog's day

This is a work of nonfiction. However, some names and identifying details of individuals have been changed to protect their privacy, correspondence has been shortened for clarity, and dialogue has been reconstructed from memory.

First Counterpoint edition: 2026

Library of Congress Cataloging-in-Publication Data
Names: Prigge, Matthew J. author
Title: Dog's day : the true story of a bank robbery, gay liberation, and toxic love that inspired a Hollywood classic / Matthew J. Prigge.
Description: First Counterpoint edition. | San Francisco, CA : Counterpoint, 2026.
Identifiers: LCCN 2026016769 | ISBN 9781640098060 hardcover | ISBN 9781640098077 ebook
Subjects: LCSH: Wojtowicz, John, 1945-2006 | Bank robberies—New York (State)—New York | Bank robbers—New York (State)-—New York | Dog day afternoon (Motion picture : 1975) | Wojtowicz, John, 1945-2006—Sexual behavior | Bisexual people—New York (State)—New York | Gay liberation movement—United States—History | LCGFT: Biographies
Classification: LCC HV6661.N72 P75 2026 | DDC 364.15/52097471—dc23/eng/20260601
LC record available at https://lccn.loc.gov/2026016769

Jacket design by Victoria Maxfield
Book design by Laura Berry

COUNTERPOINT
Los Angeles and San Francisco, CA
www.counterpointpress.com

Printed in the United States of America

10 9 8 7 6 5 4 3 2 1

To Erika,
for whom I would
gladly rob a bank

Contents

One

Q: You are one of the last great lovers?
A: Yeah. That's what wound me up [in] here.

—JOHN WOJTOWICZ, INTERVIEW IN FEDERAL PRISON, 1976

Lewisburg, Pennsylvania, is about 2,600 miles from Hollywood, but as John Wojtowicz (WAD-a-witz) eats his lunch on the afternoon of October 3, 1975, it is both as tangibly nearby as the square of cloudy orange Jell-O on his cafeteria tray and as remote and unimaginable as the surface of the moon. John is thirty years old, short, and slight with shaggy black hair and a small mustache. He wears a pale-blue prison jumpsuit numbered 76456-158 and sits alone in the auditorium of the United States Penitentiary at Lewisburg, where 1,600 prisoners are housed and the going rate for a murder for hire is two cartons of cigarettes. John eats a hamburger and stirs a cup of runny tomato soup while a pair of guards keep watch.[1]

The auditorium is a long, high-ceilinged room on the third floor of Lewisburg's main building. There is a stage at the far end, behind it hangs a worn, rectangular screen. Dirty green curtains are roughly hung over the tall windows that line the hall, blocking enough of the midday sun to give the room a ghostly ambiance. Three rows of long wooden benches can seat 1,000 people for movies or stage shows or for performances by the prison's all-inmate rock band. But on this afternoon, there is only John and the two guards.

In 1972, John robbed a bank. He had two accomplices: One fled the scene just as the robbery began, the other was shot dead by a Federal Bureau of Investigation (FBI) agent fourteen hours later on the tarmac at John F. Kennedy (JFK) International Airport. John was caught, convicted, and sentenced to twenty years in prison. The Brooklynite insisted that he was a political prisoner, that his act was not one of malice, but one of love. *I'm gay,* John had told the cops as he was holed up inside the bank, holding eight hostages. *I want this money so my wife can get the sex-change operation he needs,* he'd explained, so far ahead of the cultural times that no rules yet existed to police his language. *He'll kill himself without it, and this is all I can do to save his life.*

That wasn't entirely true, but John's relationship with the truth was as fraught, passionate, and volatile as any of his relationships. Still, it was a great story. It sold newspapers and magazines and was such a weirdly honest depiction of the human condition that Hollywood couldn't resist. Moviemakers purchased the rights to what would eventually become *Dog Day Afternoon* while John sat in jail waiting to enter a plea and while his hostages could still smell the overnight ordeal in their clothes. The story drew big names to write and direct and landed Al Pacino to play the lead. Filming started in the autumn of 1974, as John began his third year in prison. Thirteen months later, the picture was complete and John had finagled a screening of the film—which he ceaselessly referred to as "my movie"—for the prisoners at Lewisburg. After fighting it for weeks, the prison officials finally relented. They even agreed to give John a private advance screening.

John takes a seat in the center aisle, near the back. Two guards plant themselves in the row behind. John, with seventeen long years ahead of him, sits and stares forward. For the next two hours, he watches the glossy version of his own collapse, a passion play of heartbreak and death of which he stood in the center. A poster for the film is taped to a far wall. THE ROBBERY SHOULD HAVE TAKEN 10 MINUTES, it reads. 4 HOURS LATER, THE BANK WAS LIKE A CIRCUS SIDESHOW. 8 HOURS LATER, IT WAS THE HOTTEST THING ON TV. 12 HOURS LATER, IT WAS HISTORY.

John already knows this is how he's going to be remembered. The courts, the cops, the judges, the neighborhood goons who heckled him during the robbery, the gay activists who turned their backs—they could all get fucked. *This* will be his legacy.

The projector crackles to life and the screen glows black. A title card shows.

> *WHAT YOU ARE ABOUT TO SEE IS TRUE---*
> *IT HAPPENED IN BROOKLYN, NEW YORK*
> *ON AUGUST 22, 1972*

The mellow tones of a pop song fill the room, and John sees New York City in snips and snaps—a Circle Line ferryboat leaving its Hell's Kitchen dock, an overturned trash can, a clutch of daylight winos idling on the stoop of a flophouse—the mundane hum of a dog day afternoon. The melody plays on, and Elton John starts in with the opening bars of "Amoreena," singing wistfully about intimate times and lost love.

1. brooklyn and queens

She'd done it before, in front of others even, but only cloaked in the safety of Halloween. It might have raised eyebrows for anyone who noticed the pattern, but her father insisted it was just a phase. One year, she went as a flapper—the Roaring Twenties–era expression of female independence and sexuality that resulted in the kind of moral panic that should have seemed quaint by the 1950s. She wore the costume to the church social and was scolded and sent home by the minister. It wasn't so much the idea of the child—who was then known as Ernest Aron, just another of the neighborhood boys—wearing female dress as a gag. It was how flawlessly the kid seemed to play the role. As though it wasn't much of a costume at all.[2]

Years later, Liz Eden's thoughts drifted back to Queens, to the little duplex on 109th Street that she shared with her mother, Ruth, and older half sister, Barbara. This was the late-Eisenhower era, when the first wave of baby boomers were hitting puberty. It was a time of great sexual paradox for the United States. For fifty cents, you could see bare breasts in a nudist "lifestyle" movie in Times Square, and a buck bought you a physique magazine filled with nearly naked beefcakes posing with every muscle oiled and popping. The intention was obvious to anyone paying attention, but no one really wanted to admit it. The war years had ushered in a sexual revolution of sorts, fueled by the kind of slapdash horniness that only the fear of death can produce. Peace was supposed to bring a return to decency, but it was a damn hard bell to un-ring.

In the little house in Queens, Liz used to sit on the stairs and spy on Barbara and her boyfriend making out on the sofa while their mother was away. The sisters had never been close. Barbara found Liz to be "strange," something she confided to their mother, who assured Barbara that Liz's peculiarities were just a phase. "I was extremely jealous," Liz recalled of Barbara's boyfriend. "He was the most gorgeous man I had ever laid my eyes on." She was about nine years old at the time. Three years later, after a hitch in the service, Barbara's boyfriend came back home and proposed. Barbara accepted. It was not long after that when Liz saw the wedding dress, carefully laid out on her sister's bed.[3]

She had done it before, but this felt different. "By this time, I was furious at her that she could get a man and I couldn't," she said. "And I guess this was the first indication that I really wanted to be like my sister—not just like her but be better than her—that I could get a man away from another woman." She took off her boys' clothing and slipped the wedding dress over her head. She cinched it up as best she could and walked down the stairs to the living room, where the fiancé was sitting alone. At first glance, he blushed, thinking that it was Barbara entering the room. By this point in Liz's life, she had already been marked by her classmates at school. Her mannerism and speech got her labeled a "sissy." She was regularly picked on to the point of tears. But when the boyfriend saw her that afternoon, as open as she'd ever been to the world, he smiled. "You look as good as she's going to look in it."[4]

"It was so cute the way he said it," Liz recalled. "And from then on I just wanted to be a woman."[5]

JOHN STANLEY WOJTOWICZ was a year and half older than Liz. He was born in Brooklyn in 1945, the second child to John and Tereasa Wojtowicz. The elder John was a Polish American machinist, stern and quiet. Tereasa, known to all as Terry, was loud, Italian, and endlessly devoted to her second-born child. Her first child, Anthony, had been born prematurely and began suffering seizures while still a toddler. When it became clear the child was developmentally disabled, a court ruled that Terry and John Sr. were not equipped to care for the boy and, at just five years old, he was remanded to state custody. Terry would never forget how loudly the boy cried when they put him on a train bound for an upstate institution. He *howled*, and she never heard an end to it. It just faded as the train pulled away. After Anthony was gone, Terry moved all her attention, devotion, and love to her "Johnny." It was all she could do to quiet Anthony's wailing.[6]

John grew up, a journalist later noted, in a "blue collar environment populated by hitters and greasers." His Brooklyn was out of step with the march of postwar American prosperity: a densely populated urban mass of brownstones, corner taps, and mom-and-pop stores that became less essential to the new vision of the modern middle class each time a loaded-up moving truck made tracks for the suburbs. John's father was one of the "hitters." John Sr. was a hardline conservative who would not tolerate disobedience and never hesitated to punish with violence. His father's punishing ways paired with a naturally meticulous nature in young John that left the boy in near-constant motion. He did well in school, particularly in math classes. He liked to draw and collected stamps. He loved baseball and formed his own neighborhood team in Bensonhurst. John played nearly every day and kept a ledger of the team's statistics, figuring totals and averages in pencil. A series of photographs from the time—carefully kept by Terry—reveal the dark-haired grinning boy holding up baseballs with numerical inscriptions written on them. Statistical milestones, just like the photos that would run on the sports page when a revered Yankee, Giant, or Dodger had done something of note. When it was too dark or rainy or cold to play ball, he obsessed over Monopoly. He probably preferred to be the banker.[7]

But there were secrets as well. When John was very young, he was molested by an elderly man. The details are sparse, but the incident involved the man trapping John in a garage and urinating in his mouth. There wasn't much of a support system for victims like John in the 1950s. John's recollections, conveyed secondhand years later, suggest that the family tried to bring charges against the man, but were unsuccessful. Just like with Anthony, the family waited until the noise faded and moved on.[8]

John started working at age thirteen, making deliveries for a neighborhood grocer. He did his duties well and took his responsibilities seriously. He did his schoolwork, earned his pay, and was in bed and saying his prayers each night by nine o'clock. He attended Catholic school and went to church every week. He didn't linger in the streets or hang with a bad crowd. He never got caught sipping a beer or sneaking a cigarette. But John harbored feelings and impulses that both confused him and made sense. He had his first sexual experience in high school, when he seduced a male friend.[9]

In 1962, John graduated from Erasmus Hall High School in Brooklyn with an A average.* He earned a scholarship to Brooklyn College, just two miles from the Wojtowicz's Flatbush Avenue apartment, but he had a motor that wouldn't let him idle away as a mere student. Instead, he enrolled in night classes at Baruch College in Manhattan and found a job at a nearby Manufacturers Hanover Trust Bank branch. Every morning, he took the train in from Brooklyn and diligently set to his work and studies. He was the near-ideal of the postwar American youth. No one would have suggested his future was anything but bright.[10]

If John noticed any of the political and cultural shifts that were laying the seeds for what would become known as *the sixties,* they were lost on him. John ignored folk music, wouldn't touch a drug, and kept his hair short. Despite the chasm between him and John Sr., father and son shared a right-wing political outlook. As the 1964 presidential election neared, John spurned his home state governor, the centrist Nelson Rockefeller, for conservative firebrand Barry Goldwater of Arizona. In a photo from the family album, John stands proudly in front of a homemade banner declaring WOJTOWICZ AND ALL BROOKLYN WANT BARRY.† Despite being just nineteen—the legal voting age would remain at twenty-one until 1971—John campaigned hard for Goldwater and even traveled to San Francisco to attend the Republican National Convention. Another photo from

* Other notable alumni of Erasmus include actress Mae West, musicians Neil Diamond and Barbra Streisand, author Mickey Spillane, and chess grandmaster Bobby Fischer.

† Brooklyn, as it turned out, did not want Barry. Lyndon Johnson walloped Goldwater by a three-to-one margin in the borough, tallying more votes in Kings County than in any other in New York state.

Terry's album shows John's banner taped to a back wall at the Bay Area's Cow Palace while John and other young GOPers posed nearby. It was a group effort, but John's name remained on top. He would identify himself as a "Goldwater Republican" for the rest of his life.[11]

LIZ HARDLY KNEW her father while growing up. Ernest Aron Sr. was Ruth's second husband, fourteen years her senior and already forty-six years old when Liz was born. Ruth and Ernest were married only briefly and by the time Liz came along Ernest had already left the family to live with another woman. He could be a violent man but was protective of Liz in a way that hinted at a kind of acceptance. "If anybody touched me, my father would kill them," Liz said years later in an interview. But Ernest Sr. wasn't around enough to really help. Only once did she ever take her father's lead and defend herself physically against the torment. The instigator was a neighborhood kid, a "nasty little son of a bitch" in Liz's recollection. After pushing her to the brink one day, she snapped and knocked him on his ass with a hard right cross. He never bothered her again.[12]

It was always Ruth who was the stable figure in Liz's young life. She was, Liz later said, "my one and only love." Ruth gave Liz affection and the space to be herself. She overlooked Liz's poor grades in school and the occasional trouble she'd cause at home. The trouble was mostly an accidental byproduct of her wandering curiosity. To learn how the stove worked, she set it ablaze with lighter fluid. Once, looking for a cozy place to hide, she ended up falling asleep under the sink, leaving her mother to think she'd run away. She wanted to see how high she could climb—on fences, on trees, on garage roofs—and more than once needed the fire department to come get her down. She was out of step with the neighborhood boys, preferring playing house to sports or games. A regular playmate with most of the girls on the block, she was usually stuck as the "daddy" when acting out adult domestic life. "Out of necessity," Liz clarified.[13]

For a time, Liz's uncle lived with the family. He was a stern man, a former sergeant in the army. One day, after Liz won a bet with a neighbor boy, the boy had to pay his debt by running around the backyard naked. The uncle caught the two and gave Liz a beating. It was not the only beating she'd take from her uncle. "If he [had] ever found out I was a faggot," Liz said later, "he'd [have] kill[ed] me."[14]

When Liz was twelve years old, she had her first sexual experience. It was in the basement of a neighbor boy's house, where she would often go to play cards. Games of strip poker evolved into using sexual favors as prizes for the best hand. Liz beat the kid regularly, and he would have to settle their bets by jerking her off. Around the same time, Liz found herself getting aroused while watching the school football team practice. "Seein' all those guys grab their ass as they ran by," Liz recalled with a lustful sigh. "Nobody ever told me about the birds and bees, but I sure found out about 'em."[15]

It was also around that time that Liz's mother got sick. The family told Liz it was cancer, and her mother spent the next two years in bed. Liz kept near her side, alone together in the house, watching her fade away and fetching her glass after glass of E & J Gallo port. But there was no cancer. Ruth was drinking herself to death. She'd been a heavy drinker for years, and after Ernest left her, she could not summon the strength to quit. It wouldn't be until Liz was in her twenties that she learned the truth. Her father made up the cancer story so that Liz would not blame him for her mother's decline. It was a cruel and futile lie. Left alone to care for her fading mother, she had already come to hate him. Ruth died on May 27, 1961. Liz wore a suit to her funeral—the last time she'd ever wear one. The neighborhood boy, the one from the poker games in the basement, came to the service. During a somber break in the program, they snuck away to a hidden part of the funeral home and fooled around.[16]

There was some money in the family. Ruth owned their home and left it to Ernest Sr. when she died. He paid to have the house remodeled and allowed Liz and Barbara and her family to live there rent-free. He promised that when Liz finished high school, he'd hand her the deed with no strings attached. He also hired a string of therapists to help Liz deal with what he hoped was just a bad case of grief. Liz was open to therapy, but the effort quickly developed a pattern. Liz would speak with a doctor, the doctor would give Ernest Sr. a diagnosis, and the doctor would be fired. At a time when the concept of separating sex and gender was beginning to gain acceptance in the world of psychology, Ernest Sr. couldn't deal with what the doctors were telling him. "I was different, [they said]," Liz recalled. "I wasn't really a boy. I wasn't a girl, but I was definitely somewhere in between, and my mind was making itself up." The doctors also told her that she was gay. That part she'd figured out already.[17]

Liz felt no shame about her sexuality, but it did little to abate her increasing alienation from her home life. Now living with her older sister and her small family, she was—for the first time—under the regular watch of a strict authority figure. Gone were the soft touch and understanding love of her mother, which were replaced with the frustrated rule of Barbara and the distant support of a father who didn't know what to make of her. Liz suffered from bullies at school and from confusion within. And it all got to be too much. In a box of her mother's old things, she found a bottle of sleeping pills. She took it to school and, when no one was looking, swallowed the contents. She was found some time later, unconscious in a stairwell. She was rushed to a hospital and had her stomach pumped. He father sent her back to the doctors and paid out over $6,000 in medical bills, but nothing seemed to help.[18]

If she was ever going to get better, it wasn't going to happen in that godforsaken duplex in Queens. After turning sixteen, she asked her father for the deed to the house. He gave it to her. Liz told Barbara and her family to pack their things, sold the house, and dropped out. She moved in with an older woman, a police officer who had gotten to know Liz when she worked as a crossing guard at Liz's school. As Liz described it, "She was lonely, and I was lonely."[19]

Liz didn't stay long with the older woman. Along with the money from the sale of her mother's house, the estate granted her a $100 weekly allowance that would last until she turned twenty-one. She made new friends fast and kept no fixed address, jumping from sofa to sofa or bed to bed. She worked sporadically. The office scene was too uptight and service industry work was more hassle than Liz could tolerate, so she mostly stuck to beauty parlors and hair salons. She enrolled in beauty school and met a woman there, a lesbian with whom she would have a long-term relationship ("shacked up" as Liz called it, "the 'in' thing in those days") that produced two children. But Liz was no more equipped to play daddy than she had been back in the old neighborhood playing house. If she maintained any emotional connection to this part of her life, she almost never talked about it. One of her only recorded statements on the family came in 1973, when she said that her partner had since died and that she had not seen the children in years.[20]

Since leaving home, Liz had begun her social gender transition—even though no such term existed for it at the time. She was more frequently going out in women's dress and was now introducing herself as Elizabeth Eden.* She'd also begun cruising. Her favorite spot was a park in Jamaica, Queens. "It was just such a pretty place to cruise," she recalled. It was here, long after nightfall, that she was introduced to drag. By the time she turned nineteen, her after-hours scene was dominated by queens who could talk about nothing else. One afternoon in 1965, some friends coaxed her to a wig shop that shared a space with a beauty parlor on 165th Street—an area Liz called "Wig City"—and she found herself a canary-yellow wig. She tried it on and looked in the mirror. She felt unsure about what she saw.[21]

Then, from the adjoining beauty parlor, came a big voice. "She'll look absolutely outrageous in it when I get done with [her]!" Through a walkway emerged a stunning Spanish drag queen named Cookie. "My dear, you will be the talk of the ball." Liz hadn't even considered doing a drag ball—indeed no evidence survives that she had even ever attended one of the quasi-underground celebrations of queer culture before—but the big, loud words from Cookie landed hard. She wanted it. She wanted to be the talk of the ball. Liz chose an emerald-green empire-waist V-neck gown for the occasion, topped with a twelve-button mandarin collar long coat paired with green satin shoes and the canary wig. Liz made her debut at the annual Dayzee Dee's Drag

* *Elizabeth* was a nod to Elizabeth Taylor and *Eden* a reference to the terrestrial paradise.

Ball, held every year on Thanksgiving Eve in Brooklyn. It was the first time Liz had ever worn makeup. "It took me hours just to get the lashes on," she said. On the way to the ball, she was all nerves, unsure of herself and scared. "But once I got in," she recalled, "it was a sensational feeling. I can remember people turning around to ask if I wasn't really a girl."[22]

She loved it and wanted more. Eventually, she moved in with Cookie and another queen in the Bronx. Drag brought her confidence, power, and control—control over men, control over herself. The gowns and wigs that she bought for the stage became her everyday clothes. She was the talk of the ball, and she never wanted the talk to end. She became, one friend remembered, "the center of every scene." She absorbed herself in the drag community and carried around a portable record player, always ready to blast her favorite Judy Garland and Carmen Miranda tunes. And she got loud. "Loud, loud, loud," the friend recalled. "The wallpaper would curl off the walls when she started cursing."[23]

Hardly anyone called her Ernie anymore.

2. war

It would be hard to imagine a bigger square in all of New York City circa 1966 than John Wojtowicz. It was the year of *Blonde on Blonde*, *Sounds of Silence*, and *Revolver*. It was the year hippies took over the Sunset Strip in Los Angeles, baked on acid and looking for free love. It was the year of marches, riots, pinkos, and stinkos. And it was the year that John Wojtowicz, in his crew cut and collared shirt, took a job as a head teller at the Chase Manhattan branch on Park Avenue. He lived at home, where his mother washed his clothes, cooked his meals, and made sure he never left home without his lunch. He didn't waste his money and was sure to be home each evening early enough to preclude any indulgences in the nightlife.

That March, John traveled to Massachusetts for a company-sponsored ski weekend. The outing was a favor to the company's lower-level workers—a chance for them to catch a whiff of the good life. One night, in some plush common area of a New England ski resort, above the polite chatter of middle managers and account representatives, he heard a voice that took him right back home. Carmen Bifulco, just eighteen, worked as a typist in a Chase Manhattan office on Wall Street. She was a Brooklyn native and sounded like it. Her round and pretty face was topped with a brunette bouffant, and her eyes were deep and engaging. The day on the slopes had turned into an evening of drinks and parties and strangers laughing by the fireside, none of which interested Carmen. She planned on spending a quiet evening in her room. But before going there, she had to visit the restroom. John followed her inside.[1]

It was there, startled and alone inside the women's room, that Carmen met her future husband. He tried to act like it had been a mistake, that he'd just pushed through the wrong door, but Carmen didn't buy it. He told her he'd heard her accent. "You're not from here?" he teased. John was short and skinny, with eyes as interesting as Carmen's and a twisted little smile. Distinctive looking, if not handsome. Carmen was not terribly used to such attention from men. She stood five foot one, just a few inches shorter than John, but outweighed him by at least fifty pounds. She was fat and insecure. Both characteristics suited John's intentions just fine. As far as his tastes in females went, he had a preference for big. As far as his need for control, he was drawn to those whose self-loathing made them submissive. He asked for her number, and she gave it to him. "First man I ever, ever gave my phone number to in my whole life," Carmen later said. "What a disaster."[2]

A week or so later, when John picked her up for their first date, he brought along two other girls. "One of you is gonna be my lucky bride in the future," John said to the trio as Carmen got in the car. The foursome spent the night dancing at the Copacabana. By the end of the evening, Carmen was the only one who was willing to see John again.[3]

A week later, John got drafted. While some in the long-haired set were proudly and loudly setting fire to their draft cards, John accepted his conscription with pride. "I'm a Goldwater Republican," he said, "which means I'm a conservative and which also means I'm a warmonger."[4]

He was sent to Fort Gordon in Georgia for basic training and, throughout the summer of 1966, saw Carmen whenever he could get a weekend pass. Little was ever said by either Carmen or John about courtship. John only said he'd loved her from the first moment, and Carmen that she'd made the greatest mistake of her life. One sunny afternoon in August, walking with Carmen beneath a boardwalk in Far Rockaway, John found a stray beer can ring in the sand. He picked it up, turned to Carmen, and proposed. She said yes, and he slid the small piece of trash onto her finger.[5]

That fall, after resigning his job as a teller at the Chase Manhattan branch on Park Avenue and Thirty-Second Street, John was bound for Vietnam. He was so proud of his army uniform that he made his mother promise him that he would be buried in it, whether he died in the war or long after. He wanted to marry Carmen before leaving, but her family convinced her to wait until after his tour. John would say, only half joking, that it was because they hoped he'd be killed. After John left, they tried in vain to get her to break it off. He was too loud and demanding, a crazy man, no good for her. But she would not listen.[6]

Little is known of John's time in the service. While he would later claim—amid a flurry of exaggerations and outright lies about his life and crimes—that he was involved in heavy combat with huge losses to his brigade, a 1976 *Playboy* article for which John was interviewed used but a single word to describe his time in Vietnam: "uneventful." Most likely the truth lies somewhere in between. John would tell a lot of lies about his life—lies that were big, loud, and easily disproven. He told the kind of lies that would give anyone extreme pause in hearing a dramatic wartime tale. But there is no such thing as an "uneventful" year at war. Terry later described her son after the war as a changed person. "He goes from one extreme to another. From daylight to darkness," she said. "The service screwed him up. Whatever happened, I don't know."[7]

It was in basic training, at Fort Gordon, that John formed his first real relationship with another man. "One night we were sleeping in tents in the winter," John said. "And it's freezing in Georgia in the winter, and the oil burners always run out of oil. So what we did is, we would lie back-to-back together in a bunk to keep warm." One night, as John slept, his tentmate—whom he described as a "hillbilly from Florida named Wilbur"—undid John's pants and began to perform oral sex on him. John would later cloak the story in semi-comical terms, saying he was dreaming about getting a blow job only to wake and find Wilbur. He didn't really object to the situation, he merely asked Wilbur what he was doing. "Well, ain't it good?" Wilbur replied. John conceded that it was and eventually climaxed.[8]

If one studies the known lies and embellishments of John Wojtowicz, the story of Wilbur and the cold tent comes across as probably mostly true. There is the thread of dirty humor that John enjoyed folding into his stories, but none of the self-aggrandizement that marks his typical fabrications. In fact, John, in this scenario, is a character without agency. He was chosen by Wilbur because he was either telegraphing his still-hidden orientation and was seen as a likely target for a sort of coerced consent or because Wilbur perceived him as too weak to fight back and therefore someone whose consent need not be taken into consideration.[9]

However it began, it continued, and John and Wilbur became something of a couple. Eventually the two were found out but were given only minor punishments: a ban on showering with other men and a forced bit of humiliation in having to publicly hold hands. As they had during World War II and the Korean War, the army was willing to look the other way in a time when bodies were badly needed in an on-the-ground conflict.* When it became clear to John that the army was not going to discharge them for their behavior, he convinced Wilbur to resume the relationship.[10]

John returned to the States in October 1967 with a wedding date set for the end of the month. Despite the rush, it was a huge ceremony. Held at St. Rita's Church in Brooklyn, the bill for the event ran over $5,000. "The whole neighborhood was there," recalled Carmen, who had gone on a crash diet just before the wedding and felt sickly and weak throughout the service. That evening, blaming John for the costly extravagance of the whole thing, Carmen's father cornered him and demanded that he pay part of the bill. A huge fight ensued, which ended with Carmen's father slapping John and John throwing a wad of cash in his new father-in-law's face. By this point, the two families openly hated each other, and the bride and groom were taken around to the side of the building, where the priest who had just married them resided. After an airing of grievances, he offered to annul the

* In Randy Shilts's *Conduct Unbecoming*, an extensive history of LGBTQ+ people in the armed forces since Vietnam, he makes note of significant declines in the number of persons discharged for being gay during the peak years of these military actions, even as enlistment numbers spiked. He also notes that draft boards in the Vietnam era would often demand either signed affidavits from same-sex lovers or the sworn testimony of a psychiatrist before accepting a draftee's claims of being gay.

hours-old marriage. In every retelling of the story, in the memories of all who paid witness, John was the only one who objected to the idea.[11]

One of the photos taken on John and Carmen's wedding day shows the couple—Carmen glowing in a formfitting wedding gown and John looking sharp in his army dress greens—grinning playfully, John flashing the "OK" sign and Carmen with a finger to her lips. It's one of the standard, silly-pose pictures that a photographer pushes on the bride and groom, but the couple here smiles like they are really in on a secret. They had not saved their physical affections for their wedding night. Back in February, while John was home on leave, they had sex for the first time. And it unleashed something that would keep them coming back to each other long after the relationship had turned completely toxic.[12]

John had eighteen months remaining in his army commitment, so the couple undertook a journey through the various military bases on the Eastern Seaboard. John typically lived in the barracks and taught artillery instruction, while Carmen stayed in off-base rooming houses. The sex came in any spare moment, in any available space, and several times a day. In the bedroom, on the bathroom floor, at drive-ins, in the car while parked, in the car while on the freeway. John had a supercharged libido and refused to masturbate. Carmen was similarly wired and never had any complaints about their sex life. It would take little more than a demand from John, "Woman, pull those bloomers down," and they'd be at it. John even kept color-coded "sex charts" that tracked their various encounters. But there remained a reserved nature to their sex life. They almost always had sex in the dark or while not fully undressed. Carmen said later that John had never seen her completely naked.[13]

Despite a mutually fulfilling sex life, the marriage was decidedly not a partnership. John was a self-proclaimed misogynist, and in his mind, he was to rule and Carmen was to obey. He was especially controlling over her body. He kept track of her weight and her menstrual cycles. When she became pregnant with their first child in early 1968, it was John who told Carmen that she was with child. He had been collecting samples of her urine and having them tested. Not long after, they were standing in a line at the bank when he noticed a man staring at her. "Carmen, that man is staring at you," he said. "Go over there and kiss him." When she refused, he screamed at her. "When I tell you to do something, you do it!" Afraid and ashamed, she meekly approached the man, apologized, and lightly kissed him. John insisted on having sex right up until she went into labor and resuming soon after their child—a daughter named Dawn—was born. "I never could breastfeed," she said. "Johnny took it all."[14]

There were the occasional tender moments. On the twenty-first of each month, John sent Carmen a yellow rose—a monthly memento of the date they were married. He had pet names for her, "Carmen Baby" and "Jelly Belly." And for all his anger and rage, he had a surprisingly soft touch. "Whenever money was needed, he was there," Carmen recalled. "He was a sucker for a sob story, I'll tell you."[15]

Still, the yelling and fighting wouldn't stop. While Carmen never gave an indication of any physical abuse in the relationship, she suffered deeply from the way John treated her. "It was torture, really," she said later. "Pure mental abuse." John would often see himself as the victim. It was *his* feelings that were hurt when her family meddled. It was *his* duties as a husband that were undermined when she refused to listen. He called her "Mouth" when she got stubborn. She called him "Dingbat" when he was acting like a fool. Carmen was young and insecure and hopelessly attached to a man who was no good at all for her, but she was also, by her own admission, "thickheaded." She had a spark that challenged him in a way that he found very frustrating. Once, she nearly brained him with a crowbar. Carmen was in the car with John. His younger brother, Michael, sat in the back seat while John heaped abuse. She found the tool near her feet and drew it back, about to crack him across the side of the skull, when Michael leaped over the seat to grab it away from her.[16]

John was discharged from the army in March 1969 and went back to work at Chase Manhattan. After briefly living with Carmen's parents in their Liberty Avenue brownstone, John rented a small apartment on Rogers Avenue, and the family set up their first permanent home. It was a maddening spring for John Wojtowicz. The fights with Carmen grew so intense that the police were called to the apartment regularly. His career in finance—so much as he could even call it a career—was stalled. He'd never finished college, and his status as a veteran found him few favors in the working world. It was a time of disillusion, both inside the Wojtowicz home and out. Just three years before, he'd stormed off to Vietnam as a self-described warmonger. But what he'd seen there, and now saw every night on the evening news, had worn his patriotism thin. It all seemed so useless: so much death and no one with spine enough to either end the thing or commit to winning it.[17]

In short, it was a summer that made it easy for man like John to begin questioning things.

IT'S ALMOST CERTAIN that John knew what went on in Greenwich Village by the summer of 1969. Any lifelong New Yorker who kept up with things probably did. The Village had long been a haven for bohemians with open minds and little allegiance to whatever the square world felt was normal and proper. And by the 1960s, it was known as the heart of New York City's slowly emerging community of gays, lesbians, drag queens, and other sexual nonconformists. It was a place where there was room to be open, be it full-time or for a few hours in the dark of some musty bar.

Open as the Village was, there were always dangers and restraints. The places that might allow a person to truly be themselves were marked. Getting caught in these places could wreck a family or cost a man his job. And there was always legal peril. The prevailing interpretation of city ordinance against disorderly taverns essentially made it illegal for a bar to serve liquor to a gay person. This created a nightlife void that the underworld was glad to exploit. Unlikely figures in the nascent gay rights movements, mobsters opened illegal "private club" style bars that ran without city licensure but allowed gay men and women to drink, dance, and socialize. Payoffs to police kept the places open, but often in the dingiest conditions. In 1966, members of the Genovese crime family put a few grand into an old nightclub on Christopher Street known as the Stonewall Inn. By the summer of 1969, it was one of the most popular gay bars in the city.

John probably read about what would eventually become known simply as "Stonewall" a day or two after it happened, presented in a condescending tone in one of the city's straight daily newspapers. "Homo Nest Raided, Queen Bees Are Stinging Mad," a *Daily News* headline read. He would have read about a handful of cops busting into the Stonewall in the festive wee hours of a Saturday morning, another raid against a type of illegal establishment that had seen plenty of them. But this time was different. This time, the queens fought back. They linked arms and stood tall. They chanted and screamed; they threw bottles and coins. They made the cops run and hide. The Stonewall, mob management be damned, was theirs. It was where they felt like they belonged. It was sanctuary. Even in the dismissive language of the papers, it was plain to see that these people were deadly serious. "If they close up all the gay joints in this area," one veteran of the Stonewall riots told the *News*, "there is going to be all-out war."[18]

A week later (on Independence Day, no less), John Wojtowicz—the warmonger with no battle to fight—told Carmen that he wanted to cut back on their marathon lovemaking. It was the last part of their relationship that either of them still enjoyed. On the 16th, the Apollo 11 Saturn V rocket was launched in Florida, an event that set off a nationalistic buzz among the crew-cut set, the "Love it or leave it" crowd, the Nixonites. But John was distracted. Four days later, the lunar module touched down on the moon's surface, the culmination of a decades-long effort that had captivated the world. That afternoon, John and Carmen took their daughter to an afternoon baseball game. John left early for reasons he didn't explain. That evening, as the nation and the world waited on the grainy footage from the moon's surface, John went to their Rogers Avenue apartment, gathered up his things and whatever furniture he could fit into his car, and left. When Carmen got home, with eight-month-old Dawn in her arms, the place was almost completely empty. He'd even taken the baby's bed. There was a ten-dollar bill on a table near the door. It was cab fare so she could go back to her parents.[19]

3. all welcome, dress optional

It didn't start with Stonewall. Queer and transgender folks in Los Angeles resisted and threw fists at the cops in 1959 during a raid on a doughnut stand frequented by the gay community. Milwaukee's LGBTQ+ pioneers fought with servicemen who'd tried to start trouble at a gay bar called the Black Nite in 1961. The twenty-four-hour Compton's Cafeteria chain in San Francisco was a longtime meeting spot for drag queens and trans people. In 1966, after the Compton's management called the cops on a complaint of "female impersonation" one too many times, the queens fought back, trashing the restaurant and overturning a police car. There were gay rights protest marches in Chicago, Philadelphia, and Los Angeles and a nonviolent "sip-in" in New York City to protest the city's de facto ban on serving drinks to gay or trans people.

It didn't start with Stonewall, but it was different afterward.

The sip-in had been the work of New York's Mattachine Society, the local branch of one of the first American gay rights organizations. The Mattachine was a decidedly middle-of-the-road organization, with a focus on nonconfrontational acts and a moderate political philosophy. The New York group had even worked with NYPD Inspector Seymour Pine, who led the 1969 raid on the Stonewall, supporting his efforts to fight Mafia control of the city's gay bars. Just weeks after the raid and the three nights of rioting and protest that followed, the New York Mattachines held a meeting at which the society's leadership urged the community to work for the favor of the establishment and not threaten their acceptance with violent acts and words. "We don't want acceptance, goddamn it!" one young audience member shouted at the speaker. "We want respect. Demand it! We're through hiding in dark bars behind Mafia doormen. We're going to go where straights go and do anything with each other they do and if they don't like, well, fuck them!"[1]

Fuck them. It was a loud and simple statement of the post-Stonewall attitude. "They" were the beat cops who never missed a chance to hassle two men lingering too near each other on a street corner. They were the establishment liberals who'd marched for equality but couldn't be bothered to act on gay rights. They were the establishment conservatives who'd sooner blame deviancy than act on anything. And now they were the suit-and-tie, office-class gay men who'd rather see the street kids take abuse with dignity than be forced to defend the political efficacy of a brick through a pig cruiser's windshield.

Fuck them. They were also the Mafia-connected heavies who ran the few places in the city where gays, lesbians, drag queens, and gender nonconformists could drink, dance, and be open with their love and desires. In the city, the Genovese family was the major player in the gay bar scene, but the Gambino and Columbo families also had a slice. Mob money and influence kept the cops from raising hassle about things like the lack of a liquor license (the city still refused to license known gay bars), but also gave them a pass on things like health inspections and fire codes. A mob-run gay bar was a place where a queer New Yorker could be themself, but the privilege came at the cost of dank rooms, dirty beer mugs, and overpriced cocktails. The Stonewall was already a community landmark by the time it was raided in 1969, but its conditions were only tolerated because its customer base had no other real alternative.[2]

Gay New Yorkers were all too aware of the odd balancing act between the feelings of community that were fostered by these places and the bitter contempt they felt toward those who allowed these places to exist. The irony of the Stonewall raid, well-documented in David Carter's *Stonewall: The Riots That Sparked the Gay Revolution,* was that Pine and his squad were targeting the mob, not the gay community. While they exhibited few restraints in intimidating and harassing the Stonewall's patrons that evening, their real goal was to break up a suspected blackmail ring operating out of the bar. Pine had orders to act based on an investigation into a recent rash of embezzlement cases on Wall Street wherein closeted stockbrokers were threatened with exposure unless they paid extortion fees that forced them to dip into company holdings.[3]

But in the moment, when the NYPD busted in and started shouting and shoving, lining up drag queens and pulling couples apart, the bureaucratic motivation behind the action couldn't have mattered less. The people the cops hustled out into the street refused to leave. Others joined them. Someone shouted that the cops must be pissy over an overdue payoff. "Let's pay them off!" someone else shouted. Someone threw a handful of coins. Then a bottle. Then a brick. Pine and his goons ran inside the bar and bolted the door. A few people yanked a parking meter from the ground and used it like a battering ram. Windows were smashed. Someone set a fire. The next day, a message appeared on the building in white chalk lettering: *gay prohibition corrupt$ cop$ feed$ mafia.*[4]

Fuck them.

New gay rights organizations formed in the wake of Stonewall. The Gay Liberation Front (GLF) was born while the Stonewall's shattered front windows still lay in shards on Christopher Street. Its founding members spoke of revolution and claimed solidarity with all oppressed peoples as victims of "rotten, dirty, vile, fucked-up capitalist conspiracy." The GLF launched its own newspaper, *Come Out!,* and held dances as an alternative to the mob-run bars. At one such bar where a lesbian had recently been accosted by a straight man for refusing to dance with him, the GLF reversed the Mattachine sip-in tactic and filled the bar with queer folks who refused to spend a nickel. They even picked a fight with the ostensibly liberal *Village Voice.* The periodical had refused to print the word *gay* in their advertisements but referred to the "forces of faggotry" in its coverage of the riot. The GLF threatened to sue until the paper relented.[5]

In late 1969, a group of gay New Yorkers—tired of the dated worldview of the Mattachine Society yet not ready to embrace the wide-ranging alliances of the GLF—formed the Gay Activists Alliance. The GAA would focus strictly on gay issues and would use direct actions with high visibility to make its case. With placards printed with straightforward slogans like "Gay Is Proud" and "Gay Is Good," the GAA had the political acuity to direct its tactics at those with the most to lose. John Lindsay, the erudite liberal elected New York City mayor in 1965, had once been considered a possible ally to the cause. But now into his second term, he had failed to deliver. In actions that would come to be known as "zaps," GAA members staged several high-profile confrontations of Lindsay, demanding that he rein in the viciously anti-gay actions of the NYPD. They marched on city hall and insisted on a meeting. They disrupted a taping of his weekly television program. They shouted him down at a museum dedication and peppered him with loud questions at a preview performance of a Broadway show.[6]

More than just street theater, the GAA forced officials into taking a stance. Its endorsement of Antonio Olivieri, candidate for the state assembly, probably clinched his victory in an election decided by just seven hundred votes. Meanwhile, a series of protests against Governor Nelson Rockefeller led to both of New York's U.S. senators offering statements of support. Finally getting a meeting with a Lindsay aide, GAA cofounder Arthur Bell made it clear that gays were done "taking shit" and another summer of riots could be in the offing if nothing was done.[7]

JOHN WOJTOWICZ MOVED back in with his parents after leaving Carmen. Terry was glad to cover his domestic needs (and gladder still to be rid of Carmen). John Sr., who'd given up on enforcing his will and now spent most of his time at home drinking and watching television, hardly seemed to notice. Carmen moved back home too. She was crushed by John's abandonment, even more so a few weeks later when she learned she was pregnant again. She blamed herself for everything. Against everyone's advice, she begged him to return to her.[8]

The only surviving public utterance about Stonewall from either John or Liz was a claim by John in a 2003 interview that Liz had been one of the "crazy drag queens" who'd rioted that night in 1969. It wasn't true. In fact, while Liz was a known figure on the drag scene by the late 1960s, she was fairly unmoved by the more radical political aspects of the community. At Stonewall, like many of the previous gay uprisings, drag queens and gender nonconformists were major catalysts of rage. It had been the queens at Stonewall who'd refused to submit to police demands and who stirred up the crowds by resisting arrest. It had been the queens who'd formed an impromptu kick line during the mayhem, joining arms and singing silly and vulgar songs as the cops cowered. It was outright mockery, with the shoe finally on the other foot.[9]

But Liz showed little interest in revolution—before, during, or after Stonewall. Indeed, in the rare moment from this era when she mentioned politics at all, it was to offer support for Richard Nixon. While Liz was familiar with the streets and certainly faced her share of discrimination, her money provided a safety net that few other trans teenagers who'd just left home could rely on. Not only did she have places to stay and food to eat, but she could also afford cars and clothes and trips without relying on sex work or work of any kind. Liz spent the tail end of the 1960s living in a series of high-end apartments. During the fraught summer of 1969, she was living in a three-bedroom apartment in Forest Hills, a world away from the raw anger taking over the Village.[10]

An avid reader of newspapers since he was a boy, John would hardly have missed the change that was in the air. And the angst that drove that change would have felt desperately familiar to him. But he didn't seem ready just yet to join the movement. He kept on working, kept on letting his mother take care of him, and kept on seeing Carmen. A typical tryst of theirs involved going to a dirty movie in Times Square and then screwing themselves silly at the Hotel Century on Forty-Sixth Street. They were so engaged the moment she went into labor in early

1970. A son, Sean, was born, but the baby did little to change the dynamic between John and Carmen. They were still a mess as a couple. The only real change Carmen noticed in her estranged husband was that he seemed to be letting his hair grow long.[11]

Liz was also letting her hair grow long. On the advice of more experienced drag queens, she began experimenting with hormones in the mid-1960s. After a bad batch of drugs meant for zoo animals briefly turned her nipples black, she found an honest doctor. She soon began to notice physical changes that made her feel more at home in her body. Her hips widened and she grew small breasts. The hair on her arms and legs thinned to the point where it was hard to even see. Her facial hair—once so thick she'd need to shave twice on days she was performing—faded to a light fuzz, and the hair atop her head came in thick enough that she could occasionally go out wigless.[12]

By the end of the 1960s, Liz was the reigning Miss Mattachine New York and had won or placed runner-up in ten other competitions.* She had filled out at five feet ten inches tall with an elegantly slender figure and head full of curly brown hair. But she'd never lost the edge that so often made her the bright light at the center of any room. Independent of whatever was going down in the Village, Liz had long ago exhausted her tolerance for taking shit. In one of her periodic attempts at working, she'd enrolled in a beauty school and advanced through the program to the point where she was able to see the public. One day, a loud woman came in for a dye job and insisted that she not be given

* The Mattachine drag balls were a fundraising effort first organized by Lee Brewster, who went to work for the group in the late 1960s after being fired by the FBI for being gay. He would eventually take over the drag balls as his own enterprise after more conservative Mattachine members objected to the embrace of "cross-dressing."

a "faggot" hairdresser. Liz, dressed in men's clothes for the gig, was the only available stylist. The woman sat grumpily as Liz began her work. Asked if she had ever dyed her hair before, the woman spat, "I've never touched my hair in my life."[13]

"It looks like it," Liz replied.

As the woman kept on with her complaints and slurs, Liz mixed up a horrifying concoction of the strongest bleaches she could find, worked them into the woman's hair, and parked her under a heat lamp. Typically, the lamps were used for only about fifteen minutes. But after Liz flipped the switch, she went to lunch. A very long lunch. When she finally returned and began to unwrap the towel from the woman's head, nothing was left of her hair but a brittle tumbleweed that disintegrated almost instantly. The woman saw the shocked faces around her and demanded to know what color this smart-assed fruit had given her.

"Nude," said Liz. It was the end of her career as a stylist.[14]

IN THE EARLY hours of March 8, 1970, Inspector Seymour Pine and his soldiers raided the Snake Pit, another mob-run Village gay bar. While the action was again meant to target mob activity, not the community, Pine's method for avoiding another Stonewall-style revolt was to simply arrest everyone. More than 150 men were inside the bar at the time of the raid, and all were quickly moved into police vans and taken to the Sixth Precinct Station House to be booked and processed. Among them was a twenty-three-year-old Argentinian immigrant named Diego Viñales. It had been his first visit to a gay bar. Living in New York on an expired visa, he was terrified at the thought of being deported and sent home branded as a "homosexual." Somewhere on the third floor of the station, he broke away from the crowd and tried to escape out a window. As officers tried to intervene, he plummeted to the sidewalk and landed on a wrought-iron fence. A long spike on the fence pierced his abdomen, and the young man lay impaled and overwhelmed with pain. The piece of iron had to be cut from the fence in order to transport Viñales to the hospital, where he would remain for three months.

Whether Viñales was pushed or jumped mattered little. "Any way you look at it—that boy was PUSHED. We are ALL being pushed," read a GAA flyer issued just after the incident. In the days that followed, hundreds of GAA and GLF members—with hundreds more drawn to the movement by the news of the raid and its tragic aftermath—gathered in the little park across from the Stonewall and marched on the Sixth Precinct building. "Say it loud! Gay is proud!" they chanted. At the station house, dozens of officers stood guard. It was, in a backward way, a sign of respect. Even if they'd still sooner don riot gear than acknowledge the gay community's humanity, they no longer doubted that these queens and queers could rip shit up if provoked.[15]

Later that summer, just after the first anniversary of Stonewall was commemorated with a thousand-person march down Christopher Street, police stepped up harassment of suspected gay men on the Forty-Second Street boundary of Times Square. For weeks, patrols would scoop up as many as could fit into a police van and haul them to the Fourteenth Precinct Station House on Thirty-Fifth Street. The men would be booked as vagrants and turned loose, with few ever facing actual charges. In late August, a coalition of gay liberation and allied groups staged a march from Forty-Second Street to the Village in protest of the harassment. Chanting slogans and carrying signs, the marchers drew catcalls and projectiles from onlookers, but the mass kept growing. They arrived at Sheridan Square in the Village just as police were executing a raid on the Haven, a dry gay dance club. With cries of "Gay power!" the marchers and police traded blows as inmates at the nearby New York Women's House of Detention shouted in support of the marchers and threw flaming rolls of toilet paper from their windows. It took police reinforcements to finally beat back the crowd, with eighteen arrested and scores more injured. Inside the detention center, the women started their own riot and resisted for forty-eight hours before the prison was secured.[16]

By the end of 1970, the GAA had grown to the point where a permanent headquarters and community center was needed. Funds were raised and a committee settled on a decommissioned firehouse at 99 Wooster Street. A lease was signed in April 1971, and renovations installed office spaces and a dance floor. The Firehouse would be a safe space, an option for socialization outside of the seedy mob-run bars. It was a "celebration of post-Stonewall identity," wrote GAA member Wallace Hamilton. "We are. We are together. And if you don't like it, *fuck off!*"[17]

FOR ALL THE stories that John Wojtowicz told, true or not, he said almost nothing about the eighteen-plus months between the day he left Carmen and his daughter with ten dollars and an empty apartment and the afternoon in early 1971 when he first wondered into a GAA meeting in the Village. From a distance, he would have seen the gay liberation movement evolve from a smattering of fearless, bottle-tossing street kids to a genuine force for acceptance and political power. In an odd way, they reflected the Goldwater movement from seven long years before: unapologetic in their identity and unwilling to bow to polite society's expectations. It was an unabashedly *fuck-you* kind of movement. And John Wojtowicz—the opiniated loudmouth who had expected so much more from his American experience—was an unabashedly *fuck-you* kind of guy.

When John first appeared on the GAA scene, he introduced himself as "Littlejohn Basso." Basso was Terry's maiden name, an obvious pseudonym given John's antipathy toward his father and his proud identity as an Italian. Littlejohn was a cheeky, self-applied nickname. It was an unashamed reference to his small penis, the first of many instances in which he would be wide open about his sexuality to fellow GAA members.

Arthur Bell first encountered John in May 1971, just after the opening of the GAA Firehouse. "John was pleasant, spunky, a little crazy, and up front about his high sex drive," he later wrote. Most others recalled him in similar terms. Another member said that "all you had to do to get a laugh was to mention Littlejohn Basso's name." The laughs were likely a mix of derision and amusement. He could be sweet and warm, but his grasp on the political aspects of the GAA was incredibly shallow. His understanding of the movement, another member later said, went no deeper than a few slogans he'd memorized.[18]

For a time, John served on the GAA committee that welcomed new members. By design or by coincidence, the post offered John access to some of the most impressionable members of the growing movement. And John did not hesitate to take sexual advantage of his position. As he did in his relationship with Carmen, John went for partners he could dominate. Indeed, it was the sexual freedom that the movement offered that seemed to appeal most to John. He would, as several members recalled, fuck anything that moved. During one of the earliest dances at the GAA Firehouse—where a two-dollar admission got you all the soda or beer you wanted, and the lack of air-conditioning kept things sweaty and stripped—John had sex with a man on a mattress in the basement. There was talk afterward of expelling John from the group for the act, but it was chalked up to just another weird outburst from the loud little Italian guy that people had taken to calling "Crazy John."[19]

But perhaps the oddest thing about Littlejohn was his preoccupation with getting married. This coincided with his attempts to reconcile with Carmen, still his legal wife. The couple took a second honeymoon at the same resort in the Poconos where they'd honeymooned in 1966. Some GAA members recall his having had several male "fiancés" through early 1971, and at least one of those was serious enough that he asked for permission to use the Firehouse for the ceremony.[20]

At a time when sodomy was still illegal in New York and being queer could get you fired from your job or worse, gay marriage wasn't even on the radar for GAA. In fact, there was no clear consensus on whether or not it even should be. John's request for use of the Firehouse ignited a heated debate within the GAA about the merits of gay marriage. From what could have been dismissed as just another weird act from a member who everyone agreed was kind of crank, the GAA was forced to give the matter serious discussion. While the leadership of the GAA was dead set against it, seeing it as playing into the same regressive system that had excluded and dehumanized gays and lesbians for centuries, the rank and file saw merit in the radical take on straight culture and voted to let Littlejohn have his wedding. By that time, however, the relationship had already fizzled, and the point was moot.[21]

Shortly after the GAA leadership had taken their stand against him, John gave a tender and heartfelt speech in support of Arthur Evans, one of the wedding opponents, for renomination in his leadership role. He went about it, Bell wrote, in "his dumb, earnest way," saying that it was better to "love and forgive." Whatever the members of the GAA felt about him personally, John had found—in his own mind—a home at the Firehouse. He was able to be, for better and for worse, himself.[22]

As he grew more comfortable with the GAA crowd and with his new lifestyle, John made less of an effort to maintain the veneer of his old ways. He brought his infant son to the Firehouse and told everyone that he was the group's newest and youngest member. After John's mother caught him sneaking off to the Village, he came out to her and—even though she admitted she was still baffled by the very concept of gay relationships—she supported him. In April, he quit his bank job for reasons that remain unclear. In some versions of his own story, John claimed that he was fired for being gay—once even going so far into the fantasy as to claim that Jacqueline Kennedy Onassis saw him reporting for work in a beard and dress and demanded that he be canned. Whatever the reasons for his departure, it was another step away from the Goldwaterian life he had once envisioned for himself.[23]

That summer, he also came out to Carmen. She'd confronted him one afternoon after he came to pick up the kids with a hickey on his neck. "Johnny, how'd you get that hickey on your neck? Who's the broad you're going with?"

"I'm not goin' with no broad, whataya crazy?" he shot back.

And then there must have been a beat, a moment when everything clicked for Carmen. She knew at least some parts of John's gay past, and finally everything made sense.

"Oh, no," she said. "Don't tell me."

"Yeah, that's right."

"You're seeing guys?"

"Yeah."

Carmen paused and readied a dagger. It might have been a lie, but that was beside the point. She wanted him to hurt. "We're even," she said. "So am I."

Despite all he had put her through and his own self-serving interpretation of their wedding vows, John was genuinely and deeply wounded. He began to cry and left the apartment, once again a victim. Later that night, in what he swore was his first violation of Carmen's trust, he found a willing woman and took her to bed. Now, John thought, they were even.[24]

NOT LONG AFTER the GAA debate over whether to permit John to use the Firehouse for his since-aborted wedding, the marriage issue was again at the forefront. This time, however, the matter was being forced from without, and the GAA was unified in its stance. That May, an article appeared in the *New York Post* on Father Robert Clement and the gay-friendly Church of the Beloved Disciple on Ninth Street. The year before, Clement had attracted considerable attention by performing "holy union" ceremonies for same-sex couples. The article caught the ire of New York City clerk Herman Katz, whose office oversaw the issuance of marriage licenses. Katz called the *Post* and denounced Clement's actions, calling the unions "illegitimate" and threatening a lawsuit.[25]

Tabling their own debate over the merits of same-sex marriage, the GAA saw Katz's tirade as an unacceptable homophobic spewing from a city official and began work on one of its most ambitious zaps to date. GAA members would take over the city's marriage license bureau for a day and issue licenses only to gay couples. And for theatrics, they'd host an on-site engagement party, complete with cake and dancing. All they needed was a few bold members to act as their happy couples-to-be. It surprised no one that John was the first to volunteer.[26]

On Friday, June 4, 1971, just after ten in the morning, a few dozen GAA members rushed to the second floor of the municipal building in Lower Manhattan. Inside the marriage bureau office, they set up a coffee maker, put out doughnuts, and unveiled a modestly multitiered wedding cake. Atop the cake stood two pairs of same-sex plastic wedding figures and a message in frosting that read, "Gay Power to Gay Lovers." Meanwhile, GAA members roamed the hallways of the huge building, passing out invitations to their party.

The Honorable Herman Katz,
City Clerk, invites you
To an engagement reception for
Messrs. John Basso and John G. Bond
Messrs. Steve Krotz and Vito Russo
At his office
Room 265, Municipal Building
Friday June 4, 1971
At 10:00 am
All welcome, dress optional
Sponsored by:
Gay Activists Alliance

While marriage bureau employees—some less amused than others—tried to get the group to leave, a small but festive party got underway. Someone pulled out a guitar and led the group in resistance songs while others danced and snacked. The daylong event was cut short when the cops arrived, but not before the protesters fielded a number of phone calls. "Your mother and dad wanna get married?" one such call went. "Are they gay? Oh, I'm sorry, we can't help you." For the hour or so that the office was under GAA control, all callers were informed, with polite apologies, that no straight marriage licenses would be issued that day but, if they were free, they were invited to the engagement party.[27]

Outside the municipal building, the GAA's Marc Rubin told the press that "everybody in New York had better know that they can't push gay people around . . . The community's there and will stand up for its own." Back at the Firehouse, giddy from the rush, the participants cut the cake. While Steve Krotz and Vito Russo (the latter would go on to write the seminal film text *The Celluloid Closet* and cofound the Gay and Lesbian Alliance Against Defamation, or GLAAD) were romantic partners, they had no actual plans to get married. But in the corner of the Firehouse that afternoon, Littlejohn Basso and John Bond shared a piece of cake with broad smiles. John Wojtowicz had once again felt the prick of Cupid's arrow. It wouldn't last. Just two days later, Cupid would return. With a shotgun.[28]

4. boystown

The forecast called for a clear and pleasant afternoon in New York City, with temperatures in the low to mid-seventies. Rain was expected later in the evening, but there was no sense in worrying about it beforehand. The air was warm, and the smell of grilling sausage and cold beer made everyone feel at home. It was the opening day of the Feast of Saint Anthony of Padua, the annual Bronx street fair that honored the saint whose patronage included lost souls, the oppressed, and those in search of a spouse.

John, the proud Italian who was still using his mother's surname of Basso, had a cultural appreciation for the feast—for the red, green, and white trimmings and the Catholic iconography. Still riding high from the marriage bureau zap, he'd gone with a friend from the Village for an afternoon of treats and cold drinks. Liz could give a shit about Saint Anthony and religious gewgaws. She was there with three former priests who'd given up the cloth to come out as gay. They were there to cruise for young Italian men, the tall and dark type dressed casual in cut-off jeans and sleeveless tees. As it happened, John's friend and Liz knew each other. Passing in the crowd, John's friend saw Liz and pointed her out. She was dressed androgynously casual, her small breasts visible under her unisex top and curly hair bouncing. She wore makeup and stood out with her tall, trim figure and loud voice. John was struck. He had to meet her. The friend flagged Liz down. "I have somebody that wants to meet you," he said.[1]

Liz took a look at John. She liked her men young and long, tall with muscles. John had none of that. "I hate to break it to you," Liz told the common acquaintance. "But it looks like your friend has been dead at least a week." John smiled and introduced himself. He was immediately smitten—"love at first sight," he'd later call it. Liz was less taken. "He was too short, too old," she said. "And too eager." As Liz and her trio of ex-priests cruised, John followed along close behind. More annoyed than amused, Liz decided the only way they were going to lose the grinning little man was to get him laid by somebody, by *anybody*. One of the ex-priests, a man named David, agreed to take him off her hands. She handed over the keys to the little apartment she had on Tennis Street and wished them well. "Just don't get shit on the sheets," she said.[2]

Even after David took John off her hands, Liz wasn't getting anywhere at the feast. She made her way down to the area along the Hudson River on the west edge of the Village known as "the Trucks." It was a jungle of idle semitrucks and empty trailers, mostly kept unlocked, where gay men liked to meet for anonymous sex in the empty cabs and rigs. Cruising the Trucks had been a pastime of Liz's for years. "Gross fun," she called it. But the scene at the Trucks was played out that day, and Liz settled for what she remembered as a "strictly mediocre" blow job before heading home to wash off the grime.[3]

When she got back to her apartment, she was surprised to

find that John was still there, waiting. "I hope you don't mind if I change in front of you," she said. John grinned a big dumb grin. He didn't need to be asked. "I had these red underpants on," Liz remembered. "Well, he loves red and he got all turned on." John asked Liz if he could suck her off. It was one last chance to get a good fuck out of the weekend. Liz said he could, and John took her on with gusto. First once, then again. "Let me tell you," Liz said later. "If there's one thing that John did well, it's suck cock." He had won her over, in a way. She asked to see him again and he eagerly agreed.[4]

During the summer of 1971, Jim Morrison died in Paris; half a million people marched against the Vietnam War in Washington, D.C.; and the National Guard ended the Attica Prison revolt by gunning down forty-two prisoners. And in various New York City buses, gay bars, taxi cabs, subway platforms, and movie theaters John Wojtowicz and Liz Eden fucked like mad. "We did it everywhere," Liz said. "He was a big suck queen, he really was. He'd suck anything that walked." And he certainly tried to. Even as their relationship grew more serious, John was always given a free pass for action on the side. He continued to sleep with Carmen and any willing men he met at GAA functions and on the Village gay scene. Liz recalled that he could have sex up to eight or nine times a day. "I just couldn't be bothered."[5]

These were the good times. John found a tiny apartment for them to share in a rundown boarding house at 250 West Tenth Street in the heart of the Village that was so frequented by gay men that it was known as "Boystown."* John brought her a

* Built as a townhouse in 1826, the property was renovated into high-end apartments in the early 1990s and, in 2009, was restored into a single-family home and rented to grunge rock queen Courtney Love. It last sold in 2020 for nearly $8 million.

dozen red roses every week. After Liz mused on the poetic foreboding of a dying flower, he started buying her forty-five-cent velvet roses. John was over the moon for Liz and Liz, naturally thick-skinned and defensive, began to feel something similar. She thought it might be love, and why not? He treated her better than nearly any other man she'd ever been with. He did things for her before she even had the chance to ask for them. Some nights, they'd sit on the stoop of their Boystown apartment building and talk. Or they'd walk to the little park at the end of Christopher Street and stare across the Hudson at the lights of New Jersey blinking in the sweet summer air. They'd sit close and think about the future.[6]

But there were cracks. Just as he had with Carmen, John had been drawn to Liz's vulnerabilities. Liz was hardly the sexually inexperienced, shrinking violet that John cornered in the women's room back in 1966, but she was similarly starved for true affection. Liz was twenty-five years old and had been on her own in New York City for nearly a decade, spending most of that time as a sexually open social butterfly. Yet John's simple acts of attending to her needs and providing her with romantic attention were beyond anything she'd ever experienced.

Indeed, Liz's emotional bond overwhelmed other areas in which their connection was lacking. She was never terribly physically attracted to him and often derided his lack of a decent personality. John's small penis—she more than once referred to him as having "no dick"—and short stature were significant turnoffs for her.[7]

And there were signs that John wished to dominate her physically as well as emotionally. In their sex life—which bound Liz in monogamy, but not John—it was Liz who was always on the receiving end of anal sex, never John. "I suspect it was because he enjoyed being more in control, more dominant," Liz said. She went along, though, happy enough to be with him. But she was also, much like Carmen, selectively assertive. When the couple would playfully wrestle, Liz—six inches taller and roughly the same weight as John—would usually end up pinning him. "Sometimes it would get him upset," she remembered, "depending on what kind of mood he was in."[8]

"But he was very sweet, very lovable," Liz later said, "only because he had nothing else going for him, I guess."[9]

There were also money matters. Liz had nearly exhausted the money she'd inherited from her mother, blowing through an estimated $200,000 on nightlife, trips, and cars while working sparingly. John, also out of work, had to perform some mental gymnastics to square his need of money with his stubborn pride. He was able to use his good credit to secure bank loans to finance his fun in the Village, his support payments to Carmen, and the gifts he lavished on Liz. But it was Terry who paid off his debts to keep the credit flowing. It wasn't long before the sticky matters of Liz's devotion and having money to burn intertwined themselves in John's mind. And it didn't take long for him to need more than what a small bank loan would provide.[10]

DESPITE THE GAINS made for gay liberation in the wake of Stonewall, the rioting and marching had done little to chase organized crime out of the queer community. Indeed, post-Stonewall, the mob was quick to take advantage of the expanding marketplace, investing in bathhouses and bookstores that catered to gay clientele. With the built-in rage among the community over Stonewall, the Snake Pit, and numerous other incidents of police overreach, mobbed-up operators became unlikely pseudo-gay-lib activists, playing out any attack on their businesses (which often also peddled drugs or laundered cash) as anti-gay harassment.[11]

One of the biggest players on the scene was a Gambino associate named Mike Umbers. Between 1959 and 1971, Umbers was arrested at least ten times on various charges, including a grand larceny and forgery collar in 1960 that resulted in a five-year prison term. Since his release, he'd built up an impressive portfolio of Greenwich Village properties from which he dealt in everything from dirty novels to under-the-counter pornography to methamphetamines. His front operations included gay bars, bookstores, and a lithograph company that reproduced pornography imported from Sweden.[12]

As the gay liberation movement opened things up, Umbers gladly branded himself as an ally. After Stonewall, he gave a cut-rate lease on one of his properties to trans rights activist Marsha P. Johnson and her Street Transvestite Action Revolutionaries (STAR) group that aimed to help unhoused trans youth. He also launched a newspaper called *Where It's At*, which was among the first wave of gay lib publications to debut after Stonewall. "I have gay businesses and I employ gay people," Umbers told *The Village Voice* in 1971. "I started this whole empire myself and I'm doing more for the gay community than any organization."[13]

Nearly as soon as it launched, *Where It's At* was denounced as little more than a circular promoting mob-controlled businesses. And Umbers eventually evicted STAR from his building after they refused to give him a cut of the money the group made from street prostitution. Worse yet was his trade in "chicken"—a term used in the community for teenage sex partners who were not yet of legal age. He had an interest in an all-ages dance club where drugs were plentiful and older men regularly cruised for underaged prostitutes. In 1970, Umbers was arrested on a complaint made by three boys—ages fifteen, sixteen, and seventeen—who said that he'd recruited them to perform sex acts on film. At his Studio Bookstore in the Village, any man buying forty dollars worth of merchandise, and asking "Where can I score?" was presented with a portfolio of snapshots of young male "models" who could be booked for sessions that cost between twenty-five and fifty dollars per hour.[14]

Umbers also ran a seedy Christopher Street club called Christopher's End. The place was notorious for its after-hours orgies and its anything-goes all-nude strip shows. Umbers advertised the place using the tagline "Weird Sex—Now." In July 1971, just as John and Liz were settling in their tiny apartment in the Village, police raided Christopher's End in another pressure tactic against the mob. Umbers was able to reopen just a few days later, but by then even the GAA was ready to see the place shuttered. A picket was planned to protest the End's mob connections and the shady image it gave the neighborhood and the larger gay community.

The issue over the End did well to illustrate John's shallow understanding of the movement in which he had embedded himself. John liked the End and its "weird sex," and he liked Umbers. John went to the planning meeting for the picket but didn't raise any objections or speak in favor of Umbers. He sat, kept his mouth shut, and took notes. And then he went to the End and handed those notes over to Umbers. By the time the protest happened, Umbers was ready with a counterpicket of his own. Among them was a grinning John Wojtowicz holding a sign that read MIKE IS GOOD, a play on the "Gay is good" gay lib slogan.[15]

It would not be the last time John did business with Mike Umbers.

THAT SEPTEMBER, WALKING down Grand Street in Little Italy, not far from where they'd first met, John and Liz passed Marlene's Bridal Shop. An elegant white wedding dress in the storefront window caught Liz's eye. It was long sleeved, ornamented with pearl sequins and crystals, and trimmed with fine lace. With the veil, it cost over $550—about what John made in a month when he was still working. "I said I wanted the wedding gown," Liz recalled. "And he said the only way he'd buy it for me was if I wore it in a wedding and married him. So, I said, well, I'd do anything to get that wedding gown, so I said all right, I'd marry him.

"And then that December, that horrible December day, we were married."[16]

5. run like hell

John Wojtowicz never forgot a date. The dates that he met people, the dates that he fell in love, the dates people died. He celebrated not just anniversaries but what he called "month-a-verseries." He sent Carmen a yellow rose each month on the 21st (the date they were married) and sent Liz a red rose on the 6th (the date they met). He liked to note that the day he was born, March 9, 1945, presaged Hitler's death by just a month (it was actually about seven weeks). "I tell everyone I won World War II, because Hitler heard [I] was coming!"[1]

He could recite with ease the date that he and Carmen first had sex, the date of their engagement party, and the date he left her. He was quick to note things like Liz sharing a birthday with Coco Chanel or his son sharing one with Jerry Lee Lewis. He never missed a chance to commemorate a holiday and kept a mental index of birthdays and anniversaries of everyone from close friends to extended family.

It was a way of keeping time.

John was just twenty-six years old when he became engaged to Liz, but he already had foreboding thoughts about the future.

It wasn't so much death that scared him but the loss of control. He'd gotten sick in Vietnam: a bout of dysentery that made him think he might die. That was no way for a hero who wanted to be buried in his dress blues to go. And then there was Anthony, his older brother who remained under state care. He loved his brother, but the thought of being locked up as a nutcase terrified him. He knew things like that could run in the family. His mother seemed a little half-baked at times too. No doubt he knew that homosexuality was still classified as a mental illness in nearly every medical textbook. "Once they get you in," he'd later tell a reporter, "how do you get out?"[2]

Not long after he and Liz became engaged, John contracted hepatitis. As he never possessed a sturdy frame, his weight dropped to a waifish 118 pounds. For months, his health problems lingered as he tried to plan his grand wedding to Liz. Back at home, his brother Michael had developed a nervous condition and could no longer work. Terry cared for her two youngest sons as if they were children.

Meanwhile, John was still sleeping with Carmen and regularly seeing a small roster of boyfriends from the Village. One of them was Pat "Patsy" Coppola, a slender dark-haired man who considered himself to be John's "mistress." John had brought both Patsy and Liz to his parents' house at various times, sometimes having them as guests for dinner. He called Liz "Curly" and called Patsy "Dingbat," the same derisive moniker that Carmen often used on him. Terry knew who these young men were. John Sr. had no clue. Sometimes John would leave one of his lovers at home with his parents while he went out to run errands. Liz usually fell asleep in a chair. John Sr. liked Patsy but didn't know what to make of Liz.[3]

IN OCTOBER, JOHN and Liz announced their wedding plans. That is, Littlejohn Basso and Liz announced their wedding plans. While he was still hiding his sexuality to most of the people in his straight life and told none of them of his engagement, John's planned nuptials made a splash on the local gay scene. The *New York Mattachine Newsletter* ran their announcement, writing, "The former Mattachine member will be wearing a $400 creation by Marlene's Bridal Shop and Mr. Basso will wear his Army uniform . . . This wedding will be New York's FIRST drag wedding of two men."* One of John's old GAA acquaintances recalled hearing the news and joked, "We all figured if we wouldn't make this one, there'd surely be another one next week."[4]

Liz even issued a kind of press release to various media outlets, inviting them to cover the ceremony. "You may or may not be interested in what I have to say. Well, here goes . . ." the handwritten series of letters opened. "On Dec 4 1971, at 4 pm at 228 W 10 Street a Roman Catholic priest will perform a mass joining Ernest Aron to John Basso, the only difference with this gay holy union and the other is one of the guys will be in drag (girls' attire)." Randy Wicker, a journalist and gay rights activist, was among the few who attended as media. "It was certainly not something to be missed," he said afterward. "I'd never heard of such a thing in my life and neither had anyone else."[5]

The "other" holy union she is referring to was likely the marriage of Jack Baker and Michael McConnell, who became the first same-sex couple to be legally married in September 1971. Baker and McConnell lived in Minnesota, where the state

* This is the only known reference to Liz being a member of the Mattachine Society. If she indeed was a member of the group, it appears her only involvement was participation in the Mattachine drag balls.

marriage statutes made no mention of gender. After losing a court challenge to be granted a marriage license, McConnell legally changed his name from Michael to Pat Lyn. The couple applied for another license in a different county, and it was issued without question. Shortly after, they were married in a ceremony by a Methodist minister.

The Baker-McConnell marriage came amid a small wave of attempts by same-sex couples to obtain marriage licenses. Out in California, Rev. Troy Perry had already performed several gay marriage services, although none obtained legal recognition. In 1970 his Metropolitan Community Church, the nation's most forcefully gay-friendly church of the time, unsuccessfully sued the State of California (where marriage laws were similarly gender neutral) on behalf of a lesbian couple who wanted a state-sanctioned marriage. The case was eventually dismissed.[6]

It was the "drag" aspect of the Basso-Eden union that grabbed Wicker's attention. Indeed, the ceremony was a melding of the new trend in challenging the concept of traditional marriage and the long-hidden practice of queering traditional marriage by having one of the partners present themselves in legal documents as a gender that did not match what they were assigned at birth. There are numerous examples of supposed man-woman couples being "exposed" as same-sex during the nineteenth and early twentieth centuries, and certainly many more such unions went unrecognized and are now lost to history. But the Basso-Eden concept was so radical that Liz herself even seemed to have a hard time describing it. The letter is a rare example of her using her legal name while self-referring with masculine nouns from this period in her life. Wicker planned to videotape the ceremony—a technological novelty in itself—for broadcast on public television. *Drag* magazine, a slick quarterly founded in 1969, assigned a photographer to cover the event.* [7]

By November, several hundred invitations were mailed out. In elegant black type on an eggshell cardstock, it read, "Ernest Aron [Sr.] requests the honor of your presence at the wedding and reception of Liz Eden to Mr. John Basso on Saturday the Fourth of December, Nineteen Hundred and Seventy-One at What's Inn a Name Café, 228 West 10th, NYC."† John was planning for a full spread and open bar at the reception while Liz found burgundy and gold dresses for her three drag queen bridesmaids. The costs for the event had already run into the thousands, easily exhausting the $500 or so John had left in the bank. The money problems added weight to what would be a deeply stressful month.[8]

With John being a devoted Catholic and Liz occasionally expressing a nondenominational faith, the couple had tried to get Father Clement—whose blessing of gay couples had inadvertently led to the marriage bureau zap—to officiate the ceremony. But Clement flatly refused, saying that "the drag aspects and attempts at publicity made it a sacrilege." Liz then reached out to Gennaro Auricchio, a former reverend in the Society of Saint Paul who had previously counseled Liz after her first marriage fell apart. Auricchio had taken a leave of absence in the late 1960s and had ignored an order to return to the cloth in 1970, resulting in his excommunication. He was now living in the Village and

* *Drag* was founded by Lee Brewster, the same person behind the Mattachine drag balls.

† Both the invitation and press release written by Liz use the word *wedding* in reference to the ceremony but never the term *marriage* in reference to actual union. It is not known whether this was purposeful or not.

working as a librarian at New York University (NYU). Liz took John to meet Auricchio and told him of their plans, but he, too, refused to have anything to do with the ceremony.[9]

Around Thanksgiving, with no one to perform the ceremony and with John borrowing money from anyone who would loan it to him, Liz tried to take her own life. She never mentioned how she made the attempt, but it was serious enough to put her in the hospital. Auricchio visited her in the hospital, and she gave her confession. "I'm all mixed up," she told him. "I want to be a girl. I have to marry the boy I introduced you to. If you don't [do it], I'll be more successful next time."[10]

Auricchio offered a compromise. "I promised him I would perform a blessing," Auricchio said later. "I would not and cannot perform a homosexual marriage. It's an unnatural alliance. A blessing is a union between two persons who promise to be loyal to each other and, in this particular instance, it erased a deep feeling of shamefulness. Ernie felt once this was performed, his soul would be clean." He would do it, he said, to save Liz's life.[11]

A WEEK LATER, 350 people crammed into the What's Inn a Name Café to see Liz march down a makeshift aisle in her gleaming white dress with lace sleeves and a billowing cascade skirt ("Yes, I had the nerve to wear white," Liz said later). John wore his army dress uniform, a line of medals and honors on his breast. He had filled out a bit since his illness and wore his hair in a neat pageboy cut. Liz's mascara dripped in summer heat as Auricchio had her repeat after him, "With this ring I promise my heart will love you and my body will serve you." John did the same, and they slipped rings on each other's fingers. John stood on tiptoes and Liz leaned over as they kissed.[12]

Terry Wojtowicz was there, beaming from the front row, tears on her cheeks, as John and Liz embraced. "Oh, I'm gay . . . I'm happy about it," she told Wicker and his video camera. "He's my son. No matter what he does or who he's involved with, he's still my boy and I wanted to be there." Wicker asked her about the rest of the family. "Well, they don't go for it, you know, it's just one of those things," she said with a nervous laugh.[13]

Liz's father, Ernest Sr., also attended with his wife, Gertrude. His presence was a mild surprise for Liz. He said nothing for the videotape but did pose with Liz for an awkward father-of-the-bride photo. Liz and Gertrude wear grim expressions while Ernest, looking odd in a gawdy modern sport coat and old-style high-waisted trousers, gives the slightest of grins.[14]

In the stack of snapshots from the wedding that Liz kept, her expression typically registers as something between morbid and annoyed. She stares daggers at the camera as she is helped to put on her dress. She glares across the room as her veil is affixed. She can barely contain an eye roll while holding up a pair of cornea-assaulting gold lamé pillows while opening gifts. She forces a smile while cutting the cake with John. The only shot in which she genuinely seems to be enjoying herself is when she sits at the gift table, showing off a foot-long candle in the shape of an erect penis.

In the same photos, John looks every bit the man who had just married the love of his life. He stares right into the lens, his wide brown eyes glowing and a tight smile on his face. He looks so happy that he might just burst.

By the time the food was set out and the bar opened, about five hundred people were inside the What's Inn a Name, the rumor of a free meal having drawn in freeloaders from across the Village. Someone, beholden to the wedding tradition that the bride needed to take the first bite, stuck a forkful of turkey in Liz's mouth so that the feast could begin. It was the only bit of the spread she'd get. Some "guests" didn't even bother to find a seat; they just loaded a plate and left.[15]

The gifts the couple received didn't reveal a great deal of affection from the huge crowd either. While those nearest delivered on some homemaking items, it was the gag gifts—dildos and other phallic mementos—that got the most attention. But it was the silver kettle that contained the envelopes—and the cash gifts within—that gave John his only pause of the evening. He had expected (or hoped) that cash gifts would total about $2,000 and help offset a good portion of the borrowed money he'd laid out for the wedding. Totaled up, the money amounted to only about $150. Later in the night, while Terry was drunk on champagne and being carried around the room by a friend of the couple, John went from guest to guest, giving deep open-mouthed kisses. In between smooches, he leaned in close and asked his closest friends if he could borrow some money. He just needed a bit, he told them, to help keep the creditors off his back a little bit longer.[16]

Later that night, the wedding party and their well-wishers went to the GAA Firehouse for a nightcap and then bounced off to a series of bars, tooting horns and living it up. Lit up enough to be so bold, someone in the group asked the party to pose in front of the Sixth Precinct police house—the same place where Diego Viñales had gone out the window two years earlier. One of the cops shouted at Liz, "Hey, babe, is it too late to stand in for the groom? How 'bout just for tonight?" It was probably the high point of her night.[17]

Back at home, late into the night, John told Liz he wanted to give her his "virgin ass." Liz obliged him, but John couldn't get into it. He told Liz to tie him up and she did, but the whole thing ended up a disaster. Liz got off, but John couldn't. He became furious and Liz refused to untie him until he calmed down. "Considering what was to happen in the month ahead," Liz said later, "I should have left him tied and run like hell."[18]

Already deep in the hole from the ceremony, John used the last of his cash to treat the wedding party to brunch the next day. There would be no honeymoon.[19]

IT ONLY TOOK a few weeks for the union to turn violent. Sometime before Christmas 1971, John brought Liz to his parents' house for a visit. But this visit was different. Things turned when John insisted that they stay the night and—as a married couple would—sleep in the same bed. Michael, John's younger brother, objected and John responded with fists. At some point, John Sr., who until now had been ignorant (either purposefully or otherwise) of his son's relationship to Liz, called Liz a "faggot." The slur set John off. He grabbed a knife and went after his father, accidentally cutting Terry while she tried to hold him back.[20]

As it had with Carmen, marriage seemed to bring out all of John's demons. He became intensely jealous and controlling. "All I had to do was talk to another man and he would go into an uncontrollable rage," recalled Liz. More than once, he stalked and attacked men he suspected of flirting with Liz. He followed one alleged partner to Queens, bashed up the side of his car, and put a brick through the window with a note that read, "This is for Liz." The rages continued at home, where John and Liz would have arguments so loud and intense that neighbors would rush in to separate them.[21]

In January, everything came to a head. It started with another argument, no one bothered to remember what about, during which Liz locked herself in the bathroom of their little West Tenth Street apartment. John pounded on the flimsy bathroom door, demanding that she come out. Liz held a kitchen knife that she'd grabbed during the fight. As John began to splinter the door, Liz drew back and stabbed the blade through the cheap wood—once, twice, three times. One plunge nicked John and drew a tiny amount of blood. "He went berserk," Liz said later. John tore through the door, grabbed Liz, and dragged her out. He punched her and knocked her to the ground, then picked her up and threw her onto the bed. Liz laid there, sobbing. She later suspected it was her tears that finally pulled John out of his rage. "I remember the look on John's face after we calmed down," she said. "His face told me he knew he had gone too far."[22]

The police showed up shortly after and took both of them into custody, dropping them at Saint Vincent's mental hospital. It was John's first time in an institution. His stay would be short, but he would not forget it. Years later, in one of his many self-serving lies, he put the burden on Liz for the trouble. She'd locked herself in the bathroom intent on slitting her wrists, he claimed. He broke down the door out of fear for her safety. *She* fought *him*, and he was cut in the process. He was the victim, and Liz was the violent one. After Liz declined to press charges, John was released and recommended for outpatient treatment, which he quickly abandoned.* In John's self-deluded recollections, he was about to be committed when he broke free from his restraints, beat up a few security guards, and "ran the fuck out of the place."[23]

John and Liz briefly reconciled after the incident, although

* During his sentencing hearing in February 1973, John did admit that this outpatient treatment was the result of his attempting to kill Liz.

Liz knew that whatever feelings she had for John—love or something like it—were gone. It was different, she said, he was different. She put up with two more turbulent months before once again breaking things off. John, as he was now doing more and more often, simply ignored the reality of the situation.[24]

THAT SPRING, *DRAG* ran its photos of the ceremony, referring to it as "New York's first drag wedding." Indeed, the stipulation from the former Reverend Auricchio that he performed only a *blessing* and not a marriage seems to have gone unmentioned entirely by John and Liz. In a spread titled, "Here Comes the Bride," *Drag* ran a bridal portrait of Liz looking grim framed by an ornate border and another of her showing leg with a "Show Us That Garter Belt Liz" headline. "Breathtaking in her expensive 'especially made' wedding gown," *Drag* wrote, "she had everything a bride could wish for: something borrowed, something new, something old . . . AND A MAN TO BOOT!"[25]

The attention made John a minor celebrity on the scene. In March, *Gay*, a new monthly just launched by *Screw* publisher Al Goldstein, mentioned "Marryin' Man Little John Basso" as one of the notables attending a drag ball at the Hotel Diplomat. Arthur Bell, now writing for *The Village Voice*, even sought him out for a piece on gay marriage. But Randy Wicker, having decided the footage he'd shot of the ceremony was "too bizarre," shelved plans to use it for a program on public access television.* [26]

After the split with Liz, John moved in with Patsy Coppola

* John would later claim that the footage was shown on the *CBS Evening News with Walter Cronkite* on the evening of the ceremony and that the footage even made Cronkite chuckle. This is pure Wojtowicz fantasy.

and continued the sexual relationship that he had never really stopped during his time with Liz. He hung a GAY IS PROUD poster on their bedroom door and hung up a crucifix—a gift from his mother—over their bed. He also pinned up a cheeky gag poster that read YOU GET WHAT YOU PAY FOR. SATISFACTION GUARANTEED OR YOUR MONEY BACK. Underneath that last line he added FROM LITTLE JOHN in marker. Every night before bed, John would pray out loud.[27]

He also began sending Liz threatening letters. He said that she wouldn't live to see their anniversary, that she had thirty days to live, that she had twenty-nine days to live, that she had twenty-eight days. He'd find out where she was staying and leave notes topped with a skull and crossbones. It was a matter of Italian honor, he insisted. She'd been unfaithful, and he was duty-bound to kill her. In one letter, he told her that if she left the state, he would be through with her. But that as long as she stayed in New York, she was his. She considered moving to Florida, but she had found a job that she liked, working in a storeroom on Long Island. She wore men's clothes to the job and kept her hair pulled back. The people there liked and accepted her, and she liked them. But on April 4, Liz took John at his word and left a note on Patsy's door that read simply, "John, I've left for Florida, Liz."[28]

John found the note and flew into a rage. He called her work and demanded to know where she was. Someone there told him that she'd picked up her things that morning and that her father had taken her right to the airport. He called her father, and he said that he'd dropped Liz at LaGuardia and watched her board a plane. He told John that if he was smart, he'd leave her be.[29]

It was all a put-on. Liz hadn't left her job and had only

relocated to a furnished room in Queens that cost her thirty dollars a week. Her coworkers and father were in on it, all willing to do what they could to help rid her of John. She even mailed a package of prefilled postcards to friends in Florida that they could mail back to her friends in New York—postmarked evidence that could be shown to John to prove that she had left the state.[30]

It didn't work. John wouldn't give up. He sent threatening letters to her workplace and even showed up once, demanding to know where she was. He cornered one woman on an elevator and screamed that he would come back and kill her if she didn't give up Liz's new address. He concocted a plan to hitchhike to Florida to hunt her down, going so far as to pack a bindle and make a sign before Terry talked him out of it. The company felt they had no choice but to let Liz go. She stayed in Queens until her money ran out and then moved in with a friend on Seventy-Fourth Street. She grew out her eyebrows and a small mustache and started wearing glasses. The worst part of her summer hadn't even begun yet.[31]

6. no such luck

Right around the time John Wojtowicz was enjoying his minor celebrity in the Village, eighteen-year-old Salvatore Naturile Jr. was released from prison in New Jersey. Sal was a Jersey native, raised by a troubled single mother who never stayed long in one place. He had been in and out of trouble with the law since age eleven. He stole things and took drugs but left behind no evidence of being violent in his early years. He was crafty enough to once devise a plan in which he hid in a department store after closing, rang up a pair of sales on television sets, and then left the next morning with the TVs and receipts to prove he'd paid for them. Crafty enough to dream it up but cursed enough to still get caught. "He was an outlaw," said one New Jersey cop who'd arrested him multiple times. "Always in trouble and always a headache."[1]

Some might wonder if Sal ever had a chance. If his father played any role in Sal's upbringing, no one ever bothered to mention it. He died in 1969. His mother was a heavy drinker and was abusive to Sal and his two sisters. She also had trouble with the law, serving time at least twice on charges of vagrancy. In 1971, she was arrested in Keansburg, New Jersey, on some forgotten charge and given the option of sixty days in jail or leaving town and never coming back. She opted to leave, and her daughters were taken in as wards of the state. By the time Sal was released in early 1972, her whereabouts were unknown.[2]

Sal drifted to New York and settled—as much as he was ever able to settle—in the Village. He was a love-starved kid and not entirely at ease with his sexuality. He met some guys in the Village and had some affairs. Eventually he was introduced to Wallace Hamilton, a fifty-three-year-old author and playwright. The middle-aged Harvard graduate took a shining to the teenage street kid with dark hair and an inexplicably blond mustache. Hamilton enjoyed his company, and Sal found something in the peaceful afternoons he'd spend at Hamilton's apartment. He would show up irregularly and ask if he could stay awhile, promising to be quiet as Hamilton worked. He was always welcome and would usually sit and read contentedly. Hamilton later wrote that Sal just "wanted to be cared for."[3]

Hamilton described Sal as "dreamy, gentle, and affectionate." He was also charming and funny and made friends fast in the Village. One was another eighteen-year-old named Gary Badger. Sal opened up to Badger about his sexuality and his apprehensions. He also talked about his time in jail. He'd been sexually assaulted in jail several times, with at least one incident involving multiple men. Now that he had become ever-so-slightly open with his sexuality, the idea of going back to jail terrified him. He'd rather die.[4]

Sal made another close friend who had come to New York from Kentucky. The friend wanted to visit home but had a warrant out for his arrest. He and Sal cooked up a scheme in which the friend would go home in drag with Sal posing as his "husband." The two made the long bus ride down south, but the act was unconvincing, and the friend was quickly arrested. Once again, Sal was crafty but cursed. He remained stuck in Kentucky until Hamilton wired him forty dollars so he could get back home. Sal promised he would pay back the money.[5]

After returning from Kentucky, Sal found work at the Penny Candy Store on West Tenth Street in the Village. Store manager Stephen Brockelman later described Sal as "polite and always punctual." Sal worked behind the counter, peddling Turkish Taffy, Squirrel Nut Zippers, and Mary Janes for a few cents each. He always offered to cover any day-end shortages from the cash register, even though they never amounted to more than a few dimes. He was trying to go straight, but even his newfound attitude and his deadly fear of incarceration were not enough to keep him on the right side of the law. In May, he was picked up for loitering and drug possession. Two months later, he was arrested in Times Square for possession of burglars' tools. Both times, he gave his name as "Donald Matterson." The police never connected "Matterson" to Sal's long rap sheet from New Jersey. Once that summer, Sal showed up at Hamilton's apartment with a paper sack full of nickels that he'd pilfered from a vending machine on Coney Island. He swore it would be his last caper.[6]

With the regular income from his work at the candy store and his various side hustles, Sal was able to rent his own place. It was a shabby single room in a Boystown boarding house at 250 West Tenth Street. And he found a favorite neighborhood gay hangout, Danny's Dancing Bar, on Seventh Avenue South, just a few blocks from the Stonewall Inn. Danny's was a popular gay nightspot in the Village. Two of its other regulars were John Wojtowicz and Robert Westenberg.[7]

Robert Arthur Westenberg was a slender and sandy-haired

twenty-one-year-old grade school dropout, with a youthful face and narrow, evasive eyes. He was one of ten children from a broken home in Queens where money was often scarce. Robert worked occasionally as a fabric salesman in the draperies department of Boussac of France, a Third Avenue department store.[8]

Robert had regular health problems and had undergone three major operations by the time he turned twenty-one, including procedures for a collapsed lung and a dislocated spinal disc. He felt sick all the time and drank and took barbiturates. In the late 1960s, he moved in with his supervisor at Boussac of France and began a three-year relationship with the man. But Robert's late nights in the Village strained the union. He got too wild, drank too much, and had too little interest in work. At some point in the first half of 1972, Robert attempted suicide and was briefly hospitalized. By that summer, surviving on meager disability payments from the state, Robert admitted that he would have "done anything" for some real money and a chance to get out of the city. "Even kill, the way things were going."[9]

ALONG WITH EVERYTHING else that was in meltdown in his life, John was fighting with Carmen nearly every time he saw her. She by now knew that John had "married" Liz. He'd even had the nerve to show her an album of photos from the ceremony. What stung her the most was that he married her in his army uniform. "That hurt," she said later. "Because he married me in that uniform." When he showed her the photos, she shoved them away and slapped John across the face. John couldn't understand it. "I love you and I love Ernie," he said incredulously. "I just have to have one of each." He insisted to her that he was not a "homosexual" but that he was "gay," which John seems to have seen as analogous for "bisexual." During one of their fraught visits, Carmen scolded their son for playing with her purse. She said he was "being a fairy." John blew up, screamed at her to never use that word, and stormed out of the apartment. All the while, they were still having regular sexual rendezvous.[10]

John was also back on the activist scene by the summer of 1972. He'd drifted away from the GAA Firehouse, eventually dropped from the membership rolls for not attending meetings. But he'd taken up with the group's newly formed Brooklyn branch and was even elected as a GAA of Brooklyn officer. He also contributed a piece to its weekly newsletter. "As a sadist," his article began, "I try to please my partner. I try to fulfill his needs and desires, and he tries to fulfill mine. No self-respecting sadist or masochist will ever force an individual to do anything against their will." He signed the piece "Little John (Basso)" and closed it out with the plain and cheery post-hippie motto of "Try it, you'll like!"[11]

The gay liberation movement in the summer of 1972 was in a political position that would have been nearly unimaginable pre-Stonewall. In New York, over ten thousand people showed up for the third annual Christopher Street Liberation Day parade, and gay pride parades drew similar crowds in Philadelphia, San Francisco, and Washington, D.C. In D.C., the school board voted to permit openly gay teachers. Congresswoman Bella Abzug, one of the most forcefully pro-gay politicians to hold federal office at the time, made campaign stops on Fire Island and at a New York bathhouse—with many watching her speech wearing only a towel. George McGovern led the pack for the Democratic nomination for president while running campaign ads in gay newspapers outlining a seven-point plan to protect the rights of gay Americans.[12]

John's activism in Brooklyn kept him close to his parents' house, where he was now spending most of his residential time. He kept a mailbox at his old West Tenth Street apartment, where he'd pick up the welfare checks that allowed him to eke out a living. He was still borrowing money from banks, but his mother's ability to keep up with his debts was waning. Down in the Village, he owed money to people whose terms and conditions made Chase Manhattan's look downright charitable. He had one wife who saw him as an increasingly menacing mystery and another who was on the lam. He felt love for so many people—his mother, Carmen, his kids, Liz, friends, hookups, and hangers-on—and felt so often like he got nothing in return.

Oh, and John Wojtowicz was dying.

Or so he claimed.

John did indeed have intestinal polyps (he'd later be treated for them in prison) and his bout with hepatitis was a true health scare, but there is no evidence to suggest that John was ever actually told by a doctor that his intestinal issues were fatal. But at some point, over the summer of 1972, John told a select few people that he had terminal cancer. One of them, perhaps the only one to take him seriously, was John Bidonde, another young gay man drawn to the Village in the early 1970s by the promise of community. Bidonde had fled an overbearing home situation at age twenty and found a room at 250 West Tenth Street. He became friends with John and Liz and was part of their wedding party. He was, Randy Wicker wrote, one of the few in the gay community who "genuinely" liked John. He visited him when he was in the hospital with hepatitis. And John visited Bidonde, making a four-hour trek by train, when Bidonde was recovering after an operation on Long Island. He knew John could have a quick temper but at first found him mostly to be a harmless eccentric.[13]

Bidonde was a sweet kid, a strawberry-haired painter who was trusting and naive. He took John at his word when he claimed to be working with the mob. He was a bit skeptical when John showed him an article in the newspaper about a Mafia-related murder and said that he'd "set that one up," but thought twice when John flashed him a stack of bills—his "contract" rate from the hit. Bidonde said that John had tried several times to recruit him into various schemes and robberies. John once told Bidonde that if he hadn't made a success of himself by age forty, he'd knock over a bank and "retire to the Riviera and go out in style."[14]

Despite all this, Bidonde didn't truly get concerned about John until he began palling around with an eighteen-year-old kid with a mismatched mop top and mustache named Sal.

OUT OF CASH and still in hiding from John, Liz took a menial job at an uptown gay bar called the Round Table. It was a place that she knew John never visited. She worked in men's dress, her eyebrows grown in and still wearing a mustache. She'd been there only a few weeks when a friend of John's recognized her. "Ernie?" he called out. Liz reflexively turned her head and immediately knew she'd fucked up. "When did you get back into town?"[15]

It also happened to be the night that Liz dropped acid for the first time. She was on speed, too, part of a drug regimen that was becoming more and more essential to her day-to-day functionality. She tried to play it off, to make the friend think that he'd gotten some stories mixed up, that she'd never left town, that spotting her uptown was too inconsequential to warrant telling John. It didn't work. John showed up later that night, dressed in hot pants and a button-down shirt embroidered with butterflies—part of his increasingly flamboyant fashion sense. He immediately began to pledge his love aloud, making a scene that was embarrassing at best. Liz rushed into the back and broke down. She swallowed a handful of quaaludes to calm herself. A friend took her home and gave her another handful of pills, which she took without a second thought. All the while, John sat patiently at the Round Table's bar, waiting for her.[16]

In all, Liz took sixteen quaaludes that night. She ended up in the emergency room with an overdose and was discharged a few days later, frantic that John would be waiting for her when she got home. He wasn't, but she packed up and quickly moved in with a friend in Brooklyn. It didn't really matter though. He knew where she worked and showed up most nights, bothering her and declaring his love. It seemed that nothing would put him off—not ignoring him, not yelling at him, not the obvious fear and panic in Liz's eyes every time he saw her.[17]

Liz didn't like labels, but she would probably most accurately be described as genderfluid at this point in her life. She usually presented herself in public as femme but would typically appear more masculine when she worked. At home, she favored jeans and billowy shirts—a decidedly androgynous look. Her preference was to be called "Liz," and most people did so. John was a stubborn exception and would refer to her only as "Ernie."* While she would say often that she "felt" like a woman, she would generally refer to herself as being a "boy with tits."[18]

But it was in a feminine role that Liz found the most peace. "I couldn't imagine myself as a guy. I'm more at ease as a woman," she said in 1972. "When I walk out as a girl, I hold my head up,

* Liz would occasionally use her birth name too during this period.

not down, like when I go out as a man." She first considered gender-affirming surgery in 1966, when she was twenty years old, but had decided against it. That year, clinics at the University of Minnesota and Johns Hopkins became the first in the United States to offer transition surgery. By 1972, she felt as though it might have been a mistake to dismiss a surgical transition as a pipe dream. She was miserable. She'd never really been happy. Not that she could remember. And in the midst of that awful summer, she began to revisit the idea. Not because it felt practical—she was broke, after all—and not because it felt any more right than it had when she was twenty.[19]

"I knew that the only thing that would upset him was if I had a sex change. That would turn him off because he was already married to a woman," Liz said. "So I knew that if I had the sex change, he wouldn't be bothered with me anymore." And so, in late June, Liz told John that she was going to have the surgery and that he couldn't do a damn thing to stop her. "I prayed that would finally turn him off," she said. "No such luck."[20]

John had objections at first. He wanted Liz as she was, as a "boy with tits." But through June and into July, as he continued to bother her at work, he came around to the idea with an enthusiasm that crushed Liz. He knew she didn't have the money for the operation and, in his deluded and self-centered way, took it upon himself to get the cash. This would be his grand gesture that would get her back. This would be how he'd take total control. This would be his mission. By mid-July, after he went with her to see a doctor who said that the entire process would cost about $3,000, John seemed more obsessed with the idea of Liz transitioning than she ever had been. He promised her he'd have the money by the end of the month.[21]

John's newfound purpose did not change his brutal behavior toward Liz. The stalking and threats continued. The friend from Brooklyn who'd taken Liz in when she was trying to hide from John had a nervous breakdown, and Liz was certain she was heading for one too. One day at the Round Table, she finally convinced him to make some concessions. She would agree to see him socially once or twice a week if he would leave her alone the rest of the time. He agreed, but not much really changed. Liz was seeing her therapist three times a week and was taking a galaxy of pills—both prescription and otherwise. The drugs were so powerful, Liz said, "I couldn't even raise my hand if I had to go to the bathroom."[22]

At the end of July, still without the money for the operation, Liz told John she never wanted to see him again. The compromise wasn't working, and Liz just couldn't take it anymore. A day later, John showed up at the bar in a rage and carrying a gun. Liz hid in the back while John grabbed one of her coworkers by the hair and threatened to kill her if Liz didn't leave with him. The bar's manager pulled his own gun and a brief standoff ensued. But Liz was tired. Too tired to put up with things anymore. "So I'll get shot in the bar," she said. "Or get shot in the street by John. So I chose to get shot in the street by John."[23]

John drove her to a hotel by JFK Airport where he had rented a room. John had seemingly calmed down. He began to talk about death and Liz joined in. She mentioned in passing that she would prefer to pass away in her sleep, to go from this side to that without even noticing. When night fell, John gave Liz a few sleeping pills and she drifted off. But soon, caught between here and there, she heard a metallic clicking. She opened her eyes and saw a gun pointed at her face. Liz bolted upright and John put the gun away.[24]

—

LIZ'S BIRTHDAY WAS August 17. In the weeks since the incident with the gun at the Round Table—which ended up costing Liz her job—John seemed to mellow. On the 17th—a Thursday—John surprised her with $500 in cash. It was borrowed, another bank loan that allowed him to flash bills and impress people. He gave it to her and then immediately asked for it back. If she would let him keep the $500, he said, he could have the full $3,000 by the end of August. By now, the idea of having the operation had rooted itself in Liz's brain. John admitted that his feelings for her might change if she actually went through with it. And there remained that part of Liz that truly wanted to become a woman. She gave him back the money and told him as forcefully as she could that she wanted to spend the evening with her friends at a bar and that she did not want him there. He agreed but insisted that she spend the next day with him.[25]

Liz had fun that night. She dressed all in pink and drank and danced with the people she loved. She was twenty-six years old, and it was a warm and dreamy evening. The next day was hot, with temperatures in the eighties. Clouds moved in that afternoon, and the humidity dropped, leaving New York City with the most mundane of summer weather. John picked Liz up in a rented car that morning, and they spent the day together. John was angry about something trivial and going on and on about taking Liz to Puerto Rico or some such place. Her birthday was a respite, but it was also an island in a sea of misery. "All I could think about was how horrible my life was," Liz said later. "Here I was, twenty-six, and nothing was right, nor had it ever been. I was no closer to what I wanted—the sex change—and what was worse, it was nowhere in sight."[26]

Liz had already decided that morning what she was going to do.

John dropped her at her apartment early that evening and said he'd be back at 11:00 p.m. Liz went upstairs and gathered up every pill she could find. Four or five bottles of sleeping tablets, prescription drugs, and a collection of random downers that she had been given. "I started taking pill after pill, and I eventually got to where it was like M&M's—I just swallowed them a handful at a time." She threw up the first batch but kept going. She found her way to a big leather chair and melted into it. "I remember just sitting there and seeing different segments of my life coming up in front of me." A friend called and Liz picked up. The friend asked what was wrong and said that Liz didn't sound right. "I've decided to do away with myself," Liz said before dropping the receiver. The friend tried calling back again and again but couldn't get through. She called the landlady in a panic, but the door was bolted from the inside. Liz felt shocks throughout her body and made her way to the bed. "There was just no thoughts in my head, and I didn't see anything. I had seen my mother . . . so I knew this was the end."[27]

The landlady managed to break through the door around 10:30, and Liz was rushed into a squad car and taken to the hospital. She wasn't breathing upon arrival, and the doctors couldn't find a heartbeat. It was too late to pump her stomach, so they went right to the defibrillator. Her friend watched in horror as they blasted her until a heartbeat returned. She was weak but stable, battered but alive. Back at the apartment, John had arrived around 11:00. A squad car and ambulance were still at the scene. In the apartment, Liz had left a note explaining that she "was doing it because I couldn't stand John's threats anymore, that I was afraid he was going to kill me. I had seen guns in his apartment, in his car . . . I had a feeling he was going to kill me one of these nights. And so I had said I had decided to do away with myself."[28]

After John learned what had happened, he rushed to the hospital and demanded to see Liz. The staff said he couldn't see her, that she was still too groggy and that he'd have to come back in the morning. John began to scream about coming back with a shotgun if that's what it took to see her. He shoved his way into her room and found her, gaunt and half asleep, tubes running everywhere and machines buzzing and beeping. He immediately began to cry. "Why?" he sputtered. "Why did you do it? I thought things were going so well with us."[29]

Two

"He was a showman all the way."

—HOSTAGE ROBERT BARRETT,
ON JOHN WOJTOWICZ

John Wojtowicz watches as the scene settles on three men sitting in a parked car in Brooklyn. One of them, a skinny kid in a cheap shirt, cases the front of the building and reports back to the man in the passenger's seat. John makes those two right away—it's Bobby and himself. Himself! There he is, being played by Al Pacino. John is transfixed by Pacino. He loved him in *The Godfather,* the last film he saw as a free man. The other man John assumes to be Sal, even though he's a good twenty years older and doesn't look anything like him. The three make their way inside the bank and things get underway.

John notices the little differences, but he's still stuck on Pacino. He winces at the way Sonny—where the fuck did they get that name from?—struggles to tear open the box with the gun. That didn't happen. And then again when Bobby—known here as Stevie—flees the bank. Not that it didn't kind of happen like that, but there were no jokes at the doorway about Stevie wanting to take the car. *Why would he even have the keys?* John wonders. *Sal drove. Jesus Christ.*

Sonny races around, in command. He blocks out the security cameras with spray paint—they'll only turn on if the alarm is tripped—so no footage will exist in the event things go south. John was now impressed with Sonny. That was a good idea. It wasn't his . . . but now, shit, maybe it was?

There's a tall woman playing one of the tellers. John recognizes her right away. I bet that's Mouth, he thinks. Sonny swears and the woman scolds him. "We got young girls here! You could watch your language."

"I speak what I feel," Sonny says.

That's Mouth, all right.

They got the guard all wrong, John thinks. An old skinny man with asthma appears on the screen, hardly able to stand up once things get started. In real life, the guard was bigger than any of them. A young guy too. And what a whiny pain in the ass he was.

On-screen, there's no money in the vault. Sonny and Sal take what they can and are about to leave when the phone rings. Mulveney, the name they gave to the manager, holds out the receiver. "It's for you," he says.

Two minutes earlier. Two fucking minutes earlier. If they'd only been able to get out of the bank two goddamn minutes earlier. Where could John be right now? Not in the stinking heat of the biggest room at Lewisburg. Not sitting in front of two guys who'd waste no time in beating him senseless if he just happened to stand up and make a run for one of the windows. Then again, he wouldn't be up on that ratty old screen in the way of *Al Pacino* either.

But where? Brooklyn? Maybe. Puerto Rico? He'd thought about it. Would Ernie be with him? Of course he would be. Why would he let himself think otherwise?

7. he's crazy

It was hard to keep a secret in the Village. Sure, what you got into on Christopher Street might not make it back home to Jackson Heights, but between the Hudson and Broadway, your business was everyone else's too. Gary Badger, a bartender at Danny's, first heard about John's plan to knock over a bank with a gang of down-and-out street kids as early as April 1972. As many as four other gay men from the Boystown house on Tenth Street were alleged to be involved. Among them was Sal Naturile, who told one friend that it was a chance for him to "have enough money to keep [me] in ice cream for the rest of [my] life."[1]

Another eventual accomplice in the plot was Robert Westenberg, who John called "Bobby." Robert and John had known each other for more than a year at this point. They often ran into each other at Danny's, where John would spot Robert across the bar and invite himself to grab a nearby seat. Robert's friends didn't like John. It got to the point where when John spotted him, they'd tell Robert to go join John rather than bring the big-talking little man over to them.[2]

One afternoon in the spring of 1972, Robert and John were

sharing their miseries at Danny's over a few glasses of beer. Robert was living on a pitiful $97 twice-monthly welfare check and sick to death of New York City. When John mentioned that he had a plan to rip off a bank and score some real money, Robert didn't need to think twice. Two days later, John introduced him to Sal, and Robert and Sal quickly hatched a plan to take their share of loot and head out to California to open a boutique.[3]

Then the bank robbery plot went cold. For months, it seemed like just another example of John's empty bluster. But in early August, right around the time that John dragged Liz from the Round Table at gunpoint, the gang got back together. The plan was on, John said. John tried several times to get John Bidonde—the good-natured kid who'd befriended him and Liz at Boystown—to join in. Bidonde declined, but the circle of chatter about the heist widened. Shortly after, Sal visited Wallace Hamilton. He admitted that he was "cooking something up" and said it would be a score big enough to get him out west, away from all the pitfalls of the city. "All right, Sal, what's going to happen if you get caught?" Hamilton prodded. "I mean, like ten to twenty [years], right?"[4]

Sal grinned. "They're never gonna catch me," he said, forming a finger-and-thumb pistol with his hand and putting it against his temple. All Hamilton could do was to tell him to "be good."[5]

Despite all the talk, no one seemed to think the heist would ever actually come off. From John, it was just more of his pulp novel bullshit. From Robert, it was nothing more than a sweet kid trying to act tough. From Sal, it was just his offbeat sense of humor. The rumors, the gossip, the chirping—even the hushed conversations that John led with Sal and Robert listening intently, his assurances that the plot was "infallible" and that he had "backing" from someone important—through all of it, no one remembered John mentioning anything about Liz and her operation. No one remembered him mentioning Liz in connection with the robbery at all.[6]

LIZ EDEN WOKE up in the psych ward at Kings County Hospital on Saturday, August 19, 1972. She'd been pumped full of drugs and could hardly muster the strength to sit up. If she'd been able to read the paper that morning, she might have read the story of Frank Sibley Jr., a forty-three-year-old Reno man who'd pedaled a bicycle onto the tarmac at Reno Municipal Airport, rifle secured to the handlebars, and hijacked a Seattle-bound 727. He held the plane for thirteen hours and was delivered a bundle of $1 million in cash before being shot by FBI agents. He lived and was due to be charged with air piracy. Just two months earlier, a plane at the same airport was hijacked by a man who'd simply run down a United flight, gun in his hand and pillowcase over his head. Even from the psych ward, it was enough to wonder what the world was coming to.[7]

Liz mostly slept that weekend. But before being sedated, she'd warned the doctors about John. He'd insisted that he was going to break her out, that he'd get together all the men he could and storm the place if that's what it took to free her. If she had been able to tell him that she was there voluntarily, he wouldn't hear it. As she slowly began to return to her senses, she was overtaken by the horror of the place. The stench of vomit hung in the air, and patients wandered around aimlessly. One was using the floor as a toilet. Another was beating his head against the wall. Somehow, word got around that Liz was gay, and her fellow inmates became hostile. She found a friendly doctor who arranged for her to be moved to a confined ward. It was nice there. She had her own room and privileges to walk the halls and play pool. There was a calm little rec room with a television set. The doctor assigned to her was kind and helpful. She liked him.[8]

John never made good on his threats to raid Kings County and bust Liz free. He saw Carmen that weekend, taking her and the kids to a double feature of *The Carey Treatment* and *Shaft's Big Score*. By now, she'd become fully accustomed to his new style of dress—which involved equal parts flash and camp. A typical outfit included purple velvet pants and a lavender shirt. She'd seen his costume jewelry too—gaudy rhinestones and tiaras—but he usually saved that for the Village. But on this weekend, she mostly noticed the mirrored sunglasses—not because they were all that unusual but because he kept asking her about them. "Can you see my eyes through these glasses?" he asked.

"Why?" she answered. "Are you planning on robbing a bank?"[9]

Late on Saturday night, John went down to the Village. At the Fruit Juice Orgy Bar on Christopher Street, he met up with Mike Umbers, the Gambino associate and scourge of the legit gay rights movement. For $150 in cash, Umbers sold John a pearl-handled Colt Cobra .38 revolver. A week earlier, John had purchased a $35 Enfield rifle from an unknown person. These added to the arsenal that Liz had seen in his apartment and car trunk. The pistol was stolen, pilfered from a New Jersey mail truck the year before, and untraceable to anyone in the Village.[10]

On Sunday, John went to Boystown to see Robert, who was in the process of moving back in with his mother. "I have something to show you." He took Robert out to the street where he'd parked a tan Plymouth Duster he'd rented the week before from Econo-Car on Coney Island Avenue in Brooklyn. John popped the trunk and showed Robert the arsenal. It was time, he told

Robert. He knew a place where two hundred grand could be gotten: one hundred for himself and fifty each for Robert and Sal. Robert didn't even think the guns were real until he picked one up and felt its heft. "I have people to pay off," John said. "Big debts." Later on, Sal joined them, and the three made one last pitch to John Bidonde to join in. Bidonde again declined, and John treated his little dead-end gang to a matinee showing of *The Godfather*, the smash hit Mafia picture that came out earlier that spring. They all particularly liked the line about making an offer that could not be refused.[11]

That night, Sal met some friends at Danny's. Someone noticed that Sal had a .38 pistol tucked into his belt. He told his friends not to worry, that he just wanted it for a little protection. Sal ate a cheeseburger that night. He'd become pretty fond of the greasy offerings from Danny's grill. After he finished his dinner, he said to no one in particular, "Well, this is my last cheeseburger." While Sal made his cryptic goodbyes at Danny's, John loaded the trunk of the rented Duster. He packed up some toiletries and a small bundle of personal possessions, including a topaz ring and over one hundred photos and a reel of Super 8 film from his wedding to Liz. Next to that laid a Mossberg 500 twelve-gauge shotgun, an M1917 Enfield rifle, and a flashy new suit.[12]

On Monday morning, John left his parents' house, telling his mother he was going to see Liz in the hospital. She asked if he'd be home for dinner—he was always home for dinner—but he said nothing and closed the door behind him. John picked up Sal and the two went to Robert's mother's house in Queens. By now, Lorraine Westenberg knew who John was. "It struck me that there was something wrong with him," she'd later say. John had called the house several times in the previous week. Once when

Robert was out, he told Lorraine to tell Robert that he'd called and that "this means money." She did, but he wouldn't call him back. He called again, and Robert refused to come to the phone. But that Monday, he went along. They told Lorraine that they would be right back.[13]

With them in the car was a typewritten note in all caps, pounded out by John on a borrowed typewriter earlier in the day. "Dear Sir," it began,

> *Please try to relax and stay calm as you read this note no harm will come too you if you do exactly as you are told. This is a hold up. There is a bomb in the bag at my feet, if triggered the whole building and half the block will go up. The lives of all of us depends on your actions and other present. Take the vault keys and accompany us to the conference room. We will follow you. We are heavily armed and will not hesitate to kill anyone who does not do exactly as they are told. Complete cooperation is the only course. There is no reason for anyone to be injured or killed. It is all up to you.*

The final line of the note was a nod to the movie they'd just seen. "This is an offer you cant refuse." It was signed, "THE BOYS."[14]

TUESDAY, AUGUST 22, 1972, was a scorcher in New York City. The forecast had undersold the heat, predicting highs in the upper eighties. But by midday, the temps topped ninety. It was the kind of heat that brought out the stink of the city—the ruddy mash of garbage, exhaust, and stale cigarette smoke. It was the kind of day where it felt damn near impossible to find a breath of fresh air. Liz had finally come out of her medicated stupor the day before. She'd had time to assess her situation and surroundings. The encroaching fear of the psych ward was gone. The people in her confined ward were relatively peaceful. The doctors, nurses, and orderlies were all dressed in pure white and moved gently through the hallways and rooms. On Tuesdays, the ward was permitted access to a small rooftop patio for an evening barbeque.[15]

It was an unlikely time for Liz Eden to find peace. She had literally come back from the dead, but come back to what? Nothing had really changed. John was still acting like a madman, and if anything, this would make his brutal infatuation only worse. She still felt incomplete in her own flesh. She was still broke. Soft stubble pocked her face, and her hair was an unholy mess. Her eyebrow pencil had been confiscated, leaving her shaved brow bare and facial expression muted. But still, above the smell of trash bins and the gutters, looking out over Brooklyn, she felt a rare moment of ease. The air was warm, and a breeze snaked around the tenements and apartment towers, slightly ruffling the terry-cloth robe she'd cinched around her pajamas.[16]

Five miles away, on Avenue P in South Brooklyn, Robert Barrett sat at his desk signing off on a loan application and preparing to close out the day's business at branch number 252 of the Chase Manhattan Bank. Barrett was the branch manager, forty-three years old and a salt-and-pepper kind of handsome. Dolores Goettisheim, forty-eight, was the assistant manager. Dressed in a dark-blue jacket and modest skirt, she stood behind the counter helping Shirley Ball, a fifty-two-year-old teller who worked two days a week, balance the day's transactions. A handful of customers remained at the counter as the city-mandated bank closing time of three o'clock neared.[17]

The bank occupied a squat, single-level building at the corner of Avenue P and East Third Street. It was a charmless structure: whitewashed brick with a pair of ten-foot-tall picture windows on each side of the main entrance. On the far end of the Avenue P side there was a night deposit drawer. On the angled corner at the intersection, a rectangular black sign read THE CHASE MANHATTAN BANK N.A. in white, sans serif typeface. Sitting among the residences and smattering of neighborhood businesses—barbershops, pizzerias, florists—that still operated in the modestly ornate turn-of-the-century structures that lined the street, the bank building was notable only for its distinctly mundane style. The interior was similarly dull. Phony woodgrain facing on the counters and self-service islands, off-white Formica, tempered overhead lighting, plain gray fixtures. It was the kind of modernity that excited no one.

Outside the bank, three men sat in a parked Plymouth Duster. The car, a tan 1972 model, was on East Third, facing Avenue P. It was out of sight to anyone inside the bank and positioned so that with a sharp turn and no more than three traffic lights to maneuver, it could quickly hit Ocean Parkway. From there, it could run north to Highway 27 or south to the Belt Parkway, conduits out of the borough and out of danger.[18]

The men were well dressed, especially for young people. Sharkskin suits, pinstripes, and pocket squares. They each had a pair of mirrored sunglasses, but no one had yet put them on. They'd seriously considered adding glue-on mustaches to the ensemble but ditched the idea as "too much." At five minutes to three, Sal got out of the car and walked around the corner. He carried a black attaché case and had a pistol. A minute later, Robert climbed out of the two-door's back seat and nervously did the same. He carried the *Godfather*-quoting note and an old briefcase stuffed with towels—what they'd hoped would pass for an explosive. For a moment, John was alone in the car. He was not dressed for the balmy weather. The vinyl smell of a car parked in the hot sun filled his nose. He held a long wrapped box on his lap, the kind used by florists for long-stemmed roses. Inside was the rifle and the shotgun. He got out of the Duster and calmly walked around the corner and into the bank.[19]

They had done this before—tried to, anyway. The original plan for the robbery was to hit a bank on Monday, August 21. After picking up Robert, the three had driven into the city and parked the Duster outside a Manufacturers Hanover Trust branch in Lower Manhattan. One of the men, probably John, was carrying the rifle and shotgun in an old canvas duffel bag. They'd all left the car at the same time and were nearing the bank's entrance when the duffel split and the guns spilled onto the sidewalk. They threw their sport coats over the weaponry and managed to gather everything up and hustle back to the car before anyone noticed.[20]

They fled the scene, flustered but not discouraged. John drove back to Brooklyn and eventually settled on another Manufacturers' branch on Waverly Avenue. It looked like an easy hit, John said. He noted that it was the only bank in the neighborhood and probably had a lot of money in it. The three got inside this time. They'd found an old box—a long cardboard container—and stashed the guns inside. Robert held the box and the note and Sal was about to pull his gun on the manager—the cue for Robert to hand the note to the head teller—when a big, Brooklyn voice broke through the tension. "How ya doin', Bobby?" It was a friend of Robert's mother who'd recognized him and wanted to know everything from how Lorraine was doing to why Robert was dressed so nicely. Once again, they fled.[21]

Bank number three was yet another Manufacturers' branch, this time on Avenue B. John decided that for this one, he'd go in alone first to scope the place out. He'd get a silver dollar from a teller and make notes of how the place was set up. This one, goddamn it, *had* to work out. John went in and got his silver dollar. He got back behind the wheel to move the car to a better getaway spot. He had started to describe how everything would go down when—smack—he hit a parked car. The owners of the car wanted to get the police involved, but John talked his way out of trouble and, once again, the three left empty-handed. It was enough for one day. They rented a room at the Golden Gate Inn, a seedy motor lodge in Brooklyn, and vowed to try again the next day. Robert would later swear that he'd thought the entire thing was a joke until they'd started visiting banks.[22]

At Chase Manhattan Bank number 252, it was closing time. Calvin Jones, the twenty-four-year-old uniformed and unarmed security guard, had locked the doors. A handful of other customers remained in the bank. The strapping Jones, who Barrett would later describe as a "black-belt type," stood by the door, opening it as each customer left and locking it again afterward. Sal walked to Barrett's desk and sat down. He pulled out the .38 and discreetly pointed it at Barrett. He told him that this was a robbery and that he was not alone.[23]

Robert was standing at the self-service counter, looking at the withdrawal and deposit slips stacked neatly in plexiglass slots and the pens chained to the countertop with little braids of metal, nearly frozen with fear. John had gone to one of the tellers, a pleasant-looking woman standing behind a small iron cage with a nameplate that read "Mrs. Tutino." He asked if she had any gold or silver coins, and she replied that she did, thinking that he must be a collector. A woman stepped up behind him, and John pulled back to let her go ahead of him. The teller was impressed at the young man's manners. *That's a gentleman,* she thought to herself.[24]

Robert was supposed to have carried the long guns into the bank, but he'd begged off at the last moment. Now, he was supposed to hand the note to the head teller. Everyone in charge would then be aware of what was happening, and the robbery could commence. But he couldn't. He stood idle as John sidled up next to him, making out a deposit slip under a fake name. Robert noticed that John was quietly giggling. "Like he's going crazy," he later recalled.[25]

Robert wanted out. Fuck the fifty grand and fuck John. He'd taken a handful of tranquilizers that morning for courage, but it hadn't done any good. The truth was that this just wasn't Robert. He was a mixed-up kid who didn't have it in him to hurt anyone. He tried to summon the courage to flee, but nothing came. Then, he saw the police cruiser across the street.[26]

"John, look," he whispered, "cops outside." John told him not to worry. As it would turn out, the cop car across the street had nothing to do with them, but it was as much of an excuse as Robert needed. "This is crazy," Robert told John. "I can't go through with it."[27]

It should be said here that John would later talk of a sexual encounter between himself and Robert the night before the robbery that could at best be described as nonconsensual. In an interview for a 2014 documentary about his life titled *The Dog,* John said, "While we were in [the hotel], I grabbed ahold of Bobby Westenberg and I wanted to fuck him . . . [Robert said] 'Well I don't want you fucking me.' I said, 'I'm giving you

$50,000, right? You're telling me I'm not gonna get a fuck out of it? You're out of your fucking mind! Because I am getting a fuck out of this.' So then I fucked him."[28]

Robert left behind no recorded comments about anything that happened that night. The story John tells contains all the hallmarks of his usual bullshit—the humor-tinged vulgarity and an exaggerated sense of his own power over others. But it also fits with the darkest aspects of his personality—the need to dominate sexually and a complete disregard for the boundaries of others. Journalist Cliff Jahr, who wrote feature-length articles on John and the robbery for *Playboy* and *The Village Voice*, recorded in his notes that John and Robert did have some kind of encounter that night—and that Sal refused to join in. He also recorded a quote from Robert that night. "Sal, look," Robert said as John was out of the room. "He's crazy."[29]

John quietly but aggressively told Robert to hand the note to the teller, but Robert refused and walked to the door. Jones, the security guard, smiled as he opened the door and Robert breezed out onto the sidewalk, watching the cruiser out of the corner of his eye as he paced quickly back to the getaway car. Inside, he tossed the "bomb" into the back seat and stashed the note in the glove box. He stripped off his suit jacket and tie and put on a pair of the mirrored sunglasses. And he sat, waiting for whatever was coming next.[30]

Back inside, Sal began giving Barrett instructions. "Get that guard over here and have him stand there next to the wall," he said, gesturing. "Don't try anything dumb. I've got a partner over there, and he means business." Barrett had Jones move against the wall. Meanwhile, John took the withdrawal slip to the counter and asked for a mix of silver dollars and new one-dollar bills. Glancing back to Sal, he saw the position of the guard and thought for a second that the young and muscular Jones had drawn a gun on his partner. They were past the point of no return. John tore open the end of the box, pulled out the rifle, and loudly declared his intentions.[31]

Ball had her back to the counter as she totaled her day's receipts. "All of a sudden, I heard foul language, and when I turned around, I saw John with the rifle." Sal stood and raised his pistol. John pointed the rifle at the women behind the counter. For a moment, he seemed overwhelmed by the enormity of what he had just done. Barrett sat silently at his desk. Assistant manager Goettisheim and Jones stood against the wall. Ball, with young tellers Kathy Amore, Joan Saunders, Santa Strazzella, and Josephine Tutino stood motionless behind the counter. Sal asked about Robert.[32]

"The third party got chicken and ran out," John said.[33]

The note. Robert took the fucking note with him. John collected his thoughts and turned his gun on Barrett. "I don't want anybody hurt," John said. "Do what we say and everybody will be okay." John jumped over the counter and hustled the tellers away from the alarms. "Now listen, listen carefully. I want all the money. Tens, twenties, fifties, and hundred-dollar bills. No fives, no ones . . . I want all the traveler's checks and the book you list them in. I know all about the book and I want it."[34]

John had one of the tellers take the collected bills and set them on top of the register drawers. He said that he'd worked in a bank and knew about decoy bills. He asked for the decoy register and was handed a green, hardback book. He checked the list and went down the line of registers, stuffing the stacked bills into the attaché case and throwing the decoy money onto the floor. Things were moving right along.[35]

John was firmly in charge of the situation. Sal was mostly

silent, speaking only with the gun he held on Barrett and Jones. When Barrett suddenly remembered that the bank's safe deposit clerk, Maureen Andrews, was still in the restroom, John calmly told him to go get her but not to "try anything." John kept reminding the employees that he'd worked in a bank, that he knew all the things that could trip him up. But by now, just about ten minutes into the robbery, Barrett could see that these two were hopeless amateurs. "He tried to pretend he was very aware of everything that happened in a bank," Barrett later said. "He had somewhat of an idea of what was going on . . . most of it was completely wrong." The oddest damn thing was, according to Barrett, that they kept letting him answer the phone. He fielded several calls but was warned only to keep the conversations short and not to tip anyone off.[36]

John had one of the tellers estimate how much money they'd collected from the drawers. She guessed it was around $20,000 (it was actually well over $30,000). John then moved to the vault. He ordered Barrett and Kathy Amore to open the door. They did, and Barrett removed a large bag with FEDERAL RESERVE printed on the side. John tapped Amore on the shoulder with the end of his rifle and told her to grab the traveler's checks and their logbook. She looked to Barrett, and he nodded. She gathered up the items and handed them over. John put the checks into his bag and dumped the logbooks into a trash can. John lit a match and touched it to the books. Destroying the evidence, he said proudly.[37]

But there was a problem. A big problem. The canvas sack that Barrett had taken from the vault was way too light. John searched it and counted only about $4,000. This meant less than $25,000 in cash and a book of traveler's checks that would mostly likely need to be fenced for a fraction of their $175,000 face value.

This was well short of the $200,000 that John had promised Sal would be in the bank. John had fucked up.

For weeks, John had been talking big to Sal and Robert and anyone else he wanted to impress about the heist. He had "backing" in the plot, he told people. And he knew things, inside things. He was no amateur, of course; he'd knocked off banks before, worked with the mob, set people up to get killed even. And he had word through his sources of a bank that would be flush with cash after an armored car delivery.[38]

Two different bank employees would later tell the FBI that John was upset at the lack of money—indeed, the vault was almost empty. The details of this "inside information" were sparse, but it is clear that John made a show of making believe he had been betrayed by someone who had insisted to him that there would be $200,000 or more in the vault that was ready to be taken. No one remembered Sal saying a thing about the matter of the money, even though it would be a significant reduction of his share from the robbery. Perhaps he never even noticed, too involved in his role of the heavy and keeping everyone scared and well behaved. Or perhaps he was just too complacent in his place under John's leadership—the same kind of complacency that would have kept him from asking questions the day before when the three of them went cruising for a bank to rob even though John had a hot tip about a cash delivery to a specific branch in Brooklyn.[39]

The phone rang again, and Barrett picked it up. The fire John had started in the trash can began to pour smoke. "Hurry up, let's get out of here!" Sal shouted from across the room. Suddenly, a pair of men appeared at the front door. John doused the flames and shouted at Jones to go tell the two men at the door that the bank was closed. It was about twenty minutes past three now, they had all the money they could get. Every extra minute spent in the bank was just a temptation of fate. They had to go.[40]

John was so preoccupied with the fire and the strangers at the door and Sal's barking that he hadn't even noticed Barrett's phone conversation. Not that there would have been anything really worth noticing. The call was from Joe Anterio, a personnel officer at Chase Manhattan's downtown headquarters. Anterio was calling to fill an open shift for the next day at the Seventy-Fifth Street branch. He asked whether Barrett would be willing to allow Joan Saunders to fill in. Instead of Joan, Barrett offered to send a different employee. The man he named had been fired months earlier for theft.

Anterio was alarmed. "Are you in trouble?" he asked.

"Yes."

"Do you need help?"

"Yep." Barrett hung up.

Anterio immediately called Chase Manhattan's security division. Another call was placed to the bank by a security officer. This time, Goettisheim answered. She gave similarly disconnected answers and abruptly hung up.[41]

SOMEONE HAD ALREADY tried to rob a bank in New York City that day. An unidentified man had entered a Midtown bank and handed a note to the teller demanding money, but the teller replied that she did not have the authority to give him any cash. The man panicked, turned around, and quickly left. As John and Sal were taking charge in Brooklyn, Joe Corliss sat at his desk in the FBI's New York headquarters at Sixty-Ninth Street and Third Avenue. Corliss was the bank robbery desk supervisor and was on the phone with one of his roving agents trying to track down security camera footage of what would have been a strong candidate for the least compelling bank heist of all time.[42]

But overall, Corliss was a very busy man. Bank robberies had spiked starting in 1968, and in the twelve months before John Wojtowicz began to plot his caper, there had been around 2,600 bank robberies in the United States—an increase of about 120 percent from just four year earlier.* Between 1970 and 1971, there were 469 bank robberies in New York City alone. When factoring in the greater municipal areas that fell under the FBI's New York office, agents were dealing with about one new case per weekday.[43]

Just minutes after the second call to the Avenue P branch, Chase Manhattan security notified the FBI. Corliss radioed his nearest rover team and ordered them to the scene. Meanwhile, another call from Chase Manhattan to the NYPD was routed to Lieutenant Maurice Beers of the tenth district robbery squad. Beers dispatched his nearest patrol car, which arrived a few minutes later. The officer in the car noticed that the bank's shades were drawn and did not see the guard in the front door window. Two clear indicators that something was amiss.[44]

Robert was watching the bank too. He'd waited in the car for a few minutes before getting out and taking a walk around the block, trying as best he could to look inconspicuous. He stood by a bus stop, waiting with a couple of old women for the next arrival, only to wander off when it came. He kept his eyes on the bank, hoping desperately that John and Sal would walk out unharmed. He spotted a rock on the sidewalk and considered throwing it through one of the bank's big picture windows to

* Bank robberies would steadily climb from this period into the early 1990s, with a peak of nearly 9,400 bank heists in 1991.

distract the guard—whom he now assumed had captured his compatriots.[45]

Back inside the bank, John was frantically trying to figure out a way to secure the bank employees so that he and Sal could make a clean getaway. His plan had been to lock them all in the vault and later that evening, with enough distance between himself and the bank, call the police to have them let out. But one of the employees said that motion sensors inside the vault would trigger an alarm if it were closed with people inside. John and Sal and the employees dickered for a minute about how to keep them from tripping an alarm as soon as they left. One of John's ideas—poorly received by all involved—was to make everyone strip naked and lock them in the conference room.[46]

While John and the employees went back and forth, the phone rang again. Barrett answered. He listened for a moment, then said, "Yes." A few more moments passed. He glanced up at John and Sal, who were by now quietly arguing about what to do next. He turned away, "To the robber?" he asked. He listened for a bit and set the phone down on the desk. He nervously made his way to John, for the first time seriously considering the possibility that he might get shot. "Uh, believe it or not," he said softly, "you have a phone call."[47]

8. enough to send you back in time

George McGovern was doomed.

As John Wojtowicz pulled his guns in Brooklyn, McGovern was eating a steak lunch with former president Lyndon Johnson at LBJ's Texas ranch. The left wing of the Democratic Party had gotten their man a month earlier, when McGovern won an unlikely nomination as the party's candidate for president. The official party platform that year called for an immediate withdrawal from Vietnam, amnesty for war resisters, enactment of the Equal Rights Amendment, a universal income, and the use of busing to achieve school desegregation. A plank to call for gay rights was considered but rejected. Instead, the Democrats passed a resolution supporting "the right to be different."

Johnson, broken by the war and his rejection by the American populace, had largely retreated from the public eye since leaving the White House. He had let his white hair grow long and was smoking heavily, despite a recent health scare that left him sickly and weak. He knew better than to offer McGovern his full support. His name was too poisoned for that. Not that it really mattered. McGovern was already trailing President

Richard Nixon by double digits in the polls when news broke that his running mate, Missouri Senator Thomas Eagleton, had been hospitalized in the early 1960s for depression and had twice undergone electroshock treatments. After initially supporting Eagleton, McGovern changed course and dropped him from the ticket in early August. By the time he met with LBJ, McGovern was in a twenty-plus point hole.

While McGovern ate steak with Johnson and police cruisers quietly pulled into position around the Chase Manhattan in Brooklyn, delegates to the Republic National Convention absorbed curses from the few thousand anti-war protesters who'd descended on Miami Beach in hopes of reinvigorating their movement. In 1968, at the Democratic National Convention in Chicago, they had been on the receiving end of a brutal police riot that left hundreds injured and made it seem as though a revolution from the streets up might truly be in the offing. But the movement was tired by 1972. Even though the public now largely agreed that the war in Vietnam was a colossal mistake, the movement itself found little love among the silent majority. "One, two, three, four, we don't want your fucking war," they chanted at the luxury cars streaming into the convention site. Neither did the American people, but most of them also thought Richard Nixon was the best man to end it.

Later that evening, after officially being renominated as the GOP standard-bearer, Nixon and his entourage traveled to Miami Marine Stadium on Biscayne Bay, where a Young Republican rally was underway. The headliner at the event was Sammy Davis Jr., the Rat Packer and registered Democrat. Davis stopped the show to introduce Nixon, and the crowd went wild. As Nixon gave a brief stump speech, in which he declared his faith in the American Dream and made overt appeals to young voters, Davis—dressed in bell-bottom pants and a white linen shirt open to the waist—wrapped the president up from behind in a gleeful hug. It produced a remarkable image: The neurotic and pale Nixon, fingers folded and arms tight at his side, grins awkwardly as Davis leans into the embrace, a wide smile on his face as it presses against the shoulder of Nixon's plain, gray suit jacket. It was an instantly iconic photograph—a baffling intersection of race, culture, and political power that could have made sense only in 1972.

But it's not what New Yorkers would be talking about the next day.

BACK IN BROOKLYN, bank manager Barrett handed John the telephone. At his feet was an attaché case with nearly $38,000 in cash and another $175,000 in traveler's checks. It wasn't life-changing money, but it was real money. Enough to keep Sal in ice cream for a while, if not the rest of his life. Enough for John to get Liz her operation and to settle some of his outstanding debts. It was enough for the effort—if only they'd managed to get out of the bank two goddamn minutes sooner.[1]

"We've got the bank surrounded," the voice on the line said. It belonged to Lieutenant Maurice Beers. "Put down your guns and come out through the front door and things will be much easier for you." John said nothing. "Are you there?"[2]

"Yeah," he said. He paused again, then slammed down the phone. Sal asked if it was the cops. John said it was. Another long pause. "I gotta think."[3]

Barrett watched the color drain from John's face. "That look of disbelief that he gave me," Barrett said later. "That was one of the, one of the most nervous minutes of this whole affair."[4]

Indeed, that might have been the moment when it all came to an end. There was no plan for escape should the cops show up—because there would be no escape if the cops showed up. And there would be no capture. John, Sal, and Robert had all agreed beforehand: Either they get away clean or end it messy. The only acceptable options were success or suicide. Sal was most serious about the pact. He would not, under any circumstance, return to prison. He had his reasons. Robert had gone along with the plan, but—just as with his participation in the robbery—he was just going along. Back out on the sidewalk, he'd fled as soon as the cops arrived. He left the car and took the subway home. But John, running off the same delusions that had brought him into the bank in the first damn place, wasn't yet certain he couldn't talk his way out of it all.[5]

John asked Barrett if the building had a back door. He replied that it did, and John sent Sal to peek outside to see if the place was indeed surrounded. John and everyone else stood frozen for a moment. Sal returned and said that there were cops everywhere. More than a dozen patrol cars were already on the scene and fifty officers had taken positions covering both exits and every other possible angle of the building. And they'd keep coming. By now, police band radio chatter had alerted the media to the active bank robbery with a possible hostage component. Newspaper photographers and television camera operators probably knew about John and Sal's predicament before they even did.[6]

"Great," John said to no one in particular. "This is just great."[7]

Back in Manhattan, word reached Special Agent Dick Baker of the FBI that two gunmen had taken hostages in a Brooklyn bank. The regular head of the New York field office's criminal division was out of town, leaving Baker as the special agent in charge. Baker, fifty-one, was a twenty-five-year veteran of the bureau. He was tall, fit, gray haired, and handsome. Despite his present New York assignment, he still spoke with a distant twang—a remnant of his North Carolina upbringing. The attempted bank robbery earlier in the day hadn't been worth Baker's attention, but a hostage situation was different. If things devolved to the point where serious negotiations needed to take place, Baker would be the man in charge. He had plans to have dinner with his wife that evening. All day long, he'd been hoping for a quiet afternoon.[8]

Meanwhile, cops continued to stream into Brooklyn. As crews worked to set up a direct phone line into the bank, some two hundred officers and FBI agents surrounded the bank. Nearly forty squad cars were stationed around the scene, as well as a smattering of ambulances and other safety vehicles. Lieutenant Beers commandeered the Palestine Barber Shop across the street and a few doors up from the bank as a temporary command post, where he was joined by several security agents from Chase Manhattan's corporate headquarters. Neighbors and passersby began to stop and rubberneck. On one corner, a Red Cross station wagon set a table for water and coffee for the officers and agents. Men readied rifles and machine guns, pulled bulletproof vests over their heads, and prepared gas masks.[9]

Back inside the bank, Ball was trying not to let her nerves show. She couldn't yet get a read on the two men with the guns, and she did not want to show fear. At fifty, she was the seniormost hostage and felt protective of her fellow tellers. Several of them—Maureen Andrews (twenty-eight), Kathy Amore (twenty-two), and Santa Strazzella (twenty-one)—were young enough that they could have been her daughters. Dolores Goettisheim, the forty-eight-year-old assistant manager, had been working for Chase Manhattan for thirty years. A devout Catholic, she began to pray nearly as soon as the ordeal began to unfold. Josephine Tutino—the only of the hostages who did not live in Brooklyn—was forty-two. She felt the early stages of dread and trauma creeping near as John and Sal tried to figure out what to do next. Manager Barrett tried his best to keep out of their way while still trying to hold a kind of muted command over his bank. Only the guard—the burly twenty-four-year-old Calvin Jones—let his fear show. He begged them not to shoot and went on and on about his sickly mother.[10]

As the gravity of the situation set in, Ball summoned the nerve to make a request. She had to use the bathroom. She got John's attention. "I've got to go to the john," she said. John stared at her hard for a few agonizing seconds. Trust—never something that John offered liberally to others—would be needed if he was going to get through this, if everyone was going to get through this. His face softened. "Okay, let's go," he said. "You and me." He led Ball into the women's room and checked the empty stalls, under the sink, and behind the door. "Make yourself comfortable," he said and left Ball to her business.[11]

Back among the hostages, John set down some ground rules. They could use the bathroom, watch television, make phone calls—do, mostly, as they pleased. "But no tricks," he declared. Sal said nothing, continuing to level his gun at the group. Several of the hostages took a moment to use the restroom or call home, explaining what was happening, downplaying how afraid they were and admitting they had no idea when the gunmen might be through with the whole thing.[12]

Around 4:30, while the city cops were across the street installing a direct phone line—complete with a red receiver that would connect directly to Mayor John Lindsay's office—John picked up a phone and dialed Patsy Coppola. "Pat, guess what I just did . . ." John said. "I robbed a bank. Get down here quick."[13]

Shortly after, Sal took the phone and dialed the Penny Candy Store on Seventh Avenue. He was supposed to work that afternoon. Stephen Brockelman, the store's manager, picked up. In a calm, apologetic tone, Sal said he was sorry for being late and that he wasn't going to be able to make it in that day. In fact, he probably wouldn't be in for the rest of the week. "We're holding up a bank," he admitted.[14]

"Can't you just walk to the door and give yourself up, Sal?" Brockelman pleaded. He had interviewed Sal for the job months before in the living room of Joe Manganello, owner of the shop and Brockelman's neighbor. Despite Sal's past, Brockelman found him to be a kind, honest kid. "Come on, man. You know whatever you're doing won't work."

Sal ignored the advice. He had to go. "Tell Joe hi," he said before hanging up.[15]

THE OFFICERS AND agents already on the scene had made almost no progress. John's only demand thus far had been for the cops on the street—the ones with bulletproof vests and guns aimed at the bank's front doors—to move back. He appeared at the front windows of the building and shouted at a cop to clear them out. He emerged through the glass double doors, stripped down to his slacks and an undershirt in the early evening heat, and gesticulated and shouted. "Go on, you fuckin' guys, get the hell out of here," he said. "How many times do I have to tell you guys to get out of here."[16]

Word of the robbery had hit the news by now. It landed on the wires at just the right time, when drive time audiences would be looking for something to hold their attention on the commute home. Someone inside the bank turned on a radio, and chatter about the developing situation in Brooklyn poured forth. Perhaps emboldened by the attention, John reappraised his situation. It felt a lot like the marriage license zap from the year before, when he and his GAA comrades had taken over a city office and made it a spectacle. Perhaps he'd been looking at this the wrong way.

He picked up the phone and was connected to the police command center. He had a demand, he told them. He wanted to see his wife. If his wife was brought to the scene, he'd release a hostage. A cop asked where they could find his wife. "His name is Ernie Aron," John replied.

"His name?" the cop asked.

"Yeah, it's a man, so what? We're married," John said. "Three hundred people came to the wedding. They got poor Ernie penned up at Kings County Hospital, they think he's crazy."[17]

As a squad car was dispatched to Kings County, David Levin, a reporter for WCBS radio who had received word of the holdup, decided to take a chance and call the bank. Someone picked up, and he asked to speak with one of the robbers. To his surprise, John took the call. Levin introduced himself. "Is CBS Walter Cronkite?" John asked. Levin said that it was. "I like him," John replied in an even voice. Levin asked John what had happened.

"Well, we were holding up a bank, and we were on the way out till the stupid cop car pulled up in front." He spoke in a calm tone, almost as if he were talking through a tight smirk.

"What's going on now?"

"We're waiting to negotiate the release of the people so we can get outta here."

"Are you holding them hostage?"

"Yep."

"Could you tell me how you're armed?"

"Well, we have shotguns, we have rifles, and we have a bomb."

"How many hostages are you holding in there?"

"Eight or nine."

"And what are your terms for release?"

"Well, I want them to deliver my wife here from Kings County Hospital. When they deliver me my wife, I'll release one of the hostages. And then we'll negotiate from there. Every time they do something for me, I'll let one of the people go."

It was all so matter of fact to John. Levin asked for his name, and he gave it, carefully spelling out Wojtowicz. He asked where he lived, and John replied, "In Brooklyn," the same way you might answer someone at a party in the midst of a boring conversation.

"Which hospital is your wife in again?"

"Her name is Ernest Aron. It's a guy. I'm gay."

After a pregnant pause, Levin asked if—after the hostages were all released—John expected to "get his own release."

John paused and, for the first time in the brief interview, stumbled over his words. "Let's put it this way, I expect to get out of here. Now I know they're gonna get me sooner or later, but they gotta play it cool. After I release the last hostage, you know, then they can come and take us, right? There's no use in us blasting everybody in here. Because, first of all, the Supreme Court did away with capital punishment, right? That means I can kill everybody in here and throw down the gun and walk outside, and they can't shoot me and they can't give me the gas chamber. And that's why the Supreme Court's stupid."

After a bit more on Supreme Court politics, John said that he had to go and hung up.[18]

CBS aired the interview at 5:09 p.m., and from there the story took off. A bank robbery in Brooklyn in 1972 was about as interesting as a stolen bicycle, hostages added an angle but still didn't really give the story legs. But a *gay* bank robber holding hostages made it something worthy of cutting away from a regularly scheduled program. No one in the media was willing to explain why the gay angle suddenly made the story worthy of the attention usually reserved for an assassination attempt, but the straight viewing public wasn't really pressing for one anyway. It was all part of the unspoken assumption of the time that any part of straight life—even a bank holdup—was just *different* when it was part of a gay American's life.

As New York was getting home from work, kicking off its shoes and wondering what to have for dinner, news of the "admitted homosexual" holding hostages in a Brooklyn bank was all over the radio and television. Carmen had even heard a report of the robbery on her portable radio at Rockaway Beach, where she'd taken the kids to try to escape the heat, but didn't think much of it. Patsy called Terry Wojtowicz and filled her in before she could hear it on the news. They quickly met up and rushed to the scene.[19]

Gary Badger, the eighteen-year-old bartender who'd befriended Sal in the Village, heard about the robbery and caught John's name. Badger went to the Penny Candy Store, hoping to find out that Sal had finally summoned the sense to detach himself from John and his crazy bullshit. Sal wasn't there, of course, but he waited around for a while, hoping that he'd call back. Brockelman, who was behind the counter at the time, called Joe Manganello, who'd been watching the robbery unfold on television. "Sal just called," he said. "He's robbing a bank."

"Oh shit," Manganello said. "Goddamn it. The one in Brooklyn?" Manganello paused. "Close the store. If you need some cash, take it from the register. Just leave and lock the door. We'll talk when you get home."[20]

Brockelman did as instructed and headed back to his apartment, where he and Manganello would spend the rest of the night glued to the television, drinking gin and wishing for the best. Badger went to the nearest police precinct, hoping for a ride or at least directions to the bank. He knew that Sal would rather die than go back to prison. He wanted to do what he could to keep anyone from getting killed. The cops at the station had no time for Gary's concerns about his friend. They sat him down and grilled him for information before turning him loose. He found his own way to Avenue P.[21]

Back inside the bank, the phone would not stop ringing. After WCBS broke the queer angle to the situation—and made it clear that the man at the center of it all was giving interviews—nearly every media outlet in town took note. Over the course of multiple phone interviews, including at least one that was broadcast live, John continued his bizarre harangue against the Supreme Court. Two months earlier, in *Furman v. Georgia,* the court had voided all existing state laws that allowed for the death penalty.* He even claimed that he wouldn't have gone through with the robbery if not for the ruling. "This way," he told one reporter, "you don't have nothing to lose, it's stupid."[22]

John also made claims about his willingness to kill that belied his soft and measured tone and his friendly treatment of the hostages. "I'll shoot everyone in the bank," he answered a reporter who'd asked what he'd do if his demands were not met. He said he'd have the police draw names from a hat, blast a hole

* In the aftermath of *Furman,* thirty-seven states enacted new death penalty statutes, the constitutionality of which were upheld by the court in 1976. Executions resumed in 1977.

in whoever's name was drawn, and "send out the body." He made these threats at the same time as admitting his fear. He was scared, he told one reporter, "more scared than the hostages, I'm really nervous."[23]

The interviews quickly took on a standard format: Are you a homosexual? *Sure, I am, so what?* Is your wife really a man who is being held in a mental hospital? *Yeah, they've got him locked up, but they're gonna bring him to me or I'll start killing people.* You really feel that you can kill? *Yeah.* The only obfuscation John offered was giving the press Sal's alias, Donald Matterson, instead of his real name. As for his own identity: *Here's what it is, here's how to spell it, I'm from Brooklyn, I was in the service, I used to work in a bank, I've also got a female wife and two kids and . . .*

Reporter Steve Bauman broke the alleged motive for the robbery, the lead story on the Channel 5 news. "Detectives reached one of the stickup men, who identified himself as John Wojtowicz, by telephone," he relayed from the scene. "He first told them he tried the robbery to get his homosexual lover out of the psychiatric ward of Kings County Hospital. He demanded that the man he identified as his wife be brought to the bank in exchange for one of the hostages." Bauman then played the audio from a phone interview John had just given to another Channel 5 reporter. He said that he'd kill the people if he had to. And then he started in on the Supreme Court.[24]

John no doubt liked the attention from the interviews. The little man with no job and no prospects, who was once an ambitious young Goldwaterite full of energy and potential, was finally at the center of a universe beyond his own. But beyond the rush from this sudden burst of fame, John had a purpose in all this madness: He was desperately trying to save his own ass.

Certainly, it was no stretch for John to play the role of martyr.

He'd been skirting blame and aggrandizing himself long before he'd gathered up his guns and took on the Chase Manhattan Bank. Whether it was calculated or simply the only way in which his nature allowed him to react to the given situation, John—smirking into the heavy telephone receiver, gun on his shoulder and Sal waiting in the corner to act on his commands—needed the world to see that he wasn't really a bad guy, just a lovelorn idealist who'd gotten in too deep and trusted the wrong people.

First off, he needed people to know about the man he'd met at Danny's. He was well dressed, a man with a good salary and probably a wife and family somewhere far, far away from the Village. He was an executive at Chase Manhattan, a "big shot," according to John. He knew how the money moved among the bank's various city branches—what would go where, when, and how much. John was drinking with him one night, the executive dressed in the fashions of the straight world and John in hot pants, when the executive told him how a smart fellow with the right weaponry could score an easy $200,000. According to John, he was told that an armored car delivery was to bring a few hundred grand in cash to the Brooklyn branch shortly after closing that day. It was roughly the amount that he'd told Sal and Robert about—accounting for their share of $50,000 each once John took his half and paid the executive for the information. But something had gotten crossed up. The money was picked up, not dropped off. And the resulting delay in trying to figure everything out kept them inside the bank just long enough for the police to show up. In one telling of the story, to a man from the *Daily News,* John was asked for the executive's name. "I won't tell you because I'll use that for negotiating with the police," John coolly replied.[25]

Aside from John's claims to the media and, later, to the FBI (which he'd quickly recant), there is no evidence to suggest that this Chase Manhattan executive actually existed. John did gripe about the lack of money in the vault upon discovering that it was nearly empty, but the actions of John and his confederates earlier that day—before they'd settled on robbing the Avenue P branch—contradict the entire story. Why would they attempt to rob several other banks, knowing all the while of the goldmine in Brooklyn? Nor did any aspect of their preparation for the robbery—the note, the roles they were each assigned, their arms—suggest that they were planning to take down an armored car delivery. To knock off a bank was one thing, to hit a Brink's delivery of nearly a quarter million dollars and initiate a gunfight was quite another. But the basic concept of John's claim—a straitlaced and perhaps closeted banker surrendering information in a gay bar with mob ties—closely mirrored that of the kind of ongoing extortion schemes favored by Mike Umbers.

And then there was Liz. Aside from getting the cops to back off, the only demand he had yet made was to have his wife brought to him. He explained that she was at Kings County Hospital and suggested that her stay there was involuntary. Some reporters—like Steve Bauman of Channel 5—mistook this to mean that the robbery and Liz's release from the hospital were somehow connected, all part of the same plan. This, of course, held logic only if the hostages were part of the plan, which they were certainly not. Others seemed to take it all to mean that he wanted her nearby for support, perhaps as a means of facilitating a surrender. But no one yet made any connection between Liz, the money, and Liz's desire for gender-affirming surgery. John hadn't yet mentioned that to the media. In fact, it wasn't clear that he had yet told anyone that the money was for Liz and her surgery.[26]

Liz was in her room at Kings County Hospital that evening. The smell of barbecue and the thick summer air still clung to her robe. While the drugs they'd been feeding her were no longer being administered at coma-inducing levels, she was still pretty well doped and dreamy. The doctor, nurse, and the two men standing behind them appeared almost out of nowhere. The doctor told Liz that these two men wished to talk to her. The men identified themselves as FBI agents. They asked her if she had a friend named John. She said that she did. They told her that John was holding some people somewhere and that he wanted to talk to her. Suddenly, Liz was overtaken with fear. "Oh God," she thought, "these are the Mafia friends he sent for me and they're going to kill me."[27]

Liz said that if someone wanted to talk to her, they could come to the hospital. She insisted she wasn't going anywhere, not with these men, not with anyone. The doctor spoke calmly to Liz and insisted that these were indeed real FBI agents and that there was a bad situation where she was needed. The men showed their badges, but she wouldn't even look. "I couldn't see my own hand, let alone a badge," she remembered. After some cajoling and a lot of reassuring, the cobwebs began to clear, and Liz started to listen. John had been crazy all summer and this—this possible end to it all—slowly began to make sense. Liz agreed to go with them, so long as she was promised that it wouldn't get out on the ward that she was anything but a straight man and so long as the doctor, the one she liked, came with her.[28]

The nurse prepped a pair of syringes and quickly shot Liz up with a couple of doses of God-knows-what, and she was whisked off to a waiting patrol car. By the time she was eased into the back seat, she was almost completely out of it again. She was propped between a pair of agents, and in her ragdoll state, she laid her head across one of their chests. She later recalled looking up at the agent, then to the other one. *Just my luck,* she thought. Only one of the two was cute, and it wasn't the one she was draped all over.[29]

The car tailed another cop car that ran with sirens and lights blazing as they sped through red lights and weaved through traffic. Liz's head rolled back so that she was staring upward out the back. Clouds and treetops whizzed past, warm winds washed all over her from the open windows, and the hard pitch of the sirens rang in her ears. As they slowed, nearing the scene, she saw helicopters. One, then another, then another: television cameras getting pictures of the massive police presence and thousands of onlookers from above. *Helicopters?* she thought.[30]

There was another jolt of fear. *The airport.* It was where John had taken her that horrible afternoon when she'd woken up to a gun in her face. *Goddamn it,* she thought, *they'd fooled her.* She jerked away from the agents and refused to leave the car once they'd parked. They were at the airport, she insisted, these men were not with the FBI. They were friends of John's, and they were going to kill her.[31]

After some more convincing from the doctor, Liz came around. He asked her to look and focus. The crowds, the police cars, the block of storefronts and shops with their keepers clustered in their doorways. This was not the airport, he told her, this was all very real and this was all happening and they needed her help. Slowly and cautiously, she climbed out of the car. "I couldn't believe how many people were standing there," she recalled. The FBI agents led her and the doctor to the barbershop. Along the way, a newspaper photographer snapped a picture. Liz is in a terry-cloth bathrobe, tied around the waist. Her left hand clutches the robe at the neck. Her eyes are narrow and face the sidewalk. There is a man on each side of her. To her left is a plainclothes FBI agent in a striped collared shirt, a stocky white man with a bad attempt at feathered hair. To her right is the doctor, a Black man with a tight afro and a dark suit jacket with a loudly patterned tie. Liz's hand is wrapped around his as they walk. All three look worried, but she looks terrified. A few years later, thinking back on that day, Liz couldn't help but be hung up on that photo. "Ugh, what a picture," she recalled. "Enough to send you back in time . . . I look like something who done it and ran."[32]

By now, many in the crowd—which had swelled to several thousand people—had heard the reports that one and maybe both bank robbers were "admitted homosexuals," and that one had asked for his "male wife" to be brought to the scene. As Liz was led to the barbershop, the crowd reacted with a mix of cheers, boos, and catcalls. She didn't hear them. She didn't even notice John on the other side of the street. He was out in front of the bank, once again telling the cops to move back and to holster their weapons. His partner was inside, he kept reminding them, and he'd kill everyone if he had to. Just inside the barbershop, Liz happened to turn around. She finally saw John, acting as crazy as ever in his undershirt and with a rifle slung over his shoulder. All at once, it finally overwhelmed her. She collapsed.[33]

9. gunshot

It was clear by 5:30 p.m. that Dick Baker would not be dining with his wife that evening. The siege in Brooklyn was now over two hours old and the moment where John and Sal might have become overwhelmed by the realization of what they'd done and surrendered without incident had come and gone. Attention from the media and the public seemed to only reinforce John's determination to stay inside the bank. His mother, Liz, and at least one of his partners were now on the scene. And he showed no fear or trepidation at all in dealing with the city cops who surrounded the building. Indeed, it appeared that he was reveling in barking orders at the cops and watching them reluctantly do as he said. As Liz was being revived in the barbershop, Baker and Chief of Detectives Louis Cottell were on the ground in Brooklyn, working up a plan to give the FBI greater authority over the matter. Baker would act as lead negotiator, with the bureau in charge of all matters inside the bank and the NYPD taking charge of everything going on outside.[1]

Circus was the only word that came to mind when Cottell observed the scene around the bank. By his own estimate, about five thousand people were in the streets, squinting against the setting sun. It was still about ninety degrees outside, and many in the crowd seemed content to stand around and gape when the only other option was a stuffy apartment and reruns of *Petticoat Junction, I Love Lucy,* and *Hogan's Heroes* on television.* Hot dog vendors and soda cart operators had stationed themselves on street corners, and the pizza parlor just up the block from the bank reported doing record business. At a glance, the crowd was as diverse a gathering as you'd find in Brooklyn: kids, burnouts, street people, businessmen in light summer suits, and Orthodox Jews in long black coats. It seemed nearly every other person was eating something, giving the whole incident the feel of a block party.[2]

Cottell had the masses moved back, securing a block-long restricted radius around the bank. Cops on the detail looked anxious, worried that the crowd might provoke the gunmen into violence. As a whole, the group had an attitude: sarcastic and loud with a tinge of antiauthoritarian cynicism. They hooted and catcalled when John appeared on the street. They jeered the cops. They waited for something—good or bad—to happen. "We're out of our minds, but curiosity kills," one man in the crowd told a reporter. "I'd just like to see some action." But mostly the crowd stood and murmured, watching only the shadows on the curtains in the bank's huge front windows.[3]

A *New York Post* reporter spoke with a forty-seven-year-old man who was seated on the curb near a shuttered newsstand. His head of all-white hair belied his age. "I think he's scared

* These broadcasts would all end up being preempted by Channel 5's coverage of the robbery. Coverage of the Republican National Convention—as well as Channel 4's broadcast of *Snoopy at the Ice Follies*—would air unimpeded.

now. He knows he's going to do time," the man said. He was something of an authority on the matter. He'd done thirteen years, he told the reporter, for robbing a bank in Baltimore in 1949. Since he'd gotten out of prison, he had married and made a good life for himself. The man noted the police department brass idling on the sidewalk "whenever there's a big crowd," he said with a grin. "Maybe these kids," he said of the gunmen, "we ought to give them a little heart too. They didn't mug anybody off the street. They didn't hurt an individual. The insurance companies will take care of whatever is lost."[4]

BACK IN THE barbershop, Liz had regained her senses but was refusing to go see John. Terry Wojtowicz and Patsy Coppola had joined her there. Both Terry and Patsy were willing to go to the bank doors to try to talk John into surrendering, but for the moment, he wanted only Liz. She was finally convinced to speak to him over the phone when John agreed to trade the phone call for a hostage. But only after he heard Liz's voice. She agreed and someone handed her a receiver. Liz would later recall little of the conversation, the particulars lost in the haze of terror and whatever drugs she'd been shot up with at the hospital. She told him that he needed to let the people go. John said that he couldn't, that Sal wouldn't let him. She told him that he had to give himself up. John said no, that if he did that, Sal would kill everyone. He might have told her about the money, that it was for her and her operation, his lifesaving gift to her. He might have said it, but Liz didn't remember.[5]

As they spoke, the front doors of the bank opened and Calvin Jones emerged—frazzled and worn, but free. He lit a cigarette and flashed a peace sign. He'd been the only one of the hostages to beg for his release. He'd been so annoying about it that most of his coworkers were glad to see him go. Oddly enough, Liz recognized Jones. "He lived right near Dean Street when [I lived] on Dean Street . . . I saw him all the time," Liz recalled. "And he always thank[ed] me for saving his life."[6]

During their call, John had tried to convince Liz to meet him at the front door, but she still couldn't bring herself to get that close to the whole, awful situation. "How do you like this thing?" he said to Barrett after the phone call. "What I'm doing for her, and that silly bitch won't even come in here and talk to me."[7]

John's mind was a gelatinous mess, moving in all different directions at once, full of contingencies and dead ends. Sal was almost no help. He was keeping everyone in line, but whenever John considered the possibility of giving up, he just wouldn't listen. And the goddamn phone kept ringing. The more it rang, the less John seemed to enjoy answering. Cranks from all over the city were dialing up the bank just for a thrill. More than one of them claimed to be Liz, trying to catch some hot talk from John. One weird and gravelly voice kept calling back, whispering, "Kill them all," to whoever picked up. Barrett answered one such call, and the voice seemed to know that he was a hostage. "I hope they kill you all," he growled.[8]

In bits and pieces, John had opened up about Liz to a few of the hostages. He told Barrett about her. He'd confided in Ball that she badly wanted her surgery and that the money from the robbery could provide it (this was, incidentally, the only recorded instance of John mentioning the operation during the robbery). Ball remembered feeling pity for him. A mixed-up young man trying to do his best to make the person he loved happy. It wasn't that simple, of course, but John sold it in the way he spoke about Liz and the way he hung his shoulders.

The assumption would have been that John wanted to see Liz at the door for support, for help in working his way out of this whole situation, for the same reasons human nature urges one to reach out for loved ones in times of distress. But that wasn't what John wanted. The suicide pact that John had agreed to with Sal and Robert—the one that made certain there would be no capture—included Liz. The plan was for Sal and Robert to kill themselves straight away, but John would wait. He'd wait until he could get Liz out of the hospital and coax her to the front door. There, he would shoot her in the face and then turn the gun on himself.[9]

But she wouldn't come to the door. She couldn't get shot, and John couldn't move on.

Patsy was willing to see him at the door. Patsy was always willing. The young man who considered himself to be John's "mistress" spent a few minutes at the door, an FBI agent close behind him, again trying to make a case for John to surrender. John again said that he couldn't, that Sal wouldn't let him and that he couldn't leave the hostages alone with him. Whatever intentions John had had with Liz, he seemed genuinely concerned for the eight people still left inside. As the ordeal dragged on, he increasingly saw himself in the role of a caretaker. He was in it, and now he couldn't get out.

But in the minutes since he'd gotten off the phone, he'd hatched a plan. Just before he met Patsy at the door, he hid $5,000 in his pocket. Patsy was just about to leave when John called him back. "Come back, Pat," John said. "Come back here, I want to kiss you." And with an FBI agent pulling him back by the belt, thousands watching in the streets, and TV cameras broadcasting live, Patsy leaned in while John gave him a deep, open-mouthed kiss. The crowd reacted with a stunned mixture of cheers and whoops (with a few boos). Amid the embrace, John slipped the cash down the front of Patsy's pants. "Go give it to Ernie," he whispered.[10]

The kiss—perhaps the first gay kiss ever broadcast live on U.S. television—had been such a shock that no one noticed John slip Patsy the cash. It was the amount that John had promised Liz, more than enough to pay for her surgery. After he flashed the hooting crowd a few "Italian salutes"—the bend-one-arm-and-slap-your-bicep "up yours" motion—Patsy wandered back to the barbershop. In a moment when he hoped no one was watching, he called Liz aside. "Johnny told me to give this to you," he whispered and slipped the cash into the pocket of her robe. "And just as he stuck it in my bathrobe," Liz recalled, "the cops came along and grabbed it. Someone was five thousand dollars richer."[11]

JOHN'S FRUSTRATIONS—WITH THE police, with Liz, with whoever had given the bad information on how much money was in the bank—helped to humanize him in the eyes of his hostages. He was open about his life and his troubles. He talked about Carmen and his kids, about Liz, about his health. He confided to Barrett that he thought he was dying. "I'm a dead man anyway," he said more than once. He displayed genuine concern for Liz's well-being but little for his own safety. It was all for her, he'd tell them, even if he was a little short on specifics.[12]

"I'm supposed to hate you guys," Barrett told John, "but I've had more laughs tonight than I've had in weeks." John himself was often the object of amusement. The way he'd pace the floor and flail his arms when he was working on something in his head, the pitch of his heavy Brooklynese when he was trying to make a point. More than once, Barrett and others would tell him to slow down and relax.[13]

"I want people out there, I want reporters out there," John shouted at one point. "They're what's keeping me alive . . . Hey! I want to talk to Jackie Jensen. Lemme talk to Jackie Jensen."

Barrett grinned. "You want Jackie Jensen? Jackie Jensen used to play for the Yankees, John," he said, recalling the former outfielder and 1958 American League MVP. "You want *Jim* Jensen, of CBS."

"Yeah! That's him!" John exclaimed.[14]

At another point, John peeked out the front window at a police sniper. "What d'ya think of that sonofabitch?" he asked Barrett. "He really wants me; he wants me in the worst way."

Barrett laughed. "Yeah, John, I guess he does."[15]

John also formed a rapport with Ball, whose willingness to speak bluntly led John to refer to her as "Mouth," the same nickname he'd given to Carmen years earlier. "John called me 'Mouth' because I was the talkative one. It was, 'Hey, Mouth, do this' and 'Hey, Mouth, do that,'" Ball said later. "If they had been my houseguests on a Saturday night, it would have been hilarious. Especially with John's antics, the way he hopped all over the place, the way he talked . . . I really liked them both. Such aboveboard guys, they even told us they would kill us if they had to."[16]

John even continued his lamentations about the death penalty with the hostages. "Now, I can shoot you and they won't give me the gas chamber," John explained to Barrett. "But if I shoot a cop, I get it. Now I wonder: If I put a gun at your head and another gun in your hand and made you shoot the cop, would you get it?" All Barrett could do was laugh and tell John he had no idea.[17]

But if John made the evening feel like a cocktail party, Sal was the reminder of how horribly things could still possibly turn out. He said little and never put down his gun. "I thought he had the coldest eyes," Dolores Goettisheim said later. "Very blue, but very cold. Steel-like." He became agitated when John agreed to release Jones in exchange for Liz's phone call. He thought John was too willing to give the police what they wanted. When a report went out over the radio that the bank was being robbed by "two homosexuals," Sal took great offense. He knew what happened to known homosexuals in jail. He was near pathological about making sure nothing like that would ever happen to him again. More than once, he pointed his pistol at John when he felt like he was giving away too much to the cops. Soon enough, the primary concern among the hostages was that someone would attempt a swashbuckling rescue. It was in Sal's eyes. He'd never allow that to happen without a bloodbath.[18]

DICK BAKER FELT like the whole situation had gotten out of control. So long as the gunmen were still inside the bank, he felt that they had an upper hand. Attempts to negotiate with John had accomplished little aside from the release of Jones. Any willingness John had for making serious concessions was stunted by the rush of media attention and the cheers he heard whenever he appeared on the sidewalk, strutting and giving orders with a gun on his shoulder. Baker had a plan—one he knew would not be popular with either the gunmen or the hostages. He wanted to stall. Any demand, any request, any question—make them wait. Delay all decisions, counter any offer, and drag their feet. "With the passage of time, you wear down your adversary, and as time goes by, your options develop," Baker said later. "We were playing for an opening."[19]

But first Baker wanted to know about the snipers. Were they in place? Did any of them have a clear line of sight into the bank? Cottell said that they were, and that a few of them could see through the narrow gaps in the curtains with a clear view of the interior. His strategy of waiting for an opening only worked so long as the threats remained constant. If the rhetoric or actions from inside the bank were to spike, the wait-and-see part of the evening would probably be over. He hated the thought of it, the chaos and likelihood for harm to the innocent, but he needed that option of luring one or both of the gunmen near to the front of the building, in between those little gaps in the curtains.[20]

But before anyone did anything, Baker wanted to get inside the bank. He wanted to assess their arsenal and get a firsthand view of the bandits on their own turf. All the police and FBI knew about John—beyond the information he'd volunteered to reporters—was that he had no police record. They knew a bit about the man they thought was named Matterson, that he had a short and petty rap sheet, and they sensed he might be the more dangerous of the two. John was the one who liked to talk, Matterson preferred just to point his gun. John had talked of giving up but said that his partner wouldn't allow it. Baker figured that he might be able to reason with John. Matterson, on the other hand, might need to be dealt with in other ways.[21]

Sometime between 7:30 and 8:00 p.m., Baker tried to get John's attention with a police bullhorn and get him out on the street, figuring it would be easier to get inside if both men stood eye to eye on the sidewalk. There was no reply. Baker went back to the barbershop, where Liz was eating some pizza that the FBI had gotten for her, and called the bank. John answered.

"Mr. Wojtowicz?" Baker asked.

"Whaddya want this time?" John replied.

"This is the FBI. My name is Richard Baker, and I'd like to come over and talk to you."

"Yeah?" John answered. "What about?"

"John, I'm sure you're aware that your situation, and your friend's, is hopeless as it exists." Baker spoke in even, deliberate tones. He'd turned over the words he was going to use in his head beforehand, choosing each with care. "I'd like to talk with you and explain how we can end this terrible thing with no one getting hurt. Right now, the basic charge against you is armed bank robbery."

Words chosen with care, if not with complete honesty.

"Why can't we just talk over the phone?" John asked.

"John, I'd really like to talk to you on your ground. I'd like to see for myself that those people you're holding are all right, and it would be a show of good faith if you'll agree to see me." Baker spoke firmly. John might not have even noticed that he wasn't asking for anything, he was simply stating what he was about to do. "I'm across the street in the barbershop, and I'll come over, unarmed. You can watch me through the window."

"Are you the guy in the bureau? The guy that makes decisions?"

"Yes, I am," Baker said. "Chief Louis Cottell of the New York Police Department will also accompany me. We'll both be unarmed."

John said nothing for a moment, then hung up the phone. A minute later, Baker and Cottell started across the street. When they reached the sidewalk, John cracked open the front door, the barrel of his rifle was pointed forward. Both men took off their suit jackets and made a show of handing off their service weapons to an officer who gathered everything up and retreated back across the street.

"John," Baker said. "We're coming in."

This is how they were going to play it. It was an illusion of John being in charge. They acted as though everything was being done with his consent, but they would never ask for permission. For the past several hours, John had been negotiating with anyone in a uniform, asking for space, asking for time, asking for his friends. That part was now over. He'd grown frustrated with the city cops; all they seemed to want to do was shoot his ass dead. But Baker carried the aura of a man in charge—someone John could deal with. This suited Baker's plans just fine. He'd make things happen for John, but he'd never allow the situation to slip out of control. And if it did, well, he'd try to draw up to the front of the building, near one of those little gaps in the curtains.

John dropped the barrel of the gun and slowly walked backward into the lobby. Baker and Cottell moved forward. John swore a few times—everyone inside was used to that by now—and struck a pose that suggested he was ready to listen. "I don't wanna talk to the cop," John said, staring at Baker. "Only you." The two men exchanged a glance, and Baker nodded.[22]

"You have eight hostages," Baker said. "Mr. Robert Barrett and seven female tellers. I'd like to know if they're all okay."[23]

John glanced over to Barrett. He still seemed unsure of the exact body count. Barrett nodded. Aside from being a little nervous and a little sweaty, everyone inside was physically sound. They'd need to eat soon. Anything that might have been left in the break room refrigerator was gone and a few of the hostages had taken to eating the lollipops kept behind the counter and normally used as treats for kids who got bored while their parents conducted bank business. While Baker assessed the mental state of the gunmen, Cottell made a mental inventory of their arsenal: the rifle, the pistol, the shotgun—John had clearly inflated their holdings during his telephone inventories. The object of greatest concern—the bomb he claimed to have—was nowhere to be seen.[24]

John was finally ready to deal. He wanted out. Out of the bank, out of New York, and out of U.S. jurisdiction. The plan had come to him hours ago. Despite all the tough talk and bluster, he didn't have it in him to kill. Not the hostages, not himself, and not Liz. Not just yet anyway. The fact of the matter was that John would have given Liz one last chance had she actually come to the door. He'd have asked her to come away with him, to join him and escape and leave everything else (save for Sal and a few hostages) behind. Then it would be up to her to save her own life. Say yes and she'd join the gang, bound for whereabouts unknown. Say no and everyone would learn whether John could finally back up that big mouth of his.

And, in the summer of 1972, there was one glaringly obvious method of quickly and easily escaping the country. John was going to demand a jet. The United States was in the midst of what would later be cheekily dubbed "the golden age of skyjacking." With virtually no security systems in place to screen passengers, airliner hijackings suddenly came into vogue in 1968, when twenty-nine commercial planes were taken. That total matched the number of planes hijacked worldwide between 1961 and 1967. Between 1968 and 1972, a total of 305 commercial flights were interrupted by the demands of hijackers—an average of more than one per week. Using hijacking as a means of escape from the United States had worked, and worked regularly. John was sure he could make it happen. He had to make it happen.[25]

"We want out of this place," he told Baker. "I want you to arrange for a helicopter to take me and my friend and some hostages to Kennedy, and I want a plane ready to take us to another country." If Sal showed any reaction to the change in plans—if he knew about what John was going to do at all—nobody inside seemed to notice.

"That'll be impossible, John," Baker said, who had almost certainly anticipated an aerial escape as a possible demand. "The street isn't wide enough to land a machine, and the roof is too small. I can't promise you anything, but if you let these people go, let them out the front door one at a time, and then you and Matterson come out, I can tell you you'll not be harmed, and we can end this thing right now."[26]

That was not at all what John wanted to hear. He swore some more and dismissed Baker's line of thinking. Giving up was not an option, not after all this. He thought for a minute and offered a compromise. He wanted two cars to carry him, Sal, and the hostages. "I'll go in one car with four hostages and Sal will go in the other with the rest."

Baker looked confused. "Who is Sal?"

John clarified that Sal was his partner and that Donald Matterson was a name that only existed on his rap sheet. It was a light moment for those inside who had become accustomed to the gallows humor of the evening. Here was their FBI savior, the man who could make deals, and he had already been hoodwinked by the nervous little weirdo who hardly seemed to know what he was doing.[27]

Baker made something up on the fly about federal regulations forbidding the use of government automobiles in such a situation. John bought the fib, and Baker counted it as a small but meaningful win. Why would a man holding hostages in a bank kowtow to some obscure government rule? But John was quick with a rejoinder. "How about one of those airport limos? You get me a car, and I'll let one of the girls go just to show you we want to play ball."

It was something Baker could work with. He said he'd see what he could do. He would need some time, of course, but in the meantime, would John be willing to release another hostage? John said he would see what he could do. After about a half hour inside, Baker and Cottell left the bank and walked back across the street to the barbershop. They'd bought themselves some time.[28]

IT WAS AROUND this time that Carmen realized the bank robber she'd heard about on the radio was her husband. Like a million other New Yorkers, she was following the events in Brooklyn closely. She listened on the radio at the beach, on the radio on the subway ride home, and on television that evening. She'd later claim that it was only the mispronunciation of their last name—some news outlets were saying it either "water-witz" or "woj-to-witz"—that kept her from realizing it was her Johnny. She even recalled feeling bad for this family, as the news had reported several times that he had a wife and two children in addition to his gay lover.[29]

Carmen would give several different explanations over the years as to how she found out it was John who was inside the bank: She found out from Terry, who called her and wanted her to come down to the scene; she heard it from a neighbor, who shouted it across the backyard; she heard when her priest called and told her. Terry later confirmed after arriving on the scene, she "swallowed [her] pride" and called Carmen, whom she still loathed and blamed for most of John's problems. Given the toxic relationship between the two, Carmen's varied explanations of how she found out were probably an attempt to write Terry out of her memory. However she learned of John's involvement, she couldn't will herself out the door to witness the mess in person. She told Terry that she didn't have anyone to watch her two small children. Later, she also said she didn't go on the advice of her priest, who said that her presence might make John act irrationally. Terry would never forgive her for not showing up that night, another in a long list of things she'd never forgive her for. For Carmen, just the thought of seeing her Johnny in that situation—wielding a gun and causing terror—was enough to overwhelm her. Eventually, she turned off the television, took a heavy sedative, and passed out, fully aware that her husband might be dead by the time she woke up.[30]

Meanwhile, Liz and John spoke on the phone several more times. At least once, John broke down crying. She was still trying to get him to give himself up, he was still refusing on account of what Sal might do. Terry also spoke to him on the phone. She had tried earlier to get his attention on the sidewalk, to see him at the front door, but John would not meet her. "Mom, I don't know what I'm doing," he told her. "They got me." She begged him to give up, but he couldn't be moved. The cops also brought in a psychiatrist, who spent fifteen minutes on the phone with John to no avail. They even tracked down the former Reverend John Auricchio—the librarian who had overseen John and Liz's mock marriage ceremony—but John refused to speak with him. Loved ones of the hostages were also crowded into the command post, which had by now expanded into a neighboring insurance office. Shirley Ball's husband, Harry, was there. He had come to the scene right after Ball had called him at the beginning of the standoff. Pearl Saunders was there too. Her daughter Joan was inside. Pearl Saunders wept openly as she sat in the barbershop, repeating, "She's my only child, she's my only child."[31]

There were still thousands of people in the streets, and it was late enough that the crowd was starting to get a little buggy. Some smart-ass in the crowd started up a chant of "Come out, come out!" that kept everyone entertained for a while. Meanwhile, local television stations were still breaking into their programming to give periodic updates on the situation. The police referred to John and Sal as "gay lib types" and framed the robbery as an effort by John to break his lover out of a mental hospital. Terry told reporters, "[John] said he doesn't know what he's doing. He's very harmless. Not a mean kid, [just] disturbed."[32]

Inside the bank, someone put a baseball game on the radio. The Mets were hosting the Houston Astros that night, and Tom Seaver was tossing a gem. In the bottom of the eighth inning, a Jim Beauchamp base hit scored two runs to put the Mets on top, 4–2. Seaver was coming on to finish things off when the lights went out. The bank went dark, and the air conditioner croaked to a stop. John assumed a fuse had blown. But it was really the doing of Dick Baker. He wanted to put a little pressure on the gunmen to see how they'd react. The night air was still hot and thick. It could be used to the FBI's advantage. A large spotlight had been brought down to the scene to be blasted at the front of the building. They were still working on getting those limousine vans and arranging for the plane, he could tell John, but there were certain things he'd have to do without.[33]

Baker and company waited. The crowds waited. Everyone in the barbershop waited. Several minutes passed.

The gunshot took them all by surprise.

10. the black rose of death

For a terror-stricken moment, everyone inside the bank thought that John had just executed Robert Barrett. After the lights went out, John summoned Barrett to go with him into the basement to check the fuse box. The two were gone for a few minutes. Sal watched over the hostages, silent and with his gun aimed. Some chattering was heard in the basement and then footsteps. The two were back upstairs. Some more indistinct words followed and—*bang!*

Everyone jumped. Sal dashed to the back of the building to see what had happened. And then . . . laughter.

John emerged, with Barrett and Sal. "You know," John said, "I've had to take a shit for three days, and I think this thing just drove it up further."[1]

After inspecting the basement—where he realized that the loss of power was the doing of the FBI—John wanted to reinforce the basement door against a possible covert invasion. Back upstairs, he and Barrett started to shove a heavy metal desk in front of the door when—whoops—John dropped his rifle. The gun went off and left a hole in the floor just a few inches from

John's foot. It was the kind of thing that could have happened only on a night like this.[2]

John went outside to explain the shot. The crowd, still numbering in the thousands, offered a hearty ovation. The spotlight aimed at the front of the building gave John the appearance of an actor onstage, and he reveled in the role. He barked about the lights and the lack of air-conditioning and demanded an update on his vans and his airplane. The FBI offered only vague answers. John had another demand. The people inside were hungry. He wanted food, soft drinks, and cigarettes. The FBI said they'd take care of it. At their own pace, of course.[3]

Back inside, John took another phone call, this one from a reporter for the *Daily News*. He sounded weary. "They are pretty exhausted," he said of the hostages. "One girl is throwing up. One guy [Barrett] is a diabetic and needs a shot tomorrow." He talked about how Liz refused to see him and his plan for an escape to the airport. He ranted about the Supreme Court and his distrust of the police. He offered a fairly accurate assessment of the FBI's plans for waiting him out. "The only reason we're in here all these hours is because they're waiting for us to get to the point where we know we can't get away," he said. "The point is they want us to get desperate and do something desperate." Could he really kill? "Yep, I could kill."[4]

One of the *News* reporters he spoke to, Bob Kappstatter, seemed to win John's trust. John opened up a bit, speaking about his faith and that he'd briefly attended college. He talked about his time in Vietnam, saying that he'd served in a "noncombat" role. "I have a pretty good home life. Except that I hate my father. He always used to hit me." Why was he robbing a bank? "Well, a lot of things, personal and money problems . . . plus we got an offer from a guy downtown to do the job." How did he feel? "Well, it's only been six hours. It's not the longest six hours of my life . . . Vietnam was a lot rougher." What was the mood inside the bank? "The hostages are okay. They're even joking. But they're mad at the police. They want to get out of here." Was he scared? "Yes, I'm nervous, but you reach a point where it doesn't bother you anymore. I know I'm not going alone." Had he thought about dying? "No, I haven't thought about dying . . . I don't feel too good about this whole thing, but I'm not going to blow my brains out."[5]

John eventually asked Kappstatter to come down to the scene to act as a mediator between himself and the FBI. Just after getting off the phone with him, another call came through, this one from Arthur Bell, a cofounder of the Gay Activist Alliance and a reporter for *The Village Voice*. Bell had gotten a tip about some kind of gay liberation bank robbery going down in Brooklyn and called the bank to confirm the story. John picked up and said hello.

"Hello, this is Arthur Bell from *The Village Voice*. Can you tell me what's happening?"

"Arthur, am I glad it's you. This is Littlejohn."

"Littlejohn, what the hell are you doing down there?"

"I'm one of the robbers."

"Jesus Christ!"[6]

John told Bell the story about the Chase Manhattan executive and the lost promise of big money. He tried to fix the narrative about Sal, telling Bell, "Sal's not gay. I'm the only gay one here." He said that the cops wouldn't stop until he was dead or "in Attica." He told Bell that he'd pulled the job for Liz, for her surgery. It was the first instance of him telling this to anyone in the media. "That money," he said, "I wanted it for a sex-change operation for Ernie. Now I can't even see him to kiss him."

John asked Bell if he'd like to speak with a hostage. He did, and John put Ball on the line. She was more upset with the FBI than she was with John or Sal. "It's a damn shame that nothing's being done," she said. "They're backing John against a wall, and I don't know how long our luck is going to hold out." John came back and asked Bell to come down and help negotiate.[7]

The food, drinks, and cigarettes finally arrived an hour after John had asked for them. Three large pies, from the pizzeria up the block, were brought to the front door by an FBI agent. John had Ball go out the front door and pick everything up. He stood close behind her, holding a bundle of over $1,000 in cash. He'd meant the money as a tip for whoever brought the food, but with the agent already retreated across the street, he tossed the cash into the heavy night air and let the breeze make a mess of it all over the sidewalk and street. The few thousand people still on hand went wild and nearly broke through the police barricades. It was a typical John Wojtowicz move: showy, bold, generous—a distinctly crafted "fuck you" to everyone who was trying to keep the situation under control. John was starving but wouldn't eat what they'd brought. He hated pizza. But the sight of a half dozen cops, stooped over and trying awkwardly to peel the brand-new bills off the sidewalk was enough to keep him going.[8]

Bell called back, saying he was still trying to arrange with the police for transport to the scene. John was fed up with the FBI and their stalling tactics. He complained that they were going back on their promises (and that they'd brought him pizza when he preferred hamburgers). He now suspected that it was the FBI who was keeping Liz from seeing him. He gave Bell Carmen's phone number, just in case anything happened to him. He was not optimistic that he'd get out of this alive.[9]

Around 11:15 p.m., a police cruiser arrived at Bell's apartment and rushed him to the bank, picking up *Village Voice* editor Mary Nichols along the way. They were on the scene twenty minutes later and made their way through the swarms of people. But when Bell finally reached an FBI agent, they told him he would not be allowed near the bank. When he asked why, the agent only shrugged. Bell found Liz and updated her on the situation. He told her about John saying that the money was to fund her surgery. It was the first time Liz had heard anything about it. The medicated fog in her mind having lifted, she now wanted to go to the front door and see John. She wanted to make one last effort at getting him out alive. Or, failing that, one last chance to say goodbye. But Liz's doctor would not allow it. And the FBI certainly would not allow it. They had their plan. And that was not part of their plan.[10]

SO THINGS DRAGGED on and on. John and Sal were set on getting the vans and getting their plane. The FBI was trying to figure out the best possible scenario for getting them out of the bank, into some setting where it would be possible to end things as bloodlessly as possible. "Do you want to go to Moscow?" John asked Ball.

"No, I don't want to go to Moscow," she said, amused at the absurdity of it all.

"Do you want to go to Tel Aviv?"

"No, I don't want to go to Tel Aviv," she said, laughing. "What if an Arab catches me on the way there?"

"Well," John said, "wherever you want to go, girls . . ."[11]

John took bundles of cash from his attaché case and gave one to each of the hostages who would accept it. He ended up handing out over $4,000. From the same stack, he peeled off $300 and had Mouth process it as a payment on his Chase Manhattan Americard. On a night like this, why not?[12]

John and Sal decided that drawing lots would be the best way to determine who got to go free when it came time to release a hostage. Barrett refused to participate, insisting that he stay until the very end. As the evening dragged on, John and Sal's fatigue began to show. At one point, they inadvertently left the shotgun and the rifle on the conference room table while they were elsewhere. Ball and four of the other women were in the room, eyeing each other and the guns. But no one made a move. "None of us knew how to use those things," she said later. "If we had a man with us, maybe there would have been a different ending."[13]

Midnight came, then one in the morning, then two. Still, the FBI gave John nothing. Kappstatter, the *Daily News* reporter, arrived on the scene as a "neutral media observer" and tried to bridge the gap between what John wanted and what the FBI would give. U.S. District Attorney Bob Morse was also on the scene, trying to cut a deal with John on the possible charges. Kappstatter met the two at the front door of the bank. "So," he said to John, "howya doin'?"

"Howdya think?" John replied. His eyes were darting all over, his jaw was rigid. The rifle was slung over his shoulder.

Seeing that John was negotiating with someone who appeared to be in charge, Ball walked to the door and appeared behind John in the dimly lit lobby. "Enough is enough," she scolded Morse. "Do you want to trade eight lives for two? Don't stretch our luck, give them their demands!" And so commenced an unfathomably strange and brief bargaining session. The centerpiece of Morse's offer was a promise of no federal prosecution. While John thought and Kappstatter took notes, Ball spoke up. "What about state and city?" she asked. John nodded, yeah, what about state and city? The session was a bust. John turned and went back inside, leaving Ball alone with Morse and Kappstatter at the door. She could have left, but she turned and followed John. "I could have walked off," she said later. "But I couldn't have lived with myself afterwards."[14]

Sometime past 2:00 a.m., Barrett suddenly looked stricken. "You need a doctor?" John asked. Barrett was a diabetic, he'd mentioned it earlier in the evening, but he told John that he was okay. John asked for a doctor (the FBI didn't drag their feet on *that* request), and Barrett was sent out to have an examination in the back of a police car. He declined a shot of dextrose, saying he could have orange juice instead. The doctor still wanted to take him to the hospital for a cardiogram. Barrett waved the doctor off, rolled down his sleeve, and got out of the car to walk back inside the bank. Dismissing concerns about his health, he joked to the women, "I bet you never thought you'd spend the night with your boss."[15]

Meanwhile, out at JFK International Airport, a twelve-seat jet owned by the Hansa Jet Corporation had landed and was being prepared by the FBI. The plane was in from Newark, having just delivered several thousand pounds of mail to Pittsburgh. Even without the FBI's dawdling, commissioning a jet to fly to a yet-unknown destination with two armed men and several hostages on board was not a task that could be completed quickly. Arrangements for the plane had been made by Chase Manhattan's security division, and it took more than four hours to secure a plane and get it on the ground in New York. But Baker was content to let it idle there for an hour and half while John and Sal sweated it out inside the bank.[16]

It was after 3:00 a.m.—a full twelve hours since the ordeal

began—when Sal thought he heard someone trying to sneak in through the bank's back door. He fired a single shot toward the door—once again startling the hostages and agitating John to the point that he burst out on to the sidewalk, demanding answers. Most people outside hadn't noticed the shot or dismissed it as the noise of a firecracker. John was near apoplectic. An agent went inside with him to investigate the source of the suspicious noises and to get a look at the hostages. It was a beleaguered group. The gunmen were exhausted both mentally and physically. John was becoming increasingly hostile to delays and attempts by the FBI to modify his demands. Everyone seemed desperate to end this goddamn thing.[17]

It was time to put things into motion.

DEEP INTO THE evening, while they waited on the limousine van that would take them to the airport to wait on a plane that would take them God-knows-where, a handful of the hostages tried to talk Sal into surrendering. By now, the dynamic between the two gunmen was obvious. John was (comparatively) the brains and Sal was the muscle. John was engaging and animated, Sal was cold and brooding. But although he certainly instilled fear, Sal did not come across as particularly angry or hateful. What was it that was making this man—a kid still, really—so deathly committed to this dumb idea gone bad?

"We were all trying to make Sal give up," Josephine Tutino said in 2004. "We were all trying to persuade him . . . I says, 'Look, you're just a young boy, you know, we'll say to those authorities that you treated us good, that you didn't harm us. Why don't you give yourself up?'" It was the only actual conversation anyone recalled having with Sal during the entire ordeal. The only time anyone really tried talking to him. Sal told the women that he would not—could not—go back to prison. He told them about the sexual abuse. He told them he'd never allow that to happen to himself ever again.[18]

And that was that.

At 3:50 a.m., a single extended-length limo van finally arrived. It was metallic green with a fourteen-person capacity. The vehicle was parked in front of the bank and left empty, with the doors open, for John to inspect. While the van was on its way, Baker had lined up four agents and asked John to pick one to be the driver. John looked them over and selected a young agent named Jim Murphy. Murphy had already been on the scene for hours, heading down from the Manhattan FBI headquarters as soon as the call about the robbery had come in. After John went back inside the bank, Murphy was overtaken with a distinct feeling that someone was going to die that night. While the van was en route, the devoutly Catholic Murphy sought out John Auricchio. Murphy and the former reverend took a walk around the block while Murphy gave his confession. Unorthodox as it was, it brought Murphy solace in the face of whatever was coming next.[19]

John, rifle over his shoulder, called Murphy forward and ordered him to place his hands against the van. He patted him down and made a show of groping his crotch in the process. The crowd—by now as unruly and perverse as any group of Brooklynites still wide awake at 4:00 a.m. on a weeknight—went wild. Murphy felt humiliated. John ordered him back into the driver's seat and Murphy obeyed. He sat up straight, hands on the steering wheel and right foot on the brake. Hidden beneath the brake—wedged tightly underneath the floor mat—was a pistol. John searched every corner of the van, felt out every possible hidden pocket and reached inside every crevice, but never asked Murphy to move his feet.[20]

Satisfied that the van was clean, John took one chance to assert his authority. "I want all of you cops across the street," he shouted at the swarm of officers. Almost no one moved. "Don't you know what 'across the street' means?" John was worked up again, strutting and waving his arms. Someone in a suit and tie nodded, and the men moved back. He shouted some more about them all lowering their weapons. They obeyed.

"That son of a bitch," one cop muttered to another. "Can you believe it?"[21]

John ducked back inside the bank. Murphy slowly reached down to the floor mat, grabbed the gun, and tucked it behind his belt buckle.[22]

Inside, seven slips of paper were placed into a hat, six of them marked. Each of the hostages except for Barrett drew a slip. Josephine Tutino pulled the blank slip. She would stay behind. John and Sal gathered their things. John kept his rifle, Sal took up the shotgun. Barrett was handed the attaché case with the cash and traveler's checks. He joked aloud that it was his duty as bank manager to oversee the money until the last possible moment. John explained how they'd cross the sidewalk and where everyone would sit in the van. As Sal put on his sport coat, he turned to Tutino, who'd spent so much earnest time trying to get him to save himself and surrender. "I had two birthday presents," he told her. "But one was the black rose of death."

"Sal," she said, "just keep your cool."[23]

THE TWENTY FEET or so between the bank doors and the idling van would be the FBI's first chance. Snipers were in place. John came out first, his rifle to Barrett's head, their torsos pressed close together. No shot. John jumped into the last of the van's four rows. A moment later, Sal emerged, the six remaining women hostages ringing him, arms joined. No shot. Quickly and purposefully, the women split off and found their seats. Sal took the middle position in row three, a hostage to each side. John directly behind him, similarly bookended. The last three hostages filled the second row. Murphy was by himself in the front.[24]

Murphy made some small talk. "You want the windows down, I'll open the windows; you want them up, I'll close them. Whatever you want, just ask for it," he said. He saw that Sal was especially nervous, his gun aimed directly at Murphy's right ear. "Hey, careful with that gun, Sal, hold it a little higher, huh? My wife will be really disappointed if that goes off."[25]

Sal didn't budge. "Don't worry, it won't fire."

"If we go over a bump and it accidentally discharges, it's going to fire and I'm not going to be here anymore."

Sal considered it, and then slowly lowered the gun.

At 4:10 a.m., the van started slowly toward Ocean Parkway. It cut carefully through the few thousand people still on the scene, a trail of more than twenty police and emergency vehicles tailing behind. As soon as the caravan cleared the block, the mass of spectators suddenly surged toward the bank, eager to get a look at what was left behind or to hunt for souvenirs. Police blocked their way and urged everyone to go home. Terry rushed onto the sidewalk as the vehicles left her sight, fists clenched and sobbing. Pearl Saunders, whose daughter was still among the hostages, broke down in a crying fit. "Oh Lord Father, what is this?" she screamed. "Oh Lord Jesus, this is too much! Oh Lord, have mercy." Family members quickly ushered her away. A few FBI agents drove Terry home. "We'll take care of Sal when we get to the airport," one agent told her. "We'll save John." Another agent gave Liz and her doctor a ride back to Kings County. She said nothing on the way. Back at the hospital, she was given a shot that put her into a deep sleep.[26]

The caravan proceeded slowly along Ocean Parkway and then turned east on the Belt Parkway. Both streets had been closed by police and were free of civilian traffic but for the few dozen or so stray cars of rubbernecks who'd managed to hook up with the procession. Feeling no resistance from the gunmen, Murphy continued with his small talk. It noticeably lightened the tension in the van. John went on about pizza and how hungry he was. He threw Murphy a bit when he asked if they could stop for hamburgers along the way but Murphy assured him that he could arrange for something at the airport.[27]

At a quarter to five, the van arrived at the airport. Police had cordoned off a path to a gate in the chain-link fence that surrounded the property. The van crawled through the checkpoint, with a dozen official vehicles following. After all essential personnel had passed through, the gate was locked, and the curiosity seekers were told to go home. Along the long, dark passage to the little-used part of the tarmac where the plane would be waiting, Sal began to show his nerves. He gripped his gun tightly and had the hostages on either side of him scoot in closer. Murphy could sense that he'd have an opening. He asked John if he planned on taking him along for the plane trip. John said he didn't know. He could see the control slipping away. This was where it was going to end.[28]

They had gotten to the airport, another concession by the FBI for which John owed a hostage. They drew lots once more, and Kathy Amore picked the blank. She had been sitting in the middle of the second row. After she crawled out of the van, there was only an empty place between Murphy and Sal. They did another draw and Santa Strazzella pulled the blank. She'd be traded for the airplane. The rest would come with John and Sal to . . . no one seemed to know yet. John stammered something about having the hostages vote on the destination, or maybe they could elect a leader who'd decide for the group. Murphy could see that his mind was a panicked mess.[29]

John started up with the hamburgers again. He asked if they could go inside the terminal and get some takeout. It wasn't a rational thought. He hadn't had one since they'd left the bank. Sal called him off this time, saying they should all wait in the van for the plane. *The plane?* Where was the plane, John asked. Murphy saw the moment. He told John he needed to talk to Dick Baker about what happened next. He was just the littlest of the guys who'd been in the lineup from which John picked his driver. He had to follow orders too. He left the van, went around to the back, and conferred with Baker, FBI Special Agent Fred Fehl, and Cottell. By prior arrangement, the plane was being kept just out of sight from the van. It was scheduled to roll into view in about fifteen minutes.[30]

Murphy told them that they needed to end this now. If they were allowed to board the plane, which was full of armed agents, it could be a bloodbath. There was a window, he told them. The three others agreed, and they hatched a plan.[31]

Murphy got back in the van. He said the plane would be there in fifteen minutes. John and Sal had no further questions. Murphy kept up with the small talk. He took a more casual pose, half-turning on the front bench seat so that his right knee was up on the cushion. With his right hand, hidden from view to the rest of the van, he pulled his pistol from his belt and placed it in his lap. No one bothered to remember what they were talking about. It could have been baseball (the Mets had hung on to win that night) or the weather (tomorrow was sure to be another scorcher). It was entirely unmemorable, but it occupied the time. The long, long, *long* minutes until the whirr from the plane's jet engines began to move nearer. Murphy heard the plane getting closer and took the gun in his left hand, resting his right elbow on the seat back.[32]

The roar of the engines rose, and the plane slowly pulled into view. Sal and John locked their eyes on the plane—all hard noises and flashing lights and raw energy. This was it, all very real and right in front of them. They didn't even notice as Baker and Fehl approached the van from behind. Fehl went to the open window nearest to Sal on the driver's side. Baker walked to the open window on the other side, nearest to John. Cottell, who had long ago lost John's trust, hung back. While the plane pulled closer, Murphy asked Baker, "Will there be food on board for these people?"[33]

There was no food on board. He was really asking if Baker felt confident that he could disarm John.

Baker looked at John—exhausted and scared. The rifle was resting in his lap.

The plane got closer, the engines louder.

Sal stared ahead at the airplane. He'd never flown before. He never would.

"Yes," Baker answered.

On that word, Baker dove through the open window, grabbed the muzzle of John's rifle and shoved it aside. Murphy lunged at Sal. With his right hand, he pushed the end of the shotgun upward, toward the roof of the van and the fading evening stars. For half a second, Sal managed a struggle. Left-handed, Murphy thrust his service pistol forward and fired a single shot into Sal's wide-open chest.[34]

To the hostages, it sounded like a flashbulb: a pop and a burst of light, followed by a rush of motion and men screaming for everyone to get out of the way. Murphy kept moving forward after the shot. He climbed over the seats and stretched out long. John had a free hand that Murphy saw moving toward the pearl-gripped pistol in his belt. Murphy's free hand was on the back of Sal's neck as his body eased and went limp. A final breath left his lungs and rattled his lips. The hostages had fled on the sound of the shot, the doors wide open, letting in the damp morning air and the engine roars and the flashing lights. Murphy was stretched out as long as he could go, his pistol aimed dead-center between John's eyes. For a long, long moment, John's hand lingered at his waist. And then it moved away.[35]

"Don't shoot," John said in a small voice. "I give up."

It was August 23, 1972, 5:28 a.m. It was over.

GOETTISHEIM WOULD LATER call it the worst day of her life. After Sal was carted away and John taken off in handcuffs, a cousin picked her up and drove her home. She changed her clothes and put her navy-blue outfit with the modest skirt in the wash basket. She didn't bother with breakfast or a nap. She splashed some water on her face and walked to church. There was an eight o'clock mass that morning. "I had asked God for help, and he gave it to me," she said later. "I had to thank him."[36]

Three

"As much love as you might find between the two of us, I would never trust [John] to do anything right."

—GEORGE HEATH, JOHN WOJTOWICZ'S HUSBAND AND JAILHOUSE LAWYER

That damn handkerchief. John doesn't like that. Every time Sonny wants to come to the street, he waves a little white hankie to show that he means no harm. John never did that. Why would he? That's a sign of surrender. The only way he was able to go out on the street in the first place was because Sal could start blowing people away at any moment.

It was a shame, too, because John likes the scenes out on the street. The crowds love Sonny, just like they loved him—more or less. Sonny tells a city detective who's trying to work one over on him, "Kiss me." The cop is confused. "When I'm bein' fucked," Sonny explains, "I love to be kissed a lot." That's a good line. Had he actually said it? Maybe. Probably. He certainly remembers tossing all that money out the front door to pay for the pizza. That was a laugh. A real good way to stick it to all those damn cops. John likes the part where Sonny starts chanting, "Attica! Attica! Attica!" It wasn't something he would have done, but damn. That would have scared everyone shitless.

John has trouble with the women in the film. Not the hostages, really, even though aside from Mouth, none of them really seem like the real people. But his mother. Boy, did they ever do a job on his mother. Sobbing in that awful little living room while his old man made some crack about her being a sucker. Bullshit. John's mother isn't that type. A pain, maybe, and stubborn as hell, but never a blubbering nitwit like this. And Carmen.

Damn. He sees why the picture had upset her so much. And that awful girl they found to play her. That hurt.

And then there is Ernie. They call him Leon in the film. There is a little more humor at John's expense here—jumping around yelling "Happy birthday" to him. Christ, it wasn't his birthday, that was days earlier. That was before Ernie almost died. That was the reason he was locked up in the first place. John doesn't recognize the guy they got to play Ernie, but damn if he isn't a good fit for the role. That hair, the fey way he holds his hands, that voice . . . that voice is almost really his. Up on-screen, Leon breaks Sonny's heart. It feels like it's happening all over again.

John can hardly remember what he'd said when he talked to Ernie on the phone that night. Was it like how Sonny and Leon talked? It might as well have been. Why not? They fight a bit. John can imagine him and Ernie doing that. They were always doing that. But it's tender. There was always a tenderness to it. There was always love. As far as John can remember, at least. John sits there, tears welling. Leon is saying goodbye. "See ya in my dreams, huh?"

Sonny swallows. "Yeah . . . I'll write you a song." He chuckles. "I don't know. Life is funny."

"You said a mouthful, sweetheart."

And then they both hang up.

11. you never smile

It was all a rush of noise and light to Liz Eden. The weight of the drugs she had been given at the hospital had lifted, only to be replaced by the heavy exhaustion of terror and stress. "I was dying on my feet," she said later of watching the wailing sirens and spinning lights of the caravan that rushed off with John and Sal and the hostages on their doomed journey to JFK Airport. "I couldn't even see straight."[1]

And, for those civilians who remained at the scene, that was that. The gawkers wandered home, with the late-night reprieve from the brutal summer heat beginning to break. Those connected to the heist in whatever way lingered helplessly as the fate of their loved ones remained in flux. Liz was loaded back into a police car and taken back to Kings County Hospital. Back in her little room, a nurse gave her another shot. It knocked her cold until the next afternoon.[2]

On Wednesday afternoon, Liz shuffled out of her room and sunk into a chair in the common area by the television set. A news report about the robbery was playing. Through her medicated fog, Liz heard something about one of the gunmen being shot dead at the airport. She stood shakily and stared at the television. "And I don't know if it was my mind or the way they announced it, but they flashed a picture of John. They said, 'Bank robber killed at Kennedy Airport.'" She put it all together: John was dead. Liz collapsed. She wouldn't wake up again until Thursday morning.[3]

Back at JFK, Sal was already gone by the time he was laid on a gurney and loaded into an ambulance that had been waiting at the scene. He arrived at Jamaica Hospital minutes later, where he was officially pronounced dead. On his body, the FBI counted nearly $12,000 in cash, twelve shotgun shells, the keys to the rented Duster, a small stack of business cards and phone numbers for friends and acquaintances in the Village, a rent receipt for eighteen dollars signed "Donald Matterson," and a plain gold wedding band.[4]

John was in handcuffs, still standing on the tarmac with noise and hot winds washing all around when the cops started in on him. One told him that he'd wished John would have tried to run so he could have had the pleasure of shooting him. They shoved him around and used all the typical slurs of the time. The FBI and Port Authority Police took him to a holding area. They hit him and stripped him naked. They called him more names and mocked the size of his penis. An FBI agent took down his vital information: true name and aliases, his height and weight, where he'd went to high school, and what rank he'd achieved in the military. He gave his address as the Boystown apartment and said he had no home phone number. Under "Characteristics," the agent listed "admitted homosexual."[5]

On his person, John had a monogrammed wallet, his military discharge papers, a pair of credit cards, about thirty dollars in cash, an outpatient identification card from his brief time at

Saint Vincent's Hospital, his voter ID card, and a blue paper invitation listing the information for the wedding reception that he had wanted to hold at the Gay Activist Alliance Firehouse in July of 1971.[6]

In his initial interview with an FBI agent on August 23, John signed an Interrogation Advice of Rights statement and confessed—to a degree. He said the airplane escape had been Sal's idea. He blamed the cops for forcing him to take hostages. And he started to name names. He spoke cagily about the Chase Manhattan executive who allegedly supplied him with the inside information about the cash delivery that was supposed to have taken place the previous afternoon. He offered a rough description of the "big shot" who agreed to supply the information in exchange for half of the cash from the heist and even gave a first name. He identified Mike Umbers as the man who sold him the pistol and surrendered all he knew about the person who supplied the long guns. He told the agents that neither one of these people had any idea that he was going to use the guns for a bank robbery.[7]

The only person—the only real person—John truly turned on that afternoon was Robert. He was still pissed about Robert "chickening out" and handed the FBI everything he had on the kid. While Robert was lamming it on the streets, agents raided his mother's house and worked over his brother and grandmother for information. They told them that Robert was an accomplice to a murder. From a pay phone, Robert called Joe Scott, his former boss and the man whom he'd lived with for four years as a romantic partner. He needed money, Robert said, enough to get out of the country. Scott said he could get the cash and told him to come over to his apartment that evening. From there, Scott called the FBI.[8]

That evening, August 23, Robert changed his mind. Instead

of going to Scott's apartment—which was by then being staked out by an entire team of FBI agents—he went to his father's house in Ozone Park. They watched news coverage of the robbery on television. Later that evening, Robert's father went out and got his son a bottle of liquor to help him sleep. Back at Scott's apartment, the agents that were hidden in his living room, on rooftops surrounding the building, and in the backyard and basement all moved their hands to their weapons whenever someone neared the front steps. Scott asked the agent in charge what would happen if Robert tried to run. "We don't know if he's packing a gun or not," the agent said plainly. "If he runs, we're going to shoot." Scott, already a nervous wreck over what he'd done, broke down crying. Much to his relief, Robert never showed up.[9]

The next day—a Thursday—Robert considered leaving New York and hiding out in some remote corner of the country. But New York already felt like a jail cell. Cops seemed to be swarming every train station and bus depot he passed. Were they out hunting for him? Or had he just never noticed how many damn cops were in this city before? That evening, he went with his father to Scott's apartment, which the FBI had given up on staking out. Scott said he couldn't help him run. His father had tried, but it was Scott who finally convinced Robert to do what he needed to do. From Scott's apartment, Robert went to the FBI office on Sixty-Ninth Street and surrendered. Somewhere along the way, Robert learned how he'd nearly walked into an FBI ambush just a day earlier. "And I would have run too," he later admitted.[10]

FOR THE REST of the week, the straight world tried to sift through the messy drama of John Wojtowicz and his various lovers and accomplices. It's likely that the matter would have gotten a decent amount of attention even without the gay aspect to the case. John was enough of a spectacle on his own to draw eyes—the little man barking at cops and commanding the air space over Queens. And with thousands in the streets with nothing better to do with their evening and the noisy late-night parade to JFK Airport, the spectators themselves had become part of the show. Throw in his bizarre rants on the telephone and the ultimate triumph of the Good Guys at the end and you've got one of those happenings that people like to read as a symptom of some kind of societal decline or another.

But the queer angle to the story truly set it apart. Indeed, in 1972, the discussion of gay men or women in a major American newspaper was still a relatively new concept. Prior to the mid-1960s, nearly any reference to queerness in the print media was in reference to criminality—most often so in the way of police actions targeting gay gathering spots. Even this was considered too lowbrow for many publications. In Edward Alwood's study of gay people and the media, *Straight News,* he found that *The New York Times* made exactly zero references to "homosexuality" between 1953 and 1963 and did not stop listing gay and trans people in the same class of "civic undesirables" as panhandlers, addicts, and the homeless until 1968.* [11]

Even after Stonewall, the mainstream press paid the uprising far less attention than a similar event based on racial or ethnic discrimination would have received. The Stonewall Riot received scant coverage in the *Times* and was outright mocked in the *Daily News.* Even the liberal-leaning *Village Voice* used terms like *fag* and *limp-wrist* in its coverage. But burgeoning

* It would take far longer for the media to recognize the humanity of the unhoused and addicts in the same way.

gay-friendly underground publications, like the gay-run *Advocate* and the aggressively transgressive *Screw*, allowed gay reporters to cover both the riot and the causes that led to it. It wasn't until late 1969—months afterward—that *The Washington Post* dared to suggest there might be more to the story than a few fistfights and some broken windows.[12]

With the emergence of the post-Stonewall gay liberation movement, the press slowly began to recognize the gay community's humanity. Much of the movement's early activism—the GAA's zaps in particular—was aimed at reaching a mainstream audience via the media. These actions were also groundbreaking in their willingness to put names and faces to the community. Through the late 1960s, faces were obscured when gay men and women were bold enough to speak before television cameras, and the use of pseudonyms was a regular practice in the gay press. In 1971, the *Times* published an essay by novelist and biographer Merle Miller, the first time a major newspaper published the work of an openly gay writer. That summer, they covered the march to commemorate the first anniversary of Stonewall and even took the time to publish quotes from several participants.[13]

So when John Wojtowicz started telling reporters, "I'm gay, so what?" with a rifle slung over his shoulder, $30,000 of Chase Manhattan's cash in his duffel, and an army of New York City cops indulging his whims, it was not a news event for which anyone was prepared. While the more responsible accounts of the robbery opted not to sensationalize their headlines with references to John's sexuality, there was really no way to dutifully report this story in 1972 without acknowledging that John had—loudly and without shame—told the world that he was a gay man. This was, by 1972's standards, a decidedly political act and an act worthy of news coverage. However, when it came to connecting this act to the bank robbery—indeed, a decidedly political act in itself—the mainstream media, as they had after Stonewall, opted not to dig too deeply.

It was also, of course, an excuse for the media to treat the entire affair like a circus sideshow. The *Daily News*—which had just a month prior editorialized in favor of discharging gay employees from government jobs, referring the security risks of employing "fairies, nances, swishes, fags, [and] lezzes"—was the worst offender. "Weird, Man, Weird" read one *News* headline, "Gay? Well, Hostages Weren't Too Thrilled" read another. A supplemental *News* piece on Wojtowicz referred to his "strange life" and another subhead called him and Sal "Gay and Pal." Newspapers around the country carried headlines with either *gay* or *homosexual* in their headlines, and nearly every reference to Liz put quotes around the word *wife*. Even the relatively staid reporting of the *Times* included quotes around the word *affair* in reference to John's relationship to Liz, as though a queer extramarital relationship was something inherently different from a married man cheating with a woman.[14]

The first news articles about the robbery went to print while the van idled on the tarmac at Kennedy. A morning edition *New York Times* article cited an initial report that said "the release of a mental patient" was part of the motivation for the heist. A surviving account of a live report from the scene by Channel 5's Bill Jorgensen, delivered while Liz was on her way to the bank from Kings County Hospital, is the earliest known reference to this "motive" for the robbery. Jorgensen cited a telephone interview with John as the source of this information.[15]

While it is likely that John's early bluster over the phone referenced "freeing" Liz from the hospital as part of his rationale for robbery, it was clear by that evening that her release (it was not yet known publicly that she was voluntarily committed) was only a part of whatever John had hoped to accomplish. By the next afternoon, reports emerged that John had planned to take Liz with him to the airport and demand a destination where she could have her "sex-change" operation. The *Daily News* said they were bound for Algeria. The *Times* reported that they would have been off to Denmark. It wasn't until two days later that the first report connecting the money to Liz's gender-affirming surgery emerged, when *Newsday* wrote that, according to one of the hostages, John said that he wanted to take Liz to Copenhagen and use the stolen money to finance her transition. An AP story repeated the claim, but the detail was presented mostly as an afterthought. An August 31 *Village Voice* article quoted both John and Patsy as saying that *some* of the money from the robbery was to have paid for Liz's surgery, but—aside from a single mention buried in the bottom of a *Boston Globe* article on the robbery—the thought that the heist had been planned as a way to get Liz her surgery was mostly ignored.[16]

THE POST-STONEWALL ERA had seen a boom in the gay press. While just a handful of gay-focused or even gay-friendly publications existed in the late 1960s, by 1972 nearly every major city had a newspaper or, at the very least, a regular newsletter that reported on gay happenings and news. In New York, the paper of record for the gay community was *Gay*, a weekly tabloid published by *Screw* founder Al Goldstein. While the straight media mostly stopped talking about John Wojtowicz by the end of August, the robbery sparked a conversation in the gay media—and the larger gay community—that would last for years.[17]

The day after the robbery, Thane Hampton, a reporter for

Gay, typed out a single sentence on a sheet of paper. It read, "27-Year-Old Heterosexual Robs Bank, Taking 7 Hostages in 14-Hour Ordeal." He'd heard coverage of the robbery break into radio programming the afternoon before—like a presidential assassination, he recalled—and had spent the night at a gay bar where the case was all anyone wanted to talk about. He passed the sheet around to gay friends and colleagues and asked for their immediate reactions. Everyone he asked expressed some kind of anger or offense. It was only when he asked them to read the sentence again that they each realized they had subconsciously replaced "Hetero" with "Homo." "What does this prove?" he asked his readers. "Well, of course it proves that we're damn sensitive to any criticism (with good reason) . . . and the very idea of mentioning a *straight* bank robber's sexual orientation is so ludicrous, we reject the thought immediately."[18]

Hampton argued that such a "pedestrian" crime would have never gotten the press it had if not for a public need to gape at the "raw silk sensationalism" of a bank robber who just happened to be gay and have a transgender lover. "We haven't had a good Sick Degenerate story in ages," he wrote. "You can understand why they pounced on it." *Gay* went on to denounce the idea that John was a political prisoner in an editorial. "Bullshit," *Gay* wrote. "If he committed the crime . . . he is a bandit who deserves our pity, but not our glorification." Hampton went on to express worry that once John went to trial, his shame-free declaration of his sexuality would be used as an excuse for his actions. "[His lawyer could say that] Wojtowicz was a Good Boy—until the clammy hand of perversion clutched his immaculate soul . . . Very swell for Johnny, rotten for us."[19]

"The issue that concerns us," wrote Connie McConnohie in the *Gay Liberator*, "is the reported *gay* bank robbery. Was this what it was or, by the press coverage, is this what it became?" McConnohie questioned John's motivations in pushing his ill-conceived crime into the realm of the larger gay liberation movement. "One cannot help but question his motives for making these statements [about his sexuality]. Had the robbery been successful, or had they been caught later, would he have brought up the fact that he was gay?" Was the movement being used? Was John setting up his sexuality as a bargaining chip to either cash in for community support or to plead mentally ill at trial? McConnohie's article ran under the headline "The Great (?) Gay (?) Bank Robbery (?)."[20]

But some in the gay press felt that scolding the straight media and abandoning John as a member of the community was a failure to see the larger picture. The *Gay Revolution Networker* compared the act to the "first rock at Stonewall" and declared John's arrest to be the loss of his so-called freedom as a gay man in America. "'Our image!' we cry," the *Networker* wrote, "forgetting that any image that we present is just another chain they own to bind our gayness." Chase Manhattan, the piece continued, is "an awesomely overwhelming EMPIRE of theft and murder that takes pride in its wholesome family image with an open policy of discrimination against gay people . . . Two faggots walked into a branch of Chase Manhattan. They said we want your money. They took $29,000. That action upset a lot of things and even threatened their and others' lives. They didn't make it . . . Shot dead! Murdered and betrayed by the same identity with a system that has been murdering and betraying our precious gay lives since we were all born. There is no neutrality. We are either reclaiming by any bewildered means we can or we are submitting to the death march. The NY Post calls them 'those gay lib types.' SO DO [WE]!"[21]

Arthur Bell, the GAA cofounder and journalist who spoke

to John on the phone during the robbery, presented perhaps the most sympathetic voice on the matter. Covering the robbery for the *Voice*, he wrote that it was John's refusal to play to the good gay type—as defined by either the straight world or the gay one—that made his actions so hard for either side to process. "Macho tactics," Bell wrote, "are bad propaganda—be docile . . . changes take time, keep in your place, that is the thinking . . . [But], by asserting his homosexuality at a moment of truth in his life, Littlejohn was saying 'Gay Is Proud.'" Bell continued, "Like a closeted homosexual on his first public demonstration, he was shouting, 'Give me my freedom, I'm entitled to it, now I'm demanding it. The scene that's happening is pure catharsis, I'm releasing the poison gases you've helped me store in my head.'"[22]

Bell compared the robbery to the GAA's zaps, but with a "reverse macho trip" that made it too unexpected and exciting for the straight world to look away, and too forthright and dangerous for many in the gay community to embrace. "Homosexuals are supposed to be victims," he wrote. "And here's a tough-guy John Dillinger victor. Instead of demanding his lady in red, Littlejohn was asking for his transvestite in pajamas." But in the end, Bell concluded, it was but a single, doomed, and flailing act. "The difference between Littlejohn at the bank and a gay demonstrator at City Hall is that Littlejohn had the gun. But the outcome was the same—total defeat."[23]

ON THURSDAY, AUGUST 24, Liz was discharged from Kings County. She didn't want to leave, but the doctors said that they could no longer keep her. Her suicidal episode had passed. She had to move on. Still thinking that John was dead, she was given a few subway tokens and a dollar bill and sent on her way.

Unwilling or unable to return to the apartment where she had tried to take her own life, Liz called around until she got ahold of a drag queen friend—one of the bridesmaids from the wedding. He wasn't at home but told Liz how she could sneak into his apartment through a basement door. By the time she'd caught a bus, her hands were shaking so hard that she could barely pay the fare. She rode to his apartment in Crown Heights and let herself in. "And I just laid down," she said later. "Just sat there."[24]

She remained in a daze until the phone rang. It was a lawyer. The lawyer said that John wanted to see her and asked if she would come to the Federal Detention Center on West Street. Liz was baffled. She was sure that she'd heard he'd been killed. She even remembered seeing his body on television. After the lawyer explained how things had gone down at Kennedy on Wednesday morning, Liz felt a kind of relief. But not the kind she expected. "I figured, well, he's behind bars, he couldn't hurt me anymore . . . okay."[25]

While Liz was coming to the realization that John was still alive, Carmen and Patsy Coppola were screaming at each other on the sidewalk outside the West Street detention center. The pair had gone to visit John, along with Terry and Michael Wojtowicz. Also in tow was journalist and gay activist Randy Wicker, who had reached out to the family after the robbery over concerns about John getting both fair treatment in the media and a fair trial. With him were writers P. F. Kluge and Thomas Moore, who were planning to write a feature article on the robbery for *Life* magazine. Wicker had set up the piece and had secured $100 from *Life* for the use of John and Liz's wedding photos. He even paid for a telephone to be installed at the Wojtowicz home so that Kluge and Moore could keep in touch.[26]

Liz Eden and an intimate, before she met John. Liz left home in her teens and found drag in the mid-1960s. She loved the scene but couldn't be bothered with its politics. *(Liz Eden Papers at the Lesbian, Gay, Bisexual, and Transgender Community Center National History Archive)*

Robert Westenberg was a hard-luck case who was willing to do anything for enough money to get out of New York City. Robert and eighteen-year-old Sal Naturile made up the "gang" John would assemble for his heist. While John and Sal were both committed to getting away with the robbery or using their guns, Robert just didn't have it in him. He fled as the robbery was getting underway and later served two years for his role in the crime. He is pictured here at a youth offenders' facility in West Virginia. *(Eden Papers)*

Liz and John on the day of their faux marriage in December 1971. They'd met earlier that year while cruising at a street festival. Liz agreed to get married only so John would buy her the gown. Her expression here sums up her feelings about the ceremony. *(Eden Papers)*

Although the concept of Liz and John's union—described in the gay press as "New York's FIRST drag wedding of two men"—was radical enough to get the gay community's attention, it was not an attempt at a legal marriage. Gennaro Auricchio (*back to camera*), a former reverend who had previously counseled Liz, considered a "drag" wedding to be sacrilegious but agreed to perform a blessing "of a union between two persons." Liz's father, Ernest Aron Sr., is seen to the left of John. *(Eden Papers)*

John barking at the cops from the front door of the bank in Brooklyn. When a *Life* magazine article compared John's looks to those of Al Pacino, the seeds of what would become *Dog Day Afternoon* were planted. *(Getty Images)*

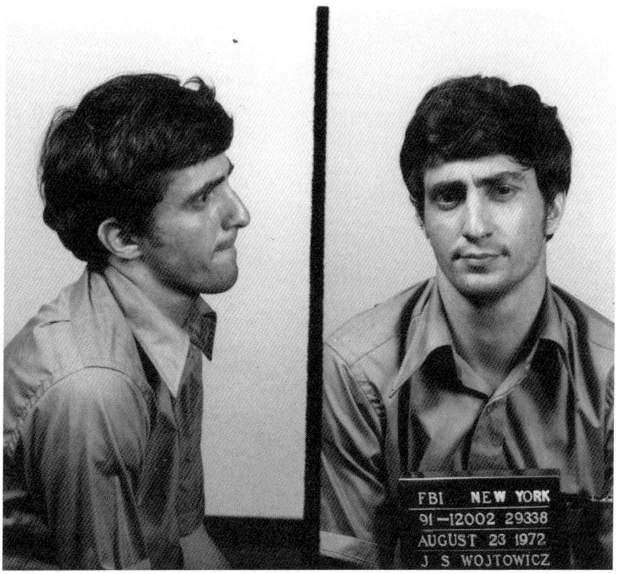

After fourteen hours with the hostages and a fatal shot to his partner's chest, John was in custody. The popular narrative of John having robbed the bank to pay for Liz's gender-affirming surgery wouldn't take hold for a few months, but he was already famous as the "gay bank robber." *(Public domain)*

Liz on the cover of London's *Gay News* shortly after the first of her surgeries. At the time, she was one of the highest-profile trans people alive, but her dreams of becoming "a superstar like Andy Warhol's Jackie Curtis or Candy Darling" would go unfulfilled. By the time *Dog Day Afternoon* was released in 1975, she was relying on sex work to make ends meet. *(Public domain)*

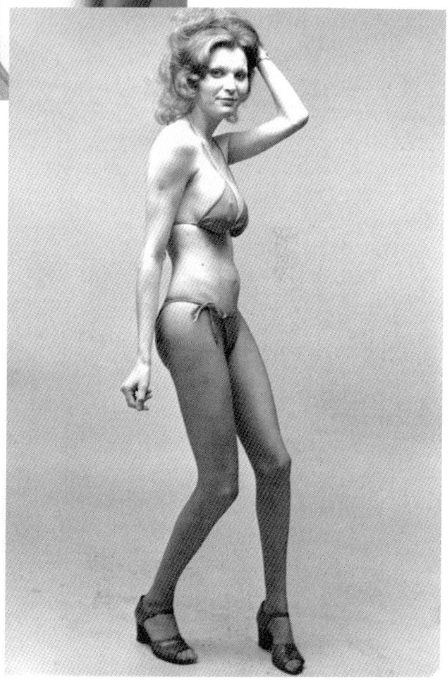

John gave Liz $2,500 from the $7,500 payment he received for the rights to his story, an amount he thought would cover the costs of her gender-affirming surgery. Over the next five years, she would have a total of fifteen operations with costs topping $60,000. "I was a shell," she'd say of her transition. "Now I'm a whole peanut." She would still, however, struggle with depression for the rest of her life. *(Eden Papers)*

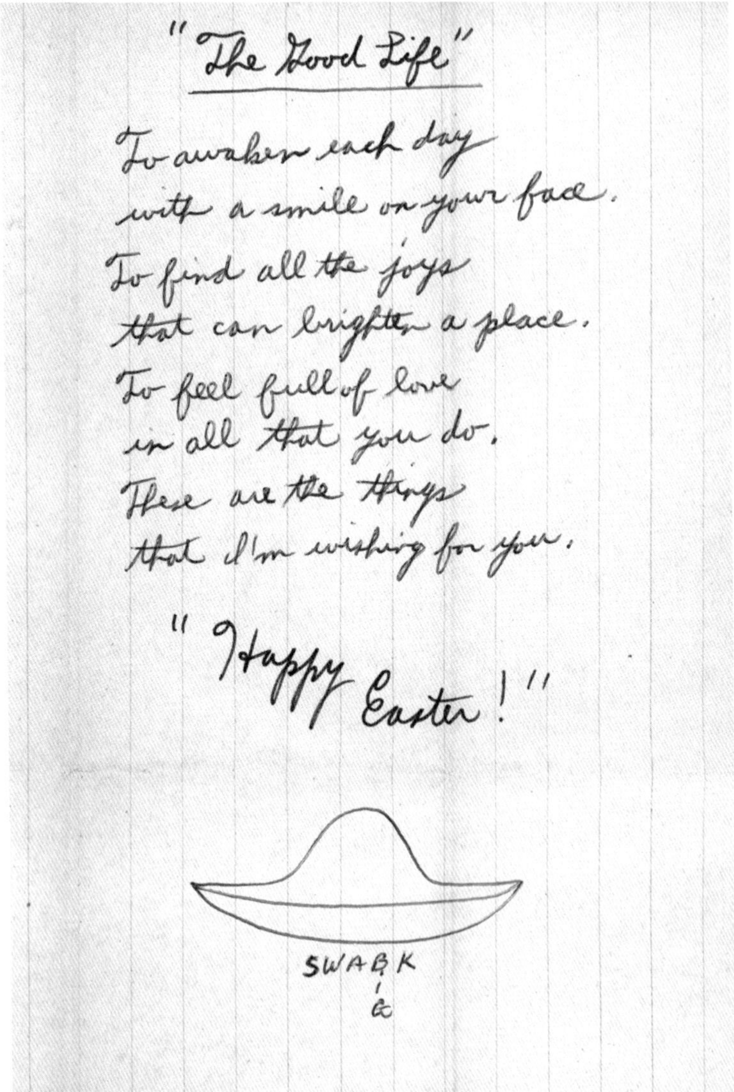

"The Good Life"

To awaken each day
with a smile on your face.
To find all the joys
that can brighten a place.
To feel full of love
in all that you do.
These are the things
that I'm wishing for you.

"Happy Easter!"

SWABK

An Easter poem written by John for journalist Randy Wicker, who covered the robbery extensively and helped facilitate the movie deal. John was a frequent letter writer while in prison, his upbeat prose belying his grim day-to-day existence as a high-profile and openly gay inmate. *(The Randy Wicker & Marsha P. Johnson Papers at the Lesbian, Gay, Bisexual, and Transgender Community Center National History Archive)*

John had hoped to make his post-prison living as a celebrity entrepreneur, once even pitching an idea of a *Dog Day Afternoon* taxi service that would run the film on a loop in the back of every cab. Here he is pictured with a friend, wearing a custom-made T-shirt outside the Chase Manhattan bank in Brooklyn that had made him famous. His dreams, like Liz's, would remain dreams. His only steady income after prison came from the state welfare department. *(Wicker & Johnson Papers)*

Despite the hell he'd put her through, Liz could never bring herself to cut John completely out of her life. While John still claimed to love her and considered her one of his several spouses, Liz's feelings for John were more rooted in pity. She never did believe that he robbed the bank for her benefit. *(Public domain)*

John, as one of his spouses saw him. George Heath, who served as John's jailhouse lawyer and later "married" him in a prison-yard ceremony, painted this in 2014. Just as with his first (and only legal) spouse, Carmen (*left*), and Liz (*top right*), John's relationship with George (*bottom right*) was often strained. "He didn't realize the consequences of things he would do or say," George later said of John.
(Wicker & Johnson Papers)

"Cocksucker! Faggot! Fairy!" Carmen screamed at Patsy. "He's probably fucked you more than he's fucked me."

"You fat whore!" he screamed back. "You're no woman to say a thing like that to me. You went with other men. You drove him crazy!"[27]

The three writers all took notes.

It was a short and tense visit. John needed $250,000 for bail. He hoped that the family and Liz could try to sell interviews. He asked Wicker to try to sell a jailhouse interview. He apologized and asked for forgiveness. Everyone involved was very tired. Carmen was cold to the idea of appearing in an interview with Liz, which John thought might have been a hot ticket.[28]

After the visit, Terry and Carmen each unburdened themselves to Wicker about the other. "I hate that bitch," Terry told him. "I swear I wouldn't go to her house if there was a death in the family, even if one of my grandchildren died. She ruined my son. It's all her fault."

Carmen scoffed at Terry's embrace of Patsy, how her mother-in-law had given him more of a chance in a few months than she'd given Carmen in eight years. "Pat is their daughter-in-law," she said. "I bet he's shitted out two kids for them already."[29]

Liz went to the detention center the next day. At the visitor's gate, she was given a special pass and waved through to the waiting room. No one bothered to ask for an ID. They all recognized her. She spent almost two hours talking with John, but none of it stuck. Reflecting on the visit years later, she couldn't remember any of the conversation. In a letter he'd written to her earlier that day—already in the mail by the time she arrived—John begged Liz not just for forgiveness but for help. "It's a chance for you to be depended upon, not the other way around," he wrote. He needed money and asked Liz to try to sell an interview. He asked if Liz would ask her father to represent him as his lawyer, even though Ernest Sr. was in business and had never been an attorney. He asked her to write to him every day. He complained that her refusal to see him at the bank had hurt him deeply. He swore that he loved her. Years later, Liz would use only one word to describe their first jailhouse meeting. "Horrible."[30]

THE FRIDAY AFTER the robbery, the Gay Activist Alliance held a discussion on the robbery at the Wooster Street firehouse, moderated by Arthur Bell. About 150 GAA members were there, double the usual attendance for an alliance meeting. Randy Wicker was there, too, as well as Barbara Trecker, a sympathetic journalist from the *Post*. Also hidden among the crowd, Bell was certain, were several undercover FBI agents. Bell opened the meeting by asking the group to discuss the differences between the robbery and the zaps of which the group was so proud. Both were illegal, but both drew attention to the cause. He was shouted down for even bringing up the comparison. "The fact is," Bell said, "we cannot dismiss the moral and ethical issues raised by the robbery. But if we could, if only we could, we could hail Littlejohn as indeed a 'gay lib type.'"[31]

Although the group was not as open to considering the act one of revolution, there was a degree of sympathy for John among the membership. The most active discussion involved the question of whether John was a "political prisoner." Some felt that the overall oppression of queer people might have driven John to do what he did. "Perhaps his life made him a criminal," one member suggested. Another recalled that he was active in the movement and referred to him as a "tender little guy."

But GAA member Marc Rubin stood up and pushed back. "I will not make a hero of John Basso," he said. "I remember him. He was a foolish little man. I want you to remember something: There is a kid who is dead and if John wanted to be a fool, why didn't he do it alone?"[32]

Deni Covello, another member, countered. "John is a political prisoner. The way the press treated it, he can't get a fair trial. No gay person can get a fair trial."[33]

The room split. Some—afraid to pay John any attention, given the recent rumors that the GAA might have played some part in the heist—wanted to ignore the matter completely. The more moderate center saw him as somewhere between pitiable and misguided and expressed interest only in supporting him in getting a fair trial. A smaller and more radical sect compared him to Angela Davis and wanted to make him a full-on martyr for the movement. After an hour-plus of heated discussion, the only consensus was that the group should push for a fair trial. "If he's going to get a fair trial, we must see that he has a gay judge," said group spokesman Charles Choset, "at least a politically gay judge. And a given percentage of the jury must be gay."[34]

"I would certainly like to know where they are going to find that 'proper percentage of open gays' and that rarest of mythological birds, the politically-gay-committed judge," Thane Hampton wrote after the meeting in *Gay*. "Hang up and call back in 1995."*[35]

A frail and jumpy-looking eighteen-year-old kid had come along with Trecker to the meeting. Near the end, he stood and introduced himself as Gary Badger. He was a bartender at

* Hampton was pretty much correct in this assessment: Deborah Batts became the first openly gay federal judge in 1994.

Danny's and knew all of those involved in the robbery, but he was particularly close with Sal. On the morning after the heist, he and Wallace Hamilton had gone to the morgue to identify Sal's body. They'd seen his eyes—open and still—and the hole in his chest where the FBI slug had pierced his left lung and heart. The room was quiet. For all the talk and opining and posturing, it was Badger who had actually seen the body of the one true victim. With tears in his eyes, he asked the group for money to bury his friend. The room remained silent.[36]

Afterward, Bell found Badger and the two began to talk. Despite his young age, Badger knew the Christopher Street scene well. He knew the characters, and he knew the players. And he knew who was behind the players. The stories he told jibed with others Bell had heard—about Mike Umbers, the Gambinos, about the money behind places like Danny's, the Round Table, and Boystown. Bell asked Badger why he was spilling all this. "Because," Badger told him, "after Sal's death, it hit me that Umbers and the Gambino people were using young kids without giving a fuck about life or death to take up money and power."[37]

The next day, the GAA released a statement on the robbery. It criticized the media's coverage of the case—the poorly conceived headlines in the *Daily News* specifically—and called for John to receive a fair trial by an impartial judge and jury. The group took no position on the crime itself.[38]

Sal's body would eventually be sent back to New Jersey, where the family—whatever could be found of it—buried him in a plot next to his father. Warner Bros. ended up covering the costs.[39]

A WEEK LATER, Bell's article—"Littlejohn & the Mob: Saga of a Heist"—appeared in the *Voice*. Spread over five pages, it laid out the details of the robbery and outlined a scenario in which organized crime figures financed and backed the plot. Bell pinned Liz's attempted suicide just before the robbery as a try to get John to call off the plan (in this version of the story, Liz had found out about John's plan the week prior—although that is almost certainly not true and there is nothing to suggest that Liz's attempted suicide had anything to do with the robbery). Umbers's surrender to police, Bell claimed, was an effort to remove himself from implication in the crime. The Gambino syndicate would get half the take—a share that was supposed to have been between $75,000 and $100,000—in exchange for their backing and information.

By the time Bell's piece ran, John had already recanted his claim to the FBI that he had been given inside info from a Chase Manhattan executive that helped him to plan the robbery. The claim was always highly dubious (again, why would they try to rob three banks before getting to the one on which they had an inside tip?), but John's invention of it suggests that there might have indeed been more to the plot than three down-and-outers looking for a payday. While Bell's claim that the robbery was "set up" by Umbers and the Gambinos is flimsy without the presence of a Chase Manhattan insider who might have had a good reason to cooperate with mobsters (recall the spree of Mafia extortions of gay Wall Street men that led, in part, to the Stonewall raid), he does draw plenty of connections between Umbers and John. It was known that John borrowed to the hilt to finance his wedding with Liz, and it was known that he was partial to Umbers despite his toxic reputation to the gay community at large. It would also eventually be proven that Umbers did indeed sell John one of the guns used in the crime (Umbers was never charged). From here, it is not too much a stretch to imagine that—while not working. While the Mafia angle would soon be disputed and the FBI would declare authoritatively that they had no suspects in the crime beyond John, Robert, and Sal, questions about John's true motivations would linger for many—including Liz Eden.[40]

THE BANK WAS closed the day after the robbery while the FBI combed through the messy scene. It reopened that Thursday—without any of the former hostages, who were each given time off to recuperate. Kathy Amore, at the insistence of her mother, decided that she could no longer work at the branch and resigned her position. She told *Newsday* that she was going to take a vacation. "I need it after what I've been through," she said.[41]

The FBI recovered over $4,000 from the hostages, the cash gifts that John had tried to give them for their troubles. The bureau totaled just over $32,100 in recovered cash from the scenes in Brooklyn and the airport. It was about $5,000 less than Chase Manhattan's internal audit reported was missing—roughly the amount that John tried to secretly hand to Liz during the robbery. Throughout the day on Thursday, curiosity seekers passed by the bank, peeking in the windows and lingering on the sidewalk. Newspaper reporters pried stories from hostages, focusing more on the weird camaraderie between the gunmen and their subjects than on the fear that overtook Amore, Josephine Tutino, and others. But even Tutino was sad when she learned that Sal had been killed. None of them, no matter how badly scared, had wanted it to end like that. Shirley Ball, the hostage John had dubbed "Mouth" for her willingness to speak her mind, was the most publicly sympathetic to the bandits. She seriously considered an offer from Randy Wicker to appear at a press conference aimed at raising money for John's bail and defense but decided against it on the advice of Chase Manhattan's lawyers.[42]

"The most important thing to do," John told Wicker on one of his visits to the West Street detention center, "is get up the bail money." He kept on Liz and Carmen, insisting that they hustle interviews through every possible medium. He wanted Wicker to open a media blitz. He still held out hope that the gay community would rally to his aid and pushed Wicker to reach out to Italian American groups and make hay on the *Voice* article alleging Mafia ties. Wicker proposed that a bank account be opened in his name at the bank he'd robbed to collect donations—a fun little showman's twist that John loved. But it all must be done quickly, John insisted. "While I am still newsworthy."[43]

Carmen and Terry were interviewed by *Newsday,* while Liz spoke with Barbara Trecker of the *Post.* Trecker's article—one of several she'd publish on the case—was surprisingly sympathetic for the mainstream media and likely among the first truly humanizing pieces of straight journalism about a trans person. Liz talked of her early life and her social transition with staggering honesty but balked when it came to telling the truth about John. She did indeed plan to have gender-affirming surgery, she told Trecker, and was only concerned about it possibly driving John away from her. It is unknown what kind of money—if any—the interviews brought in.[44]

Meanwhile, Wicker was running into brick walls trying to get the gay community to offer any support for John beyond some possible funding toward securing an unbiased jury. He had penned a lengthy article for *Gay*—mostly disputing the Mafia angle of Bell's *Voice* piece—that he hoped might stir some activist interest in the case but saw little hope for action beyond a possible zap on Chase Manhattan should they refuse to open the fundraising account for John's bail and defense. Closer to home, things were going no better. The constant bickering between Carmen and Terry made it impossible to get anyone together on anything. There would be no media blitz, no grand drive for fundraising. Wicker found it maddeningly difficult to get the family to do something as simple as opening a post office box.[45]

Back on West Street, John had fallen into a deep depression. He had started out in segregation, confined to a small cell for twenty-four hours a day—let out only to see visitors. By early September, he had been released into the general population, where he shared quarters with three other prisoners—and was a constant target for harassment and threats of sexual assault. He got one shower and one shave per week and was permitted to use the phone for five minutes each weekday. Every visit from his family or Carmen turned into a fight. No one in the gay community seemed to want anything to do with him. He was writing to Liz nearly every day, with each letter getting more desperate and more morose. He told her about dreams he had: where he got to leave the prison and be with her, where she told him that she loved him and they embraced and kissed. They seemed so real to him that he'd wake up and start to cry when he remembered where he was. He begged her to write him more, to sign her letters with love, and to send him photos of her. Specifically, one of her smiling. "You never smile," he wrote. He said she could sell his letters to make spare cash, that she should go into show business, that she could sleep with anyone she wanted to, so long as she promised to tell him about it afterward.

Liz didn't write as often as John did. She visited, but not as often as Carmen and his mother and everyone else. He'd try to call her, but she was often out. He used his television privilege time to flip through late-night news programs, hoping to see her being interviewed. He encouraged her to still try for her surgery, however it might be possible. "When they take your manhood," he wrote in one letter, "I would like to have it. They can put it in a jar vacuum sealed. It's a bit gory but I would like to have it. Even if not in here, you can save it for me." He wanted to know when she ate, what she was wearing, and what time she went to bed. He begged, begged, begged her to write him more.

In one letter, written after Liz had evidently accused John of preferring either Patsy or Carmen in some way, John asked her, "How can you say I love someone else more . . . do I have to prove you are my first and only love? I love you more than life. That's why I did what I did, all for you. When you asked me to save the people, I saved them. I couldn't surrender [and] save them . . . I'd kill myself right now if it would prove that . . . I love you more than anyone or more than life . . . I can't understand your uncertainty. If I hang myself, will you be sure then? Just say yes [and] I will." He closed by telling her that he wanted her to have her surgery as soon as possible.

12. love is a very strange thing

They called him a "hanging judge," a conservative Democrat and LBJ appointee who was known for his harsh sentencing habits. John and Robert's cases—which included charges of kidnapping, armed bank robbery, and conspiracy—had landed on the docket of sixty-one-year-old Anthony J. Travia of the U.S. District Court for the Eastern District of New York. In some circles, he was even known as "Judge Travesty."[1]

John was assigned public defender Mark Landsman as his counsel. Landsman was the former partner of Eugene Gold, who was considered among the top defense attorneys in New York City. Randy Wicker, by now acting as John's point person on all matters of public relations, thought that John had netted a great lawyer. John did not agree. "He told me to cooperate fully with the FBI. He told me to tell them everything," John complained in a letter to Wicker. "But I don't like him. He never tells me anything."[2]

During his arraignment, John pressed Landsman to raise the issue of a possible jury bias against gays, but Landsman refused. Instead, Landsman wished to use John's gay relationships as proof of his unsound mental state at the time of the robbery. John indeed wished to plead insanity in the case but hated that Landsman was equating his sexuality with mental illness. John wanted to be examined at the Federal Psychiatric Hospital in Springfield, Missouri. Landsman instead asked for a stay at Kings County, the same wretched state facility where John visited Liz just weeks earlier. Travia granted the lawyer's request, and both John and Robert were ordered to spend thirty days at Kings County to determine whether they were fit to stand trial.[3]

Just before being ordered to Kings County, John wrote a letter to the corporate headquarters of Chase Manhattan Bank. "On Tuesday, Aug. 22, 1972," he wrote, "I went to one of your branch banks in B'klyn, specifically on Ave. P. and East 3rd St." What a reader might have expected to develop into a confession, a plea for leniency and sympathy, devolved into a bizarre customer service complaint. He wrote that he had never been given a receipt for the payment he'd made (with Chase Manhattan's own money) on his Americard and that his card had never been returned to him by the teller. He made an odd reference to the NYPD and FBI not being able to find the receipt or card in their "searches" (omitting why they were searching the bank in the first place). He asked that his account be adjusted accordingly and warned that if this was not done within ten days, he would involve the authorities.[4]

On September 12, the same day the letter arrived in Manhattan and was immediately turned over to the FBI, John spent his final hours before being trucked over to Kings County to write out his last will and testament. Wicker felt that John might have been suicidal during this period, that the will was an effort to set right whatever he could before—in the face of a possible life term—either taking his own life or making a nothing-to-lose escape attempt. Landsman would later consider the will another example of John's mental instability.

The document is genuinely heartbreaking. It opened with a pledge of love to Liz. "I love you with a passion as no man has ever loved another man in all eternity." He left her $2,700 of a $10,000 life insurance policy, to be used only for her gender-affirming surgery—which was to be started within sixty days of his death, or the money would be forfeited. Any money left over from that amount would be given to Liz at the first anniversary of his death, at his grave site. Carmen would get $5,000 from the same policy, to be used for a trust fund account for his two children. "My darling wife Carmen, you are the only woman I have ever loved + you will be the only woman I ever love . . . I look forward to being once more with you + the children in the hereafter." To his children, he had these words: "I always loved you Dawn + tried to care for you as best I could. I hope you will always love Daddy + remember me. Sean, you [are] the little man of the family now + will have to look after them for me. I love you dearly + hope you will always be a good son. I ask you to watch over Ernie for me + be his friend." He left the last $2,300 of his policy and his stamp collection to his mother. "I know I have treated you badly, but I love you so much. I always hurt the ones I love + you deserve more . . . I know you could never understand how I did the things I did. But I'm me + I'm different." He told her to use the money on a vacation. He left everything else to his brother Michael and apologized to Patsy and urged him to find someone "more deserving to love you." There was no mention of John's father in the document.[5]

KINGS COUNTY WAS hell for John. He already held a deep fear of institutionalization, and his stay confirmed all his worst fears. The ward was just as bad as Liz had found it: noisy, volatile, and filthy. John's shoes were confiscated, but the ward was short on slippers, so John was left to walk around barefoot, blackening his feet from the dirty floor. His visiting periods were limited to fifteen minutes, and he had to wait in line to use a pencil to write letters.[6]

Two weeks into his stay, he had yet to see a psychiatrist. Other inmates had been waiting three weeks or more for their first session. His letters from the hospital became overwhelmingly morose and desperate. He told Wicker that he cried himself to sleep every night and was terrified that they would never let him out. He desperately wanted to go back to jail, or anywhere but where he was. Carmen, overwhelmed by the entire situation and exhausted by John's allusions and threats, told Wicker in exasperation, "If I go see Johnny, I'm going to tell him that if he intends to kill himself, he should go ahead and do it and stop keeping everybody in all this suspense."[7]

Worst of all for John, he was unable to see Liz. Leadership at Kings County did not consider her family, even after she brought a copy of the just-published *Life* article that referred to her as John's spouse. "I'm being deprived of my rights," he vented to Wicker, asking that he arrange for a massive zap on the hospital to protest his treatment.[8]

But on the outside, Wicker was getting nowhere in drumming up support in the gay community, financial or otherwise. His piece on John had run in two parts in *Gay*, but it had done little to advance the cause. He conducted an interview with Liz and promised her half of whatever he made from it. Speaking with her on September 13, Wicker prefaced a question by saying outright that John had committed the robbery to finance Liz's surgery. Liz didn't dispute the claim but also didn't elaborate on it. She dismissed claims that the Mafia was involved and disputed parts of Arthur Bell's *Voice* article and talked a bit about her and John's sex life. She mentioned the request from John for her preserved testicles and said that she'd like to capitalize on her newfound notoriety. "I'm hoping to become a superstar like Andy Warhol's Jackie Curtis or Candy Darling or one of those very good actresses," she said. She mentioned that she'd been offered the part of a transgender baker in an off-Broadway play, but she didn't think she could learn the lines in time. The article was a tawdry piece that bent toward sensationalism. Wicker eventually sold it to *Screw* for about $50. Liz was glad for her share.[9]

The Kluge and Moore feature in *Life* was published in the September 22 edition and brought the story to its largest audience yet.* Titled "The Boys in the Bank" (a play on the 1970 film *The Boys in the Band,* which was among the first mainstream films to attempt to depict gay life), the piece was largely sympathetic to John while being lighter on sensationalism than on the strange and often humorous kinship between the gunmen and their hostages. Among advertisements for Kodak Instamatics, General Electric modular homes, and Silva Thin 100s cigarettes were pictures of John and Carmen's wedding, of Terry proudly holding up John's medal-decked army dress coat, and Liz in a bouffant with dangling earrings. There was a picture of Robert Barrett and Dolores Goettisheim posing apprehensively in the bank, of Liz in her bathrobe looking like "something who done it and ran," and of John on the street in his undershirt—argumentative and gesturing—while an army of cops idles in the midday heat in front of a grocery store window display promoting forty-nine-cent quarts of half-sour pickles.

* Although *Life* had once been among the highest-circulation magazines in the country, it would cease weekly publication just three months after the article appeared.

But the lasting impact of the *Life* article came when it directly tied the money in the bank to John's desire to fund Liz's gender-affirming surgery. "I did this for you," John is quoted as saying to Liz over the phone. "So you could have your operation." The abuse, the threats, the guns went unmentioned. So did the money John owed and who he owed it to. John had yet to articulate the narrative of the robbery in such a straightforward way as had Kluge and Moore. It was a clean narrative. Landsman didn't care for the article, it would make his job more difficult, he felt. But John liked it.

AFTER THIRTY DAYS at Kings County, doctors declared John and Robert fit to stand trial, and Landsman set to working out a plea deal with prosecutors. John wrote Wicker that he had a total of one thirty-minute session with a psychiatrist while he was confined. He said the same doctor later saw Robert and revealed some of the things John had told him. He told Landsman all about this, but he couldn't get the lawyer to take up his request for a second evaluation in Springfield. John still wanted to push the insanity defense at trial, but Landsman was set on taking a plea and risking a sentence of twenty years or more.[10]

Back on West Street, John was again seeing Liz a few times a week, while trying to get Carmen and his family to do anything useful for his case. At the time, Liz was suffering from what was probably post-traumatic stress disorder—with trembling spells and bouts of sporadic crying. With the *Life* article, as well as the interview in *Screw,* the narrative that John had robbed the bank to pay for her surgery had now fully taken hold. John had seemingly backed off from his thoughts of suicide as a way of trying to make things right (Wicker had to tell him that life insurance wouldn't pay off in the case of a suicide), and none of John's other fundraising ideas had produced more than a few hundred bucks. It seemed that there would never be enough money for the operation. And Liz was secretly relieved. "I never actually wanted the sex change until I got the sex change," she said later. Even if she had been confident in going forward with the procedure, she was in no place mentally to do so. She couldn't even trust her own judgment at the moment: Did she want it, or was it just the sting of the spotlight? After all, how could she say no now that it was in all the papers? How could she let that mixed-up romantic carry a twenty-year sentence and then just change her mind?[11]

Thank God, she thought, that John was broke.

While John was still locked away at Kings County, Martin Efland read Kluge and Moore's *Life* article and was immediately smitten. Efland was a Hollywood agent who had just earned his first producer credit. A passing reference in the article noted John's resemblance to Al Pacino, the breakout star of 1972's *The Godfather*. Efland took the idea to Pacino's agent, Martin Bregman, who was preparing to produce a biopic of NYPD whistleblower Frank Serpico starring Pacino. Bregman jumped on board and found support at Warner Bros. for an adaptation of the article into a feature film. With a ready pitch and the tentative backing of a major studio, Efland placed a call to Mark Landsman.[12]

John had just been released from Kings County when Landsman told him about the possible movie deal. Landsman had little interest in getting involved and seemed to view the entire thing as an annoyance, so John got in touch with Wicker, who helped to shepherd the deal along. Wicker distrusted Landsman and had a similar disregard for Efland. After ten days of negotiations, he told John that the entire process made him depressed.

"[Efland] thinks *Boys in the Band* was a 'great movie' which really showed 'homosexuals as they are,'" he wrote to John in early November.* "He is just a straight pig exploiter out to get your release as cheaply as possible."[13]

Wicker wanted to get enough in the deal to help John hire a different defense lawyer and urged John to look into hiring an entertainment lawyer to work out the movie deal. Efland was offering a paltry $7,500, whereas Robert Stroud—the Birdman of Alcatraz—had gotten $25,000 plus a percentage of gross ticket sales when he sold the film rights to his story, and that had been a full decade earlier. Nearly everyone around John was telling him not to sign the deal. Wicker had previously raised the idea of a low-budget independent film—possibly one starring Liz as herself—but had found no one interested in funding the project. He was sure that "everyone concerned is going to hate the movie" and expected it to be centered on "maximum possible laughs at everyone's expense." Everyone else told him he should hold out for more money. Efland's stance was that the deal was what it was, take it or take off.[14]

The dissenting voice, oddly enough, came from Liz. Getting over an initial bout of dread over the prospect of getting her surgery "whether I like it or not," Liz began to change her thinking. She suddenly had agency in the matter. For the first time in God-knows-how-long, she had control over her relationship with John. He was locked away, unable to hurt her, and would be for a long time. She told him that if he *really* wanted her to get the surgery, he would take the money. She was leaving it up

* Released in 1970, *The Boys in the Band* remains a controversial landmark of gay cinema. While it was a very early example of a film centered on gay characters, it has also been derided for showing gay life as one full of misery and self-loathing.

to him, of course, but there was no doubt as to whose opinion he valued most. Had she told him not to sign, he certainly would have passed. But now she laid it out flatly for him, she turned all the newspaper articles and desperate proclamations back at him. She had felt that she couldn't turn down a chance to have the surgery after everything John had gone through. Now she made it so that he couldn't turn down a chance to pay for it.[15]

On November 30, 1972, John signed a single-page consent form, agreeing to waive all claims in relation to a character who resembled him in a film tentatively titled *The Boys in the Bank*. A letter dated the previous day from Efland to Landsman detailed that John was to receive $7,500 for the release and 1 percent of the net profits of the film.* The document signed by John, however, contained no mention of compensation. A week later, John got his check. He had Landsman give Liz $2,500 for her surgery and was convinced by Landsman to hold the remaining $5,000 as a retainer on legal expenses should the case go to trial. Similar deals with the hostages paid $600 each. Robert would eventually settle for $750. Carmen was initially given nothing, believing that the $7,500 to John was based on her cooperation. Shortly after John divvied up his payment, with nothing left for anyone but Liz and the lawyer, Wicker (who had been hired as a script consultant by Efland) took pity on her and offered her $50 for a taped interview. She used it to buy her daughter a new raincoat.[16]

LIZ REALLY COULDN'T help herself. She pointed to the mantle in her little apartment in a gay men's rooming house on Dean

* So haphazard was the arrangement with John that this letter misspelled his last name as "Woodwitz."

Street. Randy Wicker had offered to accompany her and two friends, David and Lee, to her orchiectomy—referred to by all at the time as a "castration"—in exchange for permission to write about it for *Gay*. A few months later, she would return for a vaginoplasty. "See what some friends at [Boystown] who knew John and I gave me?" It was a pair of walnuts connected by a green string. She laughed and pointed to a housemate who was standing in the doorway, a manly-looking fellow in a bush jacket and blue jeans. "It's your turn next week," she said.

He shook his head. "No thanks! I'm keeping mine."[17]

It was a chilly morning in January 1973. Much would be in the news that month: the implementation of mandatory security screening for passengers on commercial flights; the Supreme Court's ruling in *Roe v. Wade*; and the signing of the Paris Peace Accords. Richard Nixon was inaugurated for a second time, the New York Yankees were sold to a syndicate led by George M. Steinbrenner, and Lyndon Johnson died. But the biggest news in the boarding house on Dean Street was all about Liz. For the past week, most of Liz's housemates had been encouraging her not to go through with the operation. That morning, their last-ditch efforts became so annoying that Liz stormed off from the breakfast table back to her room.[18]

Twenty years earlier, Christine Jorgensen made international news when she returned to the United States after undergoing gender-affirming surgery in Denmark. The Bronx-born photographer and World War II veteran was not the first person to undergo the procedure. Dora Richter underwent the first documented penectomy and vaginoplasty in Germany in 1931. Since then, the procedure had been practiced intermittently overseas. Jorgensen brought a new wave of attention to trans identity and a new burst of demand for surgical transition. But the

American medical community largely considered such actions to be illegal—finding the removal of healthy and vital tissue to be in violation of common law against "maiming." Trans people did transition surgically in the United States over the next decade and a half but did so in such tightly bound secrecy that a cloth would sometimes be placed over the patient's face to prevent them from being able to identify their doctors should they ever be charged criminally.[19]

By 1973, after clinics at the University of Minnesota and Johns Hopkins University become the first to openly offer gender-affirming surgeries, the academic thinking held that the chances of prosecution over such procedures were mostly nil. But in practice, the long-standing legal grayness to the matter meant that the field was still too rife with predatory opportunists. Liz's roommates were all well aware of this. Nearly everyone in the house knew someone who had transitioned. There were too many horror stories, too many suicides. One former resident of the house had undergone a surgical transition and later took their own life. Liz's doctor, Benito Rish, was a plastic surgeon with a sideline in low-profile gender-affirming surgeries. Dr. Rish told Liz that he estimated that about one in three people who began the process would eventually attempt suicide. Liz laughed it off. "That doesn't worry me," she told Wicker. "I've been attempting suicide right and left without the operation, three times a day already, so what difference does it make?"[20]

As Liz left for the hospital, her housemates gathered to wish her luck, all the bad feelings from earlier forgotten. "Well, go have them cut off, baby," someone told her. "I never thought of you as really having any balls anyway."

Liz grinned. "Well, sweetheart, even with no balls, I've still got a cock a lot bigger than yours."[21]

She really couldn't help herself.

Liz had already paid $500 for the orchiectomy and another $75 for a pre-surgery psychiatric evaluation. The evaluation, which was more of a safeguard for the surgeon than the patient, lasted about an hour. Liz had never seen the psychiatrist before and would never see them again. A few days before, she visited John on West Street. He'd given her a small Virgin Mary medallion and told her that if she squeezed it tightly, he would be right there next to her. She had asked Dr. Rish about preserving her testicles for John—she had planned to keep them on her mantle next to his photo—but Rish said the law forbid him to let organs leave the hospital once removed. Good thing, said David. "You wouldn't have me as a visitor anymore if you did."[22]

Liz was in high spirits when she arrived at the doctor's office in Yonkers. She was checked in by a nurse named Terry, who was sixty-four, but—thanks to Dr. Rish's handiwork—looked twenty years younger. Liz bubbled about a possible documentary film that wanted to include her experiences and an interview she was going to do with Truman Capote (neither of these ended up happening). The nurse was happy for Liz. She asked her to sign her legal name—still Ernest Aron—as well as Liz Eden on all the paperwork. "I like to call people by their female names right from the beginning," she said with a smile.[23]

Liz's good mood vanished as soon as the injections began. She froze at the sight of all the needles—maybe twenty in all—and winced in pain at the first shot. "Doctor," she said in a panic, "maybe . . ."

"It's too late now, we've already started," Rish said.[24]

Even after the shots numbed her crotch, she could still feel the movement inside of her—the testicles being pulled out, the blood running everywhere. She squeezed the Virgin Mary so hard it nearly drew blood. Nurse Terry held her arm tightly and whispered, "Don't look down, don't look down."[25]

In the waiting area, David and Lee debated the merits of her transition. "I think Liz is having it more because John wants her to have it than because she wants to have it," Lee said. "I've known Liz for over six years. I've seen her go through very feminine stages when she wanted the operation and then go through periods where she got very butch and didn't want to think or talk about it anymore. A lot of queens, real queens, go through a sex-change phase and then get out of it. But now Liz has gotten to the point of no return."[26]

David agreed. "Liz likes to go out and pick up butch numbers, but usually she was the one who screwed *them*. It doesn't make any sense to have it cut off, she uses it too much. What's she going to do without it? I should know, I roomed with her for two months."[27]

After about a half hour, the operation was complete. Liz sat in the recovery room, trembling and crying. She was so weak that David and Nurse Terry had to help her dress. After a long, quiet car ride, the four returned to the boarding house around nine o'clock at night. A group of her housemates were sitting outside on the stoop in the cold evening air. As Liz gingerly climbed out of the back seat of Wicker's car, they stood and applauded.[28]

THE WEEK AFTER Liz's surgery, Landsman arranged for a semicovert meeting between her and John at the West Street detention center. Landsman brought her just before the regular guards were to come on duty. The topic of discussion was how John would plea. Landsman still preferred to pursue a plea bargain, John still wanted to risk the insanity defense—as did Carmen and Terry. Liz sided with Landsman. She told John that if he did not plead guilty, he could go away for life and that she might not have any interest in maintaining whatever kind of relationship they still had under such conditions. And then there was the money. Landsman, who had taken the $5,000 from the movie deal and was now acting as John's hired counsel, not a public defender, told him that if he pleaded guilty, $1,500 of that would be returned to him. What the remaining $3,500 had actually paid for went unaddressed.[29]

John had little choice but to agree to the plea. Going to trial could cost him Liz and the little bit of money that he'd been able to make for all this awful effort. Not to mention the very likely outcome of a lifetime behind bars. After he told Landsman to work out the best deal he could, the lawyer switched off the lights in the small meeting room and allowed John and Liz to have a few minutes of desperate and groping passion.[30]

On February 16, John and Robert appeared before Travia to enter their pleas. John had insisted that Liz be in the courtroom galley that day and even planned to watch her for clues on how he should answer each question from the judge. By arrangement, the charges of kidnapping and conspiracy had been dropped in exchange for a single charge of armed bank robbery. When Travia asked for his plea, John turned back to Liz. "Look at me," the judge scolded him.[31]

John, his shoulders slumped and his hands clenched so tightly they had turned white, was asked again for his plea. Landsman placed a hand on John's back. "I plead guilty, your honor." A few minutes later, Robert did the same. Sentencing was set for April 23.[32]

THE WEEK BEFORE Liz was to see Dr. Rish for her vaginoplasty, the article on her orchiectomy was published in *Screw*. Wicker had used Rish's real name throughout the piece, and the doctor was thrust into an uncomfortable spotlight from the American Medical Association and the state medical board. Rish, who would eventually be hit with a fine of several thousand dollars, refused further treatment to Liz. Under threat of a lawsuit from Liz, he referred her to another, unnamed surgeon who could finish the procedure. She underwent the operation on March 27 and spent the next week at home in terrible pain.[33]

Back on West Street, John had been put into solitary confinement after someone had called the FBI and warned that a massive protest march on the Federal Detention Center was going to attempt to break John free. Although John must have been heartened by the threat—even though it turned out to be a hoax—solitary was a stressor that added to others. Despite being told by Landsman that $1,500 would be returned to him for pleading guilty, the lawyer only gave back $1,000. He tried to fire Landsman over the matter, but Travia refused to allow him to change lawyers at this late point in the case. The $1,000 was turned over to Carmen, and John imminently told her to loan $300 to Liz, who needed some more cash to cover the final bills from her transition.[34]

And on it all went throughout April. John was refusing to speak with his lawyer. Carmen was complaining about the money Liz owed her. Terry was still on very hard times—waiting on the final $500 that Landsman owed John. Wicker was urging John and Terry to submit to interviews for the film script, but John was now demanding $3,000 to speak with anyone associated with the project. Working with Warner Bros., Landsman—who John now suspected was trying to get money from the studio behind his back—had arranged for a researcher to speak with John at West Street. The man showed up at the designated time, but John would not see him. It was $3,000 or he wouldn't tell them a damn thing, he insisted. The filmmakers wasted no time in moving ahead without him. Meanwhile, Al Pacino—who had been cast as John's character in the film—was poring over the footage that Wicker had shot of John and Liz's wedding, studying John's mannerisms and voice.[35]

Early on the morning of Monday, April 23, the day he was to be sentenced, John got out of bed and went to the bathroom area of his cell. He had given his confession at the jailhouse chapel that Saturday and had gone to mass and taken communion on Sunday. He had saved up a fistful of sleeping pills from the prison dispensary and had procured a razor blade from the canteen. While his cellmates slept, John swallowed the pills and slashed open his wrists. He was already passed out in a bloody mess on the floor by the time someone noticed. He was rushed to Bellevue Hospital, where his stomach was pumped and his arms stitched up. Given the circumstances, Judge Travia delayed his sentencing hearing from nine in the morning to two in the afternoon.[36]

That afternoon, as the last item on the judge's docket, John and Robert were brought before the court. Before they were officially called, the entire courtroom—save for Carmen, Terry, Michael, and a handful of reporters—was cleared out. Robert was called first. His lawyer admitted that Robert had been involved, but only to a minimal degree. He went over the laundry list of tragedies that had been his young life—the broken home, the health troubles, the grade school education, the confusion over his sexuality—and asked for leniency. "He knows he did wrong. He's not trying to make some cause célèbre out of his situation," the lawyer said. "You have before you a fellow who got involved with people more violent than himself . . . I think he has learned his lesson and will never be before a court again."[37]

Travia gave him two years.

It was John's turn now.

He shuffled into the room, double-chained around his waist and hands shackled. His face was swollen and raw and his arms were bandaged. Terry and Carmen knew that he'd tried to take his own life, but the sight of him—weary from whatever they'd given him at Bellevue and with his prison-issue jumpsuit still covered in his own blood—was a shock. Carmen burst into loud, painful tears, and Terry needed to be restrained from rushing toward him. "Don't tell me I can't see my son," she screamed at the guard who held her back. "What have you done to him? What have you done to him?"[38]

John was seated and had his shackles removed. "Your honor, have mercy on my son!" Terry cried. "He's all mixed up. He doesn't know what he's doing."[39]

After a lengthy back-and-forth between Travia and John about whether he wished to retain Landsman as his counsel and if he wished to withdraw his plea of guilty, John—in slow and slightly slurred speech—demurred. Landsman was still his lawyer, he asserted, and he still wished to plead guilty. After an hour recess, all involved returned to the courtroom for the sentencing. Landsman gave an overview of John's military record and his work history and noted that he had never been in trouble with the law before. "A good deal of his problems," he went on, "arise out of his taking up with this male wife of his . . . unfortunately his marriage [to Carmen] didn't do too well and he got in with persons of other persuasions, you might say."[40]

John slumped in his chair, giving no indication he was even

listening. After Landsman finished, Travia asked him if he had anything to say on his behalf before sentencing. He said that he did and shifted forward in his chair.[41]

"Love is a very strange thing," he said, speaking slowly and deliberately. "Some feel it more deeply than others. I love my wife, Carmen, my son, my daughter, my mother. And I love Ernie," he said, as usual refusing to use Liz's preferred name. "I love all of them. I care about them very, very much. Ernie attempted suicide several times before because he felt he was a woman trapped in a man's body and wanted his gender changed. I went looking for a job. Nobody would hire me because I was gay. He attempted suicide again, when I failed to get him the money for the operation I had promised him for his birthday, he took an overdose and died in the hospital, and they brought him back to life. I had promised him I would get him the money. I couldn't watch him twenty-four hours a day. Sooner or later, I knew, he would try it again and would succeed. I loved him more than he loved me. I know it was wrong to rob the bank. But what is more important, money or a human being?"[42]

It was heartfelt but mostly bullshit. It was the narrative of the *Life* article, soon to be a major motion picture, and it was the narrative that John would insist was the truth for the rest of his life. He went on a bit more, placing himself in the savior's role—not just with Liz, but again with the hostages. "I got Sal Naturile out of that bank," he said, a bit of anger rising in his voice. "I saved the hostages, not the FBI. If I had walked out of that bank, they would have all been dead. They know this."[43]

Judge Travia asked John if he was through. He said that he was. Travia told John to stand, and he did so wearily, with two guards needing to help him up. Liz wasn't in the courtroom that afternoon. She was seeing a new guy now, named Ralph. He wouldn't let her anywhere near John. "On your plea of guilty to Count Two," Travia said, no trace of emotion in his voice, "you are hereby committed for a term of twenty years."[44]

Judge Travia banged his gavel, gathered his papers, and quickly left the courtroom. As John was still considered to be suicidal, Carmen and Terry were permitted to speak with him briefly after adjournment. John displayed no emotion as they sat together. "Was I sentenced?" he asked. "Was that my sentence?" As they tried to explain to him what had just happened, John interrupted. He told Carmen that he had mentioned her and the children before he had mentioned Liz. "See, Carmen," he said. "I was in such a state my subconscious was in control and I mentioned you first. Deep down, I must care for you more." Then he muttered something about hoping that Liz wouldn't find out about what he'd said. She might get angry with him. Carmen had had enough. She told him that Liz had left him for good. She said that Liz was planning to kill herself. She told him that she was already regretting her medical transition and that she blamed him for everything. It wasn't true. But he wasn't listening anyway. He smiled, then began to laugh. There John sat, half-dead and broke, twenty years of hard time ahead of him, and the last two people in the world who truly loved him looking on with stricken expressions. He kept laughing until he ran out of breath.[45]

The next day, he was trucked off to the federal penitentiary at Terre Haute, Indiana.

13. seasons in the sun

Josephine Tutino's first impression of John Wojtowicz was that he was a true gentleman. Standing at her station in the bank on that unbearable hot afternoon in August 1972, he was asking about silver dollars. When a woman appeared behind him in line, he stepped aside and let her conduct her business first. Her impression changed when he pulled his guns and started cursing. Thirty-plus years later, and after thirteen hours as his hostage on that terribly hot night in Brooklyn, what did she think? "I really don't know. He's a puzzle. A puzzle."[1]

The piece in *Life* depicted a somewhat jovial atmosphere inside the bank. Based on that article, Warner Bros. was beginning to pour money into a film adaptation. But Tutino's experience didn't match the depiction. She had genuinely feared for her life. She remembered the fear, the heat, the exhaustion. And the hunger. Even abetted by adrenaline, they were all starving that night. So much so that they'd raided the jars of lollipops kept behind the counter. It was a heck of an odd pairing, she noticed (a devout Christian, this was the strongest language that she would use): lollipops and shotguns. Like innocence and evil.

Or like the polite young man in the suit jacket, who later became the wild-eyed bandit in the undershirt.

Shortly after the ordeal, Tutino's husband, Frank, encouraged her to put her feelings down on paper. With his help, she wrote a short song about her experience. She called it, "Lollypops and Shotguns (A Hostage's Lament)."

"I had to write it just to get it out of me," Tutino said. "All my feelings [are] there." Tutino's sons wrote the music and arrangement, and the family financed the recording and production. The Tutinos contracted a group called the Romanaires to perform the song, as well as an oddly paired doo-wop love song written by a family member called "Is It Too Late?" The record is the only known recording by the Romanaires. The family self-distributed the album and made a push to get it used in the Warner Bros. film, but it quickly sank into obscurity.

JOHN WAS JUST over two months into his sentence when he finally heard from Liz. It was a short letter, simple yet devastating. "I met a new guy named Ralph," she wrote. "He feels it's bad if I write you and so from now on, I'm not going to. Hope all works out well for you. Love, Liz. PS: Please don't bother me anymore." It was an odd summer for Liz. In a time when being trans was regarded as something between a joke and a crime against nature by most Americans, Liz had suddenly been thrust into an uncomfortable spotlight. She became, arguably, just the second American trans "celebrity" after Christine Jorgensen, who spent the early 1970s on the college lecture circuit and performing her campy nightclub act. In March, a beautiful, soft-focus portrait of Liz graced the cover of London's *Gay News*, with a headline of "Would You Rob a Bank for This Man?" She spoke at one medical conference and was a guest speaker in an NYU class taught by Professor Rosalyn Regelson, who had created one of the first pro-gay college courses in the nation. In July, Liz was a marcher of note in the fourth annual Christopher Street Liberation Day parade—one of over twelve thousand people to join the fifteen-block-long procession. "I would have worn a bikini," she told *The Advocate*, "but the silicone hasn't settled yet."[2]

When interviewed briefly by *The Advocate* at the parade, Liz felt the need to push back on rumors that she was unhappy with her transition. She was living well, she told the paper. It wasn't entirely true. She had suffered from serious complications after her vaginoplasty when the vaginal opening began to heal itself shut. She saw doctor after doctor, but they were unable to help. One put her under local anesthetic and tried to force it open using a metal dilator. The pain was excruciating. "Take the pain of castration, triple it, and you'll have an idea of the ordeal," she later said.[3]

She began to suspect that the doctor who had done the original procedure had sabotaged her in retaliation for the article that had been written about Dr. Rish and her orchiectomy. She had a hard time trusting any doctor after that. By the time she finally did find one who was sensitive to her plight, the money from John was long gone. He allowed her to pay a small amount up front, which she borrowed from a friend, and to pay the rest in installments. With a skin graft from her buttocks and a large rubber spacer (Liz, of course, would only refer to it as a dildo), the raw skin finally began to heal, and the pain subsided.[4]

Ralph, whom she had met about a month before her vaginoplasty, remained with her throughout the ordeal, but things were never the same after the surgery. Even after convincing her that she needed to cut John out of her life, they began to drift apart. "Once I was a girl, he no longer felt safe with me," she later said of the relationship. "Things were fine when I was a boy and I used to be butch in bed or bisexual in bed, it was great with him. But once I turned into a girl, it no longer suited him." About six months after the transition, Ralph and Liz split for good.[5]

AFTER THREE MONTHS at Terre Haute, John—still devastated by Liz's letter—was transferred to the federal prison at Lewisburg, Pennsylvania. Opened in 1932, Lewisburg had devolved into one of the most notorious prisons in the country by 1973. The previous year, former Teamsters President Jimmy Hoffa—just out of Lewisburg after serving fifty-eight months on a jury-tampering conviction—made a plea for prison reform before a U.S. Senate committee. He said Lewisburg was dangerously overcrowded and its men forced to work in deathly unsafe shops and factories. He'd seen men die of treatable maladies because prison medical facilities were woefully unfit. Violence was rampant, prison officials were unduly cruel, and prisoners were so beaten down by overall conditions that dignity was a rare commodity.[6]

For a prisoner of lesser stature than Hoffa—that is, every other one of the roughly 1,800 men housed there—survival at Lewisburg could be a day-to-day venture. Beatings and rapes were commonplace. Shivs were the weapon of choice at Lewisburg, and stabbings were used as retaliation for offenses both large and minuscule. Hoffa was an eyewitness to one man being stabbed seventeen times over bad feelings from a handball match. Offending the rules of the warden and his guards could get a man put into solitary confinement—known as the Hole—and left alone for weeks or months on end and made to sleep on a metal bedframe or the concrete floor. Sexual assault was almost a rite of passage for new prisoners. In the rare instances when such actions were punished, both the victim and his attackers would get sent to the Hole.[7]

This is what John was thrown into in July 1973. And it would have been hard to find a worse match for the chaos at Lewisburg. John was small, loud, semi-famous, and openly gay. He became an immediate target.

Shortly after his arrival at Lewisburg, Frank Pierson—who'd been hired to write the screenplay for *The Boys in the Bank*—wrote John a letter detailing his credentials, which included two Academy Award nominations, and asked for an interview. John replied in a rambling, six-page letter that relayed all his miseries. The threats of rape and violence against him were constant. The heartbreak from Liz's letter had left him near suicidal. He was desperate to return to Terre Haute, where he had been treated much better. He felt that all those he'd trusted in the case—Wicker, Landsman, Liz—had let him down. He expressed his love for Carmen, for his kids, and still for Liz. "I have faith in you + I feel you are a good and trustworthy person," John wrote. He hardly mentioned the film. The letter made it clear he wasn't particularly interested in the film at the moment. He just badly needed a friend. Someone outside of his worn-out band of family and hangers-on. And he asked him to, if he should happen to see her, pass along his undying love to Liz. And he asked for money.[8]

He never would give Pierson an interview.

BY DECEMBER, JOHN had settled in somewhat in Lewisburg. After splitting with Ralph, Liz had reconnected with him, boosting his bottomed-out morale. He was working unloading trucks and had television privileges that allowed him to watch movies at night. He was fastidious about his mail, keeping records of when each letter was sent and when each was received. He was sleeping better. The tranquilizers helped. On December 4, John wished Liz a happy second wedding anniversary. "We have had some great times together and also some very bad times," he wrote, "but honey the good times outdo the rest by leaps and bounds." He wrote her bad poetry ("What is the ocean without land to fall upon, what is the mountain without the sky above, what is a seed without the sun to make it grow . . .") and gave her backhanded compliments ("I know I'm all you have and you need me more than you admit to even yourself . . ."). He wrote that everyone was against them, but it was all fueled by misunderstandings and jealousy. He continued to talk of love and death, both his own and her own. If she still wanted to die, he wrote her, she could come visit him. "I will hold your hand and kill myself before your eyes. As the blood drains from me, then you [will] realize how much I really and truly love you. Then I will wait for you to do the same . . . if after I do this and you decide not to die, don't feel guilty."[9]

He signed his letters, "SWABK" (sealed with a big kiss) and wrote their names together in hearts and included crude stick figure drawings of Liz posing nude on a pedestal.

On Christmas Day, 1973, John was attacked with a pipe in the prison laundry and sexually assaulted by three other inmates. He reported the incident, which only made things worse. He was held in solitary confinement afterward. The guards told him it was to prevent him from retaliating or killing himself. He eventually had what he called a "nervous breakdown" and was briefly transferred to a psych ward in Leavenworth—a seven-hour ride by bus. He explained all this in a letter to Liz written on January 13, 1973, in between lengthy passages about death and an attempt to settle a dispute between Liz and Carmen over a keepsake box that Carmen was supposed to be holding for them. By this point, Liz hadn't written to him in almost two months.[10]

In mid-January, John was returned to Lewisburg and the general prison population. Liz wrote to announce that she had a new boyfriend, a well-built young man named Wayne. John replied that he had commissioned a portrait of her from a fellow inmate who'd taught himself to paint. It cost him a fortune, and he said it could take a month or more to figure out how to smuggle it out to her. He wished her and Wayne the best but added, "I know in your heart you do love and need me more than you will ever admit to even yourself. A time will come when you feel alone and sad. Then you will turn to me again and start writing again."[11]

IN JANUARY 1974, Robert was granted parole after sixteen months of his two-year sentence. Given credit for his time served on West Street, Robert was sent to Tallahassee after sentencing and found it to be a world apart from the lockup in Manhattan. He was young and unblemished, and rumors grew from the tangled bits of news that followed him south from the trial. Word in the penitentiary was that Robert was the transgender figure in the bank robbery, with some even believing that he had already transitioned physically. He got all the wrong kinds of attention. He constantly got notes from fellow prisoners: *I want to be your friend; I love you; I will kill for you.* After a brawl erupted in the yard over who would get to "claim" him as their own, he was accused by prison officials of "swishing around" and advertising his sexuality in order to get attention. He was doing nothing of the sort. The only thing on his mind was survival.

Eventually, prison officials found it all too much to deal with and he was transferred to the Robert F. Kennedy Youth Rehabilitation Center in Morgantown, West Virginia.[12]

A photo exists of Robert from his time in West Virginia. He stands on the lawn of the facility, building and sidewalks behind him, looking not unlike a young man posing in a suburban park. He wears a sweater and bell-bottoms; his long hair is combed over to one side and he has a faint mustache. A pensive look clouds his face, a look of distrust aimed out at the whole world. But the situation in West Virginia proved far preferable to Florida. Morgantown housed mostly first-time offenders and it was coed. "No sex pressure there at all," Robert later said. And security was lax enough that, if so willing, a couple could sneak into the nearby woods for a quick romp.[13]

He took classes in West Virginia, advancing up to the eighth grade. He learned some basic photography and worked with fabrics. "I got a just sentence," he told *Gay* after his release. "I don't understand those people who insult me and say, 'How could you have become involved in a thing like that.' I was just a naive, dumb kid who didn't know any better. I'm a lot smarter now." In late 1973, he was transferred back to Manhattan, where he stayed at a community treatment center and was permitted to leave during the day to look for a post-release job. On March 1, 1974, he was released without restrictions. Shortly after, in an interview with Randy Wicker that would never be published, he was asked what he'd do now if someone like John came to him with a chance to make a quick $50,000. "I'd tell him to go fuck himself," Robert answered.[14]

He had kept in touch with John and Liz and even heard from Terry every so often. But even as a free man, he still wasn't able to find his place in the world. The movie people had offered him $2,000 for the rights to his part of the story while he was still awaiting trial, but he'd turned it down on his lawyer's advice. Better to hold out, the reasoning went. In April 1974, they offered him $750 almost as an afterthought. He took it without hesitation. "I was so broke, I would have taken $20," he later admitted. The money went fast. By the summer, he was flat busted again. He couldn't find work, and he got kicked out of his apartment. He borrowed from friends to find another place, a vermin-infested walk-up in Chelsea. He was still sickly, he was still depressed, he still wanted desperately to get out of New York. Within months of his release, he attempted suicide twice.[15]

A two-year retrospective about the robbery by Barbara Trecker ran in the *Post* in the fall of 1974. Shirley Ball read all about John's troubles in prison, Liz's new life as a woman, and Robert's dead-end despair. She gathered up some winter clothes and tracked down Robert's fleabag apartment. She paid a visit, chatted for a bit, and handed over the clothes in a small care package. Winter was coming, she thought, and the poor kid might not have enough to keep himself warm.[16]

AS ROBERT BECAME accustomed to the hard knocks of freedom, Liz and Wayne fell in love, moved in together, and got engaged. It would be a real wedding this time, legal and binding. Wayne even bought her an engagement ring—something that John, for all the money he'd spent on Liz, had never bothered to do. John kept writing her. He said that she and Wayne had his blessing, even though it is almost certain she never asked for it. In February 1974, Liz wrote to Carmen to tell her, "You've won." Liz was sick of all the petty back-and-forth, all the pissing and moaning about the money and the keepsake box. "I won't write much more to John," she continued. "Not because you want me to stop, but because I'm engaged."[17]

Sick of it, but sick of it on her own terms.

John continued to write to Liz. He kept hearing Terry Jacks's "Seasons in the Sun" on the prison radio, and it reminded him so deeply of their relationship that he wept whenever it came on. He got in trouble again and had to do two weeks in segregation. Whatever the trouble was, it cost him some of his few friends. During his time in the Hole, he wrote love songs and sappy poems on the walls of his cell in pencil. Once out, he caught part of the 1963 Elizabeth Taylor film *Cleopatra* on television and cried. It had been Liz's favorite. And he kept writing to her. He sent her a handmade Valentine's Day card, love notes, and song lyrics he'd copied down from the radio. He had a frame for the portrait he'd commissioned made in the woodshop and scrawled tiny lines of poetry along the back of it. He said that he knew she was depressed and complained bitterly that she didn't reply often enough or say enough complimentary things about the notes he'd sent her. He wrote out a long list of letters—their numbers and the dates he mailed them—and demanded that she check off each that she'd received.[18]

Throughout April, he wrote her almost daily. Nothing like the long and rambling letters from before. These were single-page, often single-sentence notes. I love you, I need you, I want you, you are my life, and on and on. By now, her relationship with Wayne had ended. She didn't jump back into things with John. She'd still write periodically. And John wrote her too. But it wasn't the same. Fifty-plus years later, a stack of John's letters can still be found in a small box in the archives of the Lesbian, Gay, Bisexual, and Transgender Community Center in Greenwich Village. They sit among a small collection of Liz's things—paperwork, legal forms, photographs—that were donated to the archive by one of her friends. Even if she'd never answered the letters, even if they were a dark annoyance at best and abusive at worst, even if she'd never really come to a satisfying answer on whether she'd ever really loved him, she kept them. Through hard times and good, a dozen planned careers that never took off, and too many moves to count—she hung on.[19]

IN THE SUMMER of 1974, John met someone. George Heath was similar to John in a handful of ways. Both were bisexual men in their twenties, both were legally married to women and had children, both were New Yorkers serving time for bank robbery. But their differences went much deeper. John was impetuous and loud: more talk than action, but more action than thought. George was a strategist. He had thoughtful eyes, but there was a hardness behind them. John tried to survive on the inside by making people like him, the same way he did back in the Village when he was making up bullshit tales of banditry and blowing through money as quickly as he could borrow it. George, eight years into his term, had learned that it was better to be feared than liked. George transferred into Lewisburg in 1974 as a man not to be fucked with.

George had just gotten settled at Lewisburg when he took John as his "old lady." This type of relationship was typically built through coercion, but George was an atypical "daddy." He liked John but could see that his actions made him a wide-open target. In an odd attempt to appear mentally unbalanced, John told prison officials shortly after his sexual assault that he was pregnant. He even had a small baby bed built in the carpentry shop. Behavior like that might have made him a tolerable nuisance on Christopher Street, but in Lewisburg it could get you killed. "He didn't realize the consequences of things he would do or say," George said of John when he first met him. "He was just there and not there mentally."[20]

The couple was equally mismatched physically. John had gained a bit of weight in prison and grown a small mustache. He wouldn't have looked out of place at a suburban Rotary Club meeting—a cheaply cut mod-style mop of black hair, painter's brush facial hair, and a slightly puckering gut. George was tall and angular—a build that had made him a natural when he was on the drag scene years earlier. He was of Irish and African American heritage, with olive skin, lustrous dark hair, and wide eyes. Just as soon as the sinewy newcomer took John as "his," the threats against him receded.[21]

Just two weeks after John and George met, John proposed and George accepted. That day, they were "married" by a fellow inmate in the prison yard. A few weeks later, George was convicted on a charge of carrying a knife, something he suspected might have been retaliation from prison officials for the slapdash marriage ceremony. George would have been up for parole within the year, but the knife charge pushed that back to 1978. The newlyweds now found themselves with a lot more time than they had expected. And what to do with all that time?

George didn't have much of a formal education but possessed a sharp natural intellect. On the inside, he had developed himself as a formidable jailhouse lawyer, even working on his own case to earn a sentence reduction—now undone by the knife charge. John's attempts to work on his own sentence ranged from the pathetic (he half-intended the pregnancy bit to make a case for insanity—far after such a defense might have been useful) to the delusional (he had his mother working on a case for a presidential pardon), but George saw right away that there might be grounds for a reduction in his sentence. It would take time, but that was now the one thing that John and George had aplenty.[22]

AS GEORGE AND John became attorney and client, screenwriter Frank Pierson was hammering out the screenplay for what was now being called *Dog Day Afternoon*. The script, as it existed in the summer of 1974, still used all the real names of those involved, save for bank teller Kathy Amore, who had declined to sign a release. There was a conversation between John and Sal that made it plain that murdering Liz was a part of the suicide pact they'd agreed on prior to the robbery. Sal's sexual abuse in prison was graphically detailed, and his character was bloodthirsty to a near sadistic degree. Pierson also wrote a scene in which Wicker's video footage of John and Liz's wedding would be recreated and used in a lengthy television segment that the hostages would watch in the bank.

The draft most heavily deviated from reality in the end of the hostage ordeal. Instead of agent Jim Murphy—a white man who John had picked from a group of FBI men—driving the van and ending Sal's life, it was a Black agent—working undercover as an employee for the airport van service—who drove them to JFK Airport and executed the fatal shot. And then there was John, trapped by the FBI with his gun pinned down just after seeing Sal die. In reality, he surrendered meekly and asked agents not to shoot. In the script, he begged them to end his life.

The script was rife with homophobia, not in Pierson's depictions of the queer characters, but in the world in which the story existed. The word *faggot* appeared dozens of times, most often used by the crowd of onlookers who amassed around the bank during the ordeal. At one point, after John and Liz have a conversation in the street in front of the bank, a chant of the word breaks out, prompting John to pull a hostage from the bank and put a gun to her head, demanding that the crowd shut up. But Pierson also allowed space for gay voices in the script. After John's arrest at the airport, a montage of nameless members of a nameless gay rights organization spoke about John and the robbery—both lauding him and condemning him. He also included a scene where John and Liz share a long goodbye kiss at the door of the bank. The crowd roars and Liz throws a "fuck-you finger" to the disapproving mass.

Back in New York City, paperback novelist Leslie Waller took a draft of Pierson's screenplay and quickly pounded out two hundred pages that would hit stores before the end of the year. Both Randy Wicker and Liz had made abortive attempts at publishing books about the robbery, but it would take the promise of a soon-to-be-released motion picture and a pulp fictionist's crude and raw approach to finally get the story—or something loosely based on it—into print.

The novel's Littlejoe Nowicki protagonist (no real names are used in the book) is brooding and hateful. He hates his wife. He hates his mother. He really hates his father. Littlejoe is disgusted by fat people, disdainful of women beyond their use as sex objects, and makes no attempts to develop any redeeming qualities. His one joy is Lana, a trans woman badly in want of a "sex change" and generally willing to do anything for a buck or a free drink. She threatens to kill herself unless she gets what she wants, so Littlejoe recruits a teenage psychopath named Sam and—acting on a tip from a bank executive—plans to rob a Chase Manhattan branch said to be full of cash. The two find a driver (Robert's character is completely absent) and take the bank, only to find just $5,000 in the vault. The only significant break from Pierson's script is the baffling decision by Littlejoe to hold the employees in the bank overnight so that they can try to hit the next morning's armored car cash delivery. But before any of that can develop, the cops surround the place and the story plays out more or less along the lines set down by Pierson, with a couple of sexual assaults thrown in to give readers their dollar and a half's worth of grit and thrills.

But by the time the book—which would be published under the name "Patrick Mann" to keep it separate from Waller's more serious work—was tantalizing the creep set, Pierson's version of John had lost the roughness around his edges and become more identifiable, more likable. And as the studio had the production drop nearly all the real names from the script, John Wojtowicz became Sonny Wortzik. The rage from the earlier incarnations of the character remained, but Sonny did a better job of controlling himself. He was more polite and gentlemanly, he was more vulnerable, he was funnier without actually laughing himself. His relationship with Liz—now known only as Leon—softened. No longer was killing her part of the plan. The abuse Sonny had heaped was still mentioned but not demonstrated. Their two meetings on the street—in which chants of "Faggot!" were the background noise—were replaced with a single phone conversation.

AL PACINO JUST couldn't make up his mind about *Dog Day Afternoon*. He liked the script and wanted to work with Sidney Lumet again, but he was tired and felt isolated in Hollywood. He had never felt comfortable in the movies and wanted badly to go back to the stage. He took the role, changed his mind, then was back in, then changed his mind again. Just before production was about to begin, Lumet and Pierson went to Pacino's house in Los Angeles and found the actor crawling around on the floor and barking like a dog. "Al, what the fuck is this?" Lumet asked.[23]

Pacino felt like everything in his life was out of control. He was struggling to deal with his newfound fame and was more and more often using drugs and liquor to cope. And now he couldn't make up his mind about this damn role. Lumet would later say that the specter of being the first major star to play a gay man added to Pacino's worries—although Pacino himself would claim that this bore no weight on his decision (or lack thereof).* Eventually, Lumet was able to talk Pacino back into the picture, convincing him to channel all his fear and uncertainty into the role. Sonny would have been feeling something very similar while he was sitting in that damn car outside the bank.[24]

Even as the casting came together, Pierson struggled to accurately portray the character of Sonny. The problem was that everyone he talked to, it seemed, described John Wojtowicz as an entirely different person. It got to the point where he didn't think he could do the project justice and considered quitting—if only he hadn't already spent the advance. The breakthrough came when he looked for common elements in what he'd been told about John. From there, a character finally emerged. "I thought of John as a kind of magician," Pierson later wrote. "[He] tried mightily to bring to life the dreams and ambitions of the people he loved, in the belief that once fulfilled and made whole by the completion of their hopes they would be able to give back to him the love he gave so copiously to them." But John would inevitably

* In his 2024 autobiography, *Sonny Boy*, Pacino said that by 1974 he'd been living in Greenwich Village since his teens and had so many gay friends and colleagues that he didn't consider the queer aspect of Sonny's character to be "groundbreaking or unusual."

fail at such attempts. And then would come the messy outburst of rage, anger, and rejection.[25]

It was a good read on John, and it nicely framed the motive for Sonny's robbery: He needed to get the money for Leon, whom he loved deeply in his own, flawed way. If Sonny could do this for Leon, it would fix all their problems. If Sonny could pull this off, Leon would love him as much as he loved Leon. Lumet had his actors rehearse for three weeks before he even touched a canister of film. He encouraged them to improvise as they pleased within the framework of Pierson's script. He largely abandoned the hostage characters, having the actors cast in those roles create their own interpretations. They embraced the challenge, opting to wear their own clothes instead of costumes and developing an on-set camaraderie bred from long hours and the shared mission of survival. Nearing the end of rehearsals, he called in Pierson, who rewrote his script around the troupe's improvisations.[26]

Filming began in early September in Brooklyn. An old auto body repair shop was converted into the First Brooklyn Savings Bank. Lumet used all-natural lighting—fluorescents, police spotlights, emergency flood lights—and shot his scenes with a natural affect that gave the end product the feel of a documentary or newsreel. A scene in which a news broadcast aired clips from Sonny and Leon's wedding was cut. Too visually jarring, Lumet decided. Another scene in which Sonny and Leon were to meet at the bank door and share a kiss—a modified version of the kiss that John and Patsy shared (Patsy refused to sign a release)—was similarly suspect. Pacino argued against it, feeling that it was too exploitative. Lumet, himself worrying how audiences would react, agreed and axed the scene.[27]

Over six chilly nights, hundreds of New Yorkers turned out to play the gawking mass in the streets. For the scene in which gay rights marchers descend on the bank in support of Sonny, Lumet cast actual gay rights activists.* A young actor named Chris Sarandon was cast as Leon. While Leon's screen time is limited, the role was perhaps the film's most vital. Sarandon, who'd never had a film role before, was advised by Lumet during rehearsals to play Leon with "a little less Blanche DuBois and a little more Queens housewife." To help guide his process, Sarandon had a gay friend of his organize a dinner for him with a few trans people. As they all ate spaghetti, Sarandon asked lots of questions and listened intently.[28]

The last of the night scenes to be shot was the climactic showdown at Kennedy. Lumet needed to call in a favor from New York Senator Jacob Javits to secure permission to film at Kennedy and, even with the senator's backing, had only one night to shoot the arrival of the caravan, the creeping of the purloined airliner, and the final fatal moments of the ordeal. And it was in those final moments—when the agent at the wheel killed Sal (via a more cinematic shot to the forehead) and Sonny's weapon was secured and a revolver placed to his head—that the most significant change from Pierson's original draft was made. No longer did Sonny beg for death. He now, as John had done, meekly asked to live. Sonny wasn't a killer. He was a scared and mixed-up kid. As Lumet filmed Pacino being pulled from the van, shoved against its hood, and read his rights, he had already made more sense of the entire story than John ever could.

* One of those extras was a young Harvey Fierstein, the gravelly-voiced character actor and Broadway star.

14. hollywood

With $3 million of Warner Bros. money spent, six reels of Hollywood magic in the can, and an advertising campaign crafted to include no more allusions to gay and trans people than the average rollout for a new brand of toothpaste, the straight media finally started to give a shit again. They checked in on Carmen and the kids, who were scraping by on welfare in a four-room apartment in East New York. They checked in on Robert, who was glad for the warm clothes that Shirley Ball had given him but had little else going for him. They checked in on Liz, whose legal name was still Ernest Aron because she couldn't afford the fee to have it changed. And they checked in on John, who'd developed such a fear of abandonment that he asked letter writers to address him as "Littlejohn" or "Johnny" so he wouldn't have to feel the sting of reading "Dear John" whenever he opened his mail.[1]

Barbara Trecker came back, writing a retrospective about the robbery and the coming film for the *Post*. Jerry Parker did the same for *Newsday*. Cliff Jahr, a pioneering gay entertainment journalist, visited Lewisburg and interviewed John extensively—the first interview he'd given in three years.* There was little ambiguity in these stories. The movie folks had tossed a few bills at each of the battered have-nots involved and split back to Hollywood without a thought for what was left behind. "I have the feeling," Terry Wojtowicz told Parker, "that [the movie people] got what they wanted from us and that's it."[2]

For anyone who'd gotten it, the movie money was long gone. Carmen was receiving $350 a month in welfare benefits. She sold Avon at Christmastime to help with gifts for the kids and worked part-time scooping ice cream at Carvel in the summers, but any money she made on the side was deducted from her welfare. The kids—now five and seven—slept in a windowless corner of the apartment, decorated by bright and cheery wallpaper held up with Scotch tape.[3]

A few months before the release of the film, Warner Bros. went back to a handful of the principal figures in the robbery and offered them cash to sit for interviews for a promotional documentary. They offered Carmen $600. She countered with $1,500 and the studio quickly accepted. And then there was another release for her to sign—one with more restrictive language than the original slip she'd signed for *The Boys in the Bank*. The language of the release, which she signed without much thought, made any legal actions by her against the studio much more difficult. She gave her interview and Warner shelved it, releasing only a few minutes of audio as part of a "special radio featurette" that hardly seemed worth the effort and expense. "Maybe they're trying to screw us because we're just little people," she told the *Voice* about the whole affair.[4]

Warner had also approached Liz about the documentary. By 1975, she lived in a three-room hotel room where the junkies and

* Jahr would later write the articles in which both Elton John and Janis Ian first publicly acknowledged that they were gay.

pimps stomped and shouted in the hallways all night long. She got about $200 a month in disability money. Near the end of the month, when the money ran out, she turned to street walking. She estimated that her transition had so far cost over $15,000. The offer from Warner went as high as $3,500 for a single interview. It would have been the first money that anyone involved with the production of the film had paid her directly. But she was also suspicious of why the studio was suddenly being so generous. She told them to shove it and called a lawyer.[5]

In late September 1975, the same week *Dog Day Afternoon* was released, *Fifty-One Newsmagazine*, a New York alternative weekly, featured Liz on their cover with an accompanying article titled, "The Great Transexual Rip-Off." In it, Liz claimed that when she signed her release for the film, she was under the impression that her cooperation would not only provide all the funds needed for her surgery but also provide John with the money for a topflight defense attorney. Martin Efland countered this by saying that Liz signed the document in a "sound frame of mind" and with a lawyer present. Both claims are dubious. If Liz expected more money from the deal beyond the $2,500 she got from John's payout, she hadn't mentioned it until now—despite chances to do so. While Liz's mental state when she signed her release cannot be known, all involved agree that no lawyer was present to advise her. The only other signature on the document is that of Randy Wicker, who was acting both as an agent for Efland and as a notary public.[6]

But even by the time the article appeared, the point was mostly one of pride. Over the summer, Liz had gone ahead with her suit against Warner Bros. for her portrayal in the film. Oddly enough, her claim for damages was based on the film "defaming" her by portraying her as a "homosexual man." The sex with John prior to her transition was immaterial, she said, as she was already living as a woman at the time. "The relationship stemmed from the fact that he liked to suck," Liz said, "and I had a good dick at the time." The intercourse that resulted from those encounters was "natural," Liz insisted, regardless of whether or not she still had a penis. "That wasn't homosexual. I wanted to get my rocks off. I wanted a man."[7]

The suit was flimsy (not to mention surprisingly progressive in its gender politics while still being oddly homophobic), but Warner settled for a reported $6,000 on the $1 million claim. Her $2 million suit against the publisher of the paperback would end up getting thrown out.[8]

NOT THAT IT would have mattered in her lawsuit, but no one picking up the issue of *Fifty-One* with her photo on the cover would have ever mistaken her for Chris Sarandon in *Dog Day Afternoon*. Tall and long-limbed, she posed with an effortless glamour in devil-red nail polish and a snug button-down that bared her midriff and stretched open to tease her thirty-eight-inch chest. A caption on one photo paraphrased the Rolling Stones album from a few years before: "Liz Eden: Getting her yah-yahs out."

Lost in the mess over money and her displeasure with the film and book was that Liz finally felt comfortable in her own skin. "I was a shell," she told *Fifty-One*, "now I'm a whole peanut." She was working on an autobiography, dictating it aloud to Richard Barraclough, a magazine writer. The working title of the project, which would never be finished, was "Liz: The Wife of the Gay Bank Robber." She earned money go-go dancing and made a handful of noncredited contributions to the gay-focused magazine *Michael's Thing*. She generally enjoyed the attention that men gave her, still enamored with the idea that she could draw lustful stares from guys who had no idea that her knockout physique was only a few years old. By the time the movie came out, she was in only sporadic contact with John. "I don't want to remember my old life at all," she said.[9]

She'd also met a seventeen-year-old kid named Tony. "He's kinda short and dark and cute and hot and Italian-looking," she told Cliff Jahr. When the journalist raised an eyebrow, she shot back, "But don't say it. I know who that sounds like." As for John, whatever affections she once felt had soured. She no longer felt that she owed him for the surgery. She no longer felt that she owed him anything. "If he was getting money for my operation," she told *Fifty-One*, "he would have just taken twenty thousand. That would have been enough." Everyone in the Village knew John was deep in hock to some very bad people, she said. "They probably just told him to pay up or else."[10]

Just before the opening of the film, Liz had an expense account dinner with Jahr at an Eighth Avenue restaurant. She went on about Tony as she ate her London broil, she even thought that maybe she'd announce their engagement at the premier. Jahr asked her if she still loved John. "Never did," she replied. "I must have told him a thousand times."[11]

CARMEN CRIED WHEN she first watched *Dog Day Afternoon*. It wasn't the depiction of her husband that did it, but that of herself. Angela Wortzik, the character based on Carmen, is indeed one of the film's weaker points.* Susan Peretz, in the first

* In a review of the film for *Jump Cut*, Karyn Kay speculated that Lumet may have purposely framed the characters of Angela and Sonny's mother as shrill and unreasonable to push the stereotype of overbearing women causing men to "become" gay.

major role of a character acting career that spans from *Barney Miller* to *Murder, She Wrote*, plays the role wonderfully and does a dead-ringer impression of Carmen's cutesy Brooklynese. But her purpose in the film is mostly to absorb Sonny's rage. Carmen's insecurities wouldn't allow her to see past the character's physical appearance and the brief depiction of her low-rent living situation. "Am I that repulsive?" she asked. "Is my apartment as awful as that girl's was?"[12]

Jim Murphy, the FBI agent who killed Sal Naturile, saw the film in a packed house on the Upper East Side. He shrank in his seat when his on-screen counterpart, played by Lance Henrikson, fired the fatal shot. The crowd booed. He was bothered most by the portrayal of Sal as being so naive. Not long after, a family member who knew his role in the case scolded him. "How could you shoot that guy?" they wanted to know.[13]

Randy Wicker enjoyed the film overall but was disheartened by the portrayal of gay life. In an unpublished review of the picture, Wicker criticized the idea of robbery as a means of saving Leon's life. He seemed to dismiss Leon's transness, saying that the concept was a "throwback to the '50s" when it was assumed that all gay men really just wanted to be women. He also criticized the scene in which the crowd of gay-libbers march to the bank in support of Sonny. "The demonstrators are a mixed crew but more motley and 'obvious' than most gay activists," he wrote, evidently unaware that Lumet cast real-life activists.[14]

The critics almost all loved it. It was another winner for Lumet, another master class by Pacino, and a breakout for Sarandon. But for all the raves and all the attention, apart from Liz's lawsuit, few of those involved bothered to preserve their opinions for posterity. None of the hostages bothered to broadcast their opinions, or if they did, no one bothered to print them. Robert's only hope for the picture was that it be a good depiction of gay life. No one knows if it met these expectations.

Of course, the one person involved with the robbery who was truly anticipating the film couldn't just go and buy a ticket. John's eagerness for the film's release was more than just narcissism. He knew that the film would likely be the final burst of publicity his case would receive. As the buzz around the picture grew, and as journalists like Cliff Jahr came calling, he'd have one last chance to rally the public—to rally *his* public—to his cause.

Over the summer of 1975, John and Jahr conducted an ongoing correspondence that culminated in Jahr visiting John at Lewisburg. John had just won permission for Warner to screen the film inside the prison. Warner had always been open to the idea—at one point he even talked of sending Al Pacino along to introduce the picture—but Lewisburg officials squashed the plan and only relented when John made a stink about the matter in the gay media.* At the time of the visit, John had only read a copy of the script that Warner sent him. He had already absorbed the narrative, put forth in the *Life* article and the script, that the robbery was an "act of love" as reality. And to this he began to heap more exaggerations and outright lies.[15]

He told Jahr that he and Sal had planned to go right from the bank to Kings County Hospital to get Liz out of custody—by force if necessary. He said that Sal was willing to go in "with

* Although it was absolutely the kind of thing that John would make up, there was a real prospect of Pacino visiting Lewisburg to meet John and introduce the film. But prison officials refused to even consider it. At one point, they even had to reprimand John for adding Pacino to his visitor list.

guns" if they wouldn't let her out.* He said that he had been the one answering the phones during the early part of the ordeal and even approved a loan (to "someone with a long Polack name—one of my people"). He said that the police were so threatening that at least two of the hostages asked for—and were given—guns to help protect the bank against invasion. He said that New York City Mayor John Lindsay called the bank personally and said that he would order the cops to charge into the bank and kill anyone it took to end the standoff.[16]

When Jahr followed up with John after the visit, questioning him on the parts of his story that didn't quite add up, he chuckled. "Sometimes the parts I can't remember I make up." When Jahr relayed John's most outrageous claims to Robert Barrett, the branch manager could only shake his head. "He tells a beautiful story. Maybe he should have written the screenplay."[17]

In the run-up to the Lewisburg screenings—which would include a private lunchtime show for John and two general population screenings, John would not shut up about the movie—"*my* movie" as he never failed to call it. It created a lot of buzz on the inside. But once again, John was getting ahead of himself. George must have seen it coming. The prison officials probably saw it coming too. It was likely why they didn't want to show the damn thing in the first place. When they gave John what he wanted—what he was demanding—they probably had an idea of what would come next.

* This is, once again, absolutely the kind of thing John would invent. However, no one ever knew for sure what John, Sal, and Robert had planned to do immediately following the robbery had they actually pulled it off. While a trip to the hospital to try to get Liz to join them seems reasonable, the idea that Sal would have been willing to risk death or capture to facilitate her release is ludicrous.

John had his private lunchtime screening on Friday, October 3, 1975. That night, the picture was shown to more than one thousand of his fellow inmates. John said the men loved the film. They cheered him on and booed the police. "That's how to do it, John!" someone shouted out as Pacino's Sonny bossed the cops, kicked and screamed. There was a lot of laughter too. That bugged John a bit. He'd never wanted this thing to be a comedy. One inmate walked out when Sonny was revealed to be gay. "I'm not watching this faggot movie," he shouted over the dialogue as he stormed out. But when Sonny dictated his will—one of the scenes that had moved John to tears earlier in the day—the house went deadly silent. The room also went quiet at the very end, when Sal—bullet hole in his forehead—is carted off and John is placed under arrest.[18]

It was a strained silence.

John didn't notice the tension. Not at first. Not when his fellow inmates wouldn't stop asking him questions about the film. Not when they started to call him "the Dog" in place of his hard-to-pronounce last name. But eventually, the anger the film had generated became impossible to miss. Some of it was because of John's sexuality. What a man did on the inside to take care of his own needs was one thing, but to carry on like that while a free man was still a toxic thought to a huge portion of the Lewisburg population. Some of it was all the attention that John drew. It bred envy. Why should this little punk, this soft little man who might be dead by now without George's claim on him be so goddamn celebrated?

And some of it was how the movie depicted his relationship with Sal. Although the film clearly showed Sonny rejecting an offer from the FBI to "take care of Sal" in order to end the standoff, Sal still took one in the head and Sonny still survived. For plenty of men at Lewisburg it was less of a stretch to see themselves in Sal's place—the dopey con just in it for the money and willing to do whatever it took to avoid going back to the cooler—than it was see themselves as the queerly lovelorn Sonny.[19]

John's relationship with George became strained after the screenings. John felt that George wasn't taking his input about his appeal. George no doubt felt that John was interfering with his work. In late October, John shoved an inmate who had grabbed George by the hair and the inmate socked John in the mouth before things were broken up. George yelled at him for getting involved. Later, the inmate and some friends had words with John and hit him twice. George did nothing to retaliate. John wrote Carmen that the whole chain of events "really broke my heart." He felt that they were drifting apart.[20]

About a month after the screening, someone firebombed his cell. The distance between him and George may have been a factor, making John a more appealing target. But the film and the attention it brought was likely more than enough reason to draw heat. George helped him clean up his cell. John tried to downplay the event a bit in a letter home to Carmen, signing it "your loving and smoky husband," but his fear was very real.

A few months later, his cell was robbed. He reported the incident—he had to, he claimed, because so many documents related to his ongoing legal matters were taken—which again just made things worse. Another firebombing soon followed and by mid-January, John had been put into "protective custody"—a friendly term for segregation. For two months, he was confined to a six-by-nine-foot cell for twenty-three hours per day. His mail was heavily censored. He was permitted access to a radio, but no television, no newspapers, no books.[21]

John wrote Carmen regularly from segregation, his letters

glossing over his loneliness and fears with John's own version of self-centered banality. He asked about her weight and cited "our primary goal" for her slimming down to 169 pounds. He offered words of comfort about the death of Carmen's uncle and then asked her if anyone in her family had seen his movie and if they mentioned anything about it at the funeral. He talked about the fan mail he received. He asked about Carmen's Avon sales and told a crass Avon-related joke.* He mentioned Liz, bragged that he wasn't sending her a Valentine's Day card, and said that Liz had blown her chance with him. He quasi-apologized for yelling at Carmen during a recent visit but still blamed her for provoking him. "Who else should I take it out on?" he asked.[22]

John had a dream while in segregation. In it, Carmen was standing behind a podium at Madison Square Garden. Twenty-five thousand people filled the place, all screaming and cheering. A chant rose from the mass: "Free Little John! Free Little John! Free Little John!" Carmen stepped forward and spoke. "Each and every one of you here must go out into the streets and get all your relatives, friends, strangers, and even your enemies to sign petitions asking the president to pardon and free Little John." The crowd erupted as thousands of blank petition forms fluttered down from the ceiling. They called on President Gerald Ford to commemorate the nation's bicentennial by pardoning John Wojtowicz for his "act of love." He detailed the dream in a letter to Jahr, who had published a piece on John in the *Voice* and was now working on one for *Playboy*. John asked him to have petitions printed and to begin circulating them. "Before you know it, you'll have hundreds, thousands, and millions of

* "What is black and blue and goes ding-dong? A beat-up Avon lady." This was not the first time he'd told her that "joke."

signatures . . . It's going to be one of the greatest campaigns in the history of this great county."[23]

Jahr didn't even believe in the idea enough to sign his own name to the makeshift petition sheet that John had drawn up in his letter. But he did want to help. He hoped that the forthcoming *Playboy* piece—as well as the bump of notoriety John was sure to get from the upcoming Academy Awards, where *Dog Day Afternoon* was up for six trophies—could help him with his legal efforts.* That is, if John didn't get himself killed first. Most of all, he wrote John, he needed to knock off the bullshit and be straight about what had happened and what he had done. "Goddamn," he wrote John in a forceful note, "don't be sly with me anymore."[24]

George found John to be a similarly frustrating client. He was working hard on his appeal, but John kept bringing up the hopeless presidential pardon idea. An outside counsel was working on securing John's share of the profits from the film's production company. While John had a verbal agreement to receive 1 percent of the film's profits, the deal was never put into writing. Martin Bregman and Martin Efland, in an act that was downright charitable by Hollywood's standards, agreed to give him the 1 percent anyway. But John insisted on 2 percent of the profits, an idea that had been floated but never seriously discussed. Meanwhile, his chummy relationship with the prison guards (he would sign autographs for them) and the small stacks of fan mail he received from notices he put into gay newspapers made him a continued target for harassment.[25]

In June 1976, after months of requests for transfer, John was shipped from Lewisburg to the federal prison in Lompoc,

* The film ended up winning just one Oscar, for Pierson's screenplay.

California. Lompoc wasn't quite the concrete hellhole that Lewisburg was, but it was a lot farther away from home. Carmen, who still dutifully visited John—and took an overnight bus trip each time to do so—would no longer be able to see him. Finally beginning to thaw on the matter of John's sexuality, she even wrote an article about her experiences with the federal prison system for the gay newspaper *Join Hands*. "They are all the same," she wrote. "The officials treat him like dirt." At each stop, John was made to endure extra scrutiny because of his profile and orientation. Rules against contact with visitors were enforced on John and his guests, but few others. Their kids were singled out for scolding by the guards. Her letters to him were returned unopened.[26]

John was also published not long after transferring to Lompoc. Following the release of *Dog Day Afternoon*, he was contacted by *The New York Times* with an offer to write a review of the film.* He wrote the piece and submitted it, but the *Times* Arts and Leisure editor William H. Henan refused to print it. "The problem is that I just don't believe you have profoundly come to grips with the motives for your crime, and the complex relationship between art and reality," Henan wrote back to John. John eventually got *Gay Sunshine: A Journal of Gay Liberation* to run the review in late 1976, and a handful of other gay periodicals ran a reprint of the piece. It was even picked up by the film journal *Jump Cut* in 1977. *Jump Cut* titled the article, "Real Dog Day Hero Tells His Story."

John criticized the film for ignoring the "real reason" behind the robbery—that it was not just to get the money for Liz's

* The *Times* offered him $250 for the review. John countered with a demand for $2,000 that the paper flatly refused.

gender-affirming surgery, but that it was to save her life. He said that Liz would have remained committed to Kings County indefinitely if he had not gotten her the money. He said that Sal was unarmed when the FBI killed him. He said that the film suggested that he sold out Sal to save his own life. He had some more legitimate gripes as well. He disliked the admittedly cheap depictions of his mother and Carmen—although he took an unnecessary shot at Susan Peretz, calling her "ugly and greasy looking." He noted that much of the dialogue between Sonny and Leon was invented (it was), and that the conversation between Sonny and his mother was not true to life (it wasn't). He also spent considerable wordage on his plight in prison, the abuses he'd endured, and his various legal battles. He closed by reciting the prayer used in Alcoholics Anonymous, an adage that he said he tried to live by: "God, grant me the serenity to accept the things I cannot change, the courage to change the things I can, and the wisdom to know the difference."[27]

IN 1977, LIZ posed nude for the adult magazine *Club*.* The pictorial ran with an article Liz had written with Richard Barraclough titled, "TS (and It Doesn't Mean Tough Shit, Either!)." John, still cranking away at his legal work despite now being half a continent away from George, filed a lawsuit to stop the distribution of the issue, claiming that Liz's descriptions of their sex life violated

* Liz had previously posed nude in an issue of *The Female Impersonator*, appearing shortly after her orchiectomy in a series of photos with a man identified as a "boyfriend." In her excellent multipart series "The Herstory of Liz Eden" at *Trans Ascending*, Anni Arbour cites Liz's *Club* appearance as the first time a trans woman had ever appeared nude in a cis men's magazine.

his right to privacy. A judge dismissed the suit for technical deficiencies within the document—including the fact that John had neglected to sign it.[28]

The *Club* piece gives a brutally honest account of their time together—the sex, the arguments, the violence. It makes it clear that there was no love left in the relationship by the time John took his guns into the bank. It makes it clear that the biggest threat to Liz's life wasn't her lack of money but John himself. Still, she admits having pity for him. "He got the royal shaft, anyway you look at it," she wrote. "He is now doing 20 years in a California federal penitentiary while others who make his crime look like petty theft are sipping scotch and soda in the comfort of their own homes thanks to social position and smart lawyers."

She included graphic descriptions of her various surgeries and her sex life since their completion. She was still enjoying sex and was among the minority of surgically transitioned women who could achieve orgasm. She talked about Tony and their home life—"It's a loose lifestyle, but that's just the way we like it"—about his work and her hustling and about the stability she'd achieved. "I've just turned 30 and am happier now than I ever thought I would be. I have a man I love, a few close friends, and peace of mind. That's more than many and I'm grateful. Now all I have to do is hang onto it all . . . In the meantime, if you see me on the avenue, give a whistle. I love it!"[29]

But the letters John was still getting from Randy Wicker told a different story about Liz. John still asked about her, and Wicker was still hearing rumors and gossip. She was still making her usual rounds through the gay scene in the Village. Lee, the friend who'd gone with Wicker and Liz to her orchiectomy, said that she was often depressed and was using downers with increasing regularity. "And privately [she] admits she frequently regrets having the operation," Wicker wrote. "However, she won't admit this publicly, of course."[30]

A few months later, Wicker wrote to John, "I only hear bizarre stories about Liz." He'd heard that Tony had gone to jail and that she'd briefly stayed with his family but had since been kicked out. The last he heard, she was living in a condemned building in the Bronx with an underaged lover. "My," Wicker wrote, "life does get stranger and stranger."[31]

IN EARLY 1977, John settled with the filmmakers over his share of the profits from the movie. The deal gave John 1 percent of total net profits—which would mean an immediate payment of over $35,000. Lawyers for the filmmakers estimated that this portion would eventually total somewhere between $120,000 and $150,000. Even after paying off his lawyers—even his jailhouse husband, George, wanted about $12,000 for his work on the case—it would leave John far more than he would have gotten had the cops not shown up on that God-awful hot afternoon back in Brooklyn.[32]

George had spent most of the previous year drafting an appeal of John's sentence. The crux of the argument was that John had not received effective counsel and that Landsman had pressured him too greatly to enter a guilty plea that, when it came to sentencing, won John no concessions from the state. George also argued that John himself had not been in a competent state on the day of his sentencing. George and John filed the appeal in September 1976. The "statement of case" portion of the filing claimed that John's decision to rob the bank came about after Liz's birthday suicide attempt, that he'd recruited Sal and Robert that weekend, that the whole thing was so spontaneous and full of passion that it was doomed to failure. George filed, and John waited.[33]

While he whiled away his time at Lompoc, someone opened fire on Christine Freund and her fiancé, John Diel, as they sat in a parked car late one evening in Queens. Diel survived, but Freund did not. A little over a month later, Virginia Voskerichian, a Columbia University student, was shot and killed while walking home in the same area. In April, another couple sitting in a parked car was attacked by a gunman. Both were killed. The press had been referring to the murderer as the ".44 caliber killer" for his weapon of choice, but when a letter found at one of the murder scenes was signed "Son of Sam," the newspapers quickly picked up on the new moniker. With letters taunting the police and more shootings in June and July, the case became a national sensation, and New Yorkers spent a panicked summer wondering when he would strike next. To the relief of all, a dumpy postal worker named David Berkowitz was arrested for the murders on August 10 and confessed to everything the next day. And on August 12, John Wojtowicz lost his nest egg.

Right after Berkowitz's confession, New York governor Hugh Carey signed into law a bill that had just been rushed through both houses of the state legislature. The bill would become known as the "Son of Sam law" and allowed for the creation of a crime victims board that would be empowered to seize any money earned through book sales, movie deals, or other media depictions of a crime by the perpetrator of that crime. The money would be held in a special fund for a period of five years, during which victims of said crimes would have the chance to file suit and claim a portion of the cash. The bill's origin was a single sentence in a news article that state senator Emanuel Gold read during the hunt for Son of Sam that suggested that the killer "stood to get rich" by selling his story after he was captured.[34]

The first action taken by the newly created board was to collect a $40,750 payment from Warner Bros. that would have otherwise gone to John Wojtowicz. The collection of John's money was almost an afterthought. It was not even clear if the state could seize the money, given that the deal had been made before the law was passed. But a court ruled that the payment was fair game, although they shortened the period for claims from five years to just one. Berkowitz, incidentally, would eventually sign a book deal but voluntarily gave all royalties to his victims' estates.[35]

In September 1977, as classified ads in newspaper from each of New York State's sixty-one counties asked readers, "Are you the victim of a crime committed by John Wojtowicz in August 1972 at a Chase Manhattan branch bank in Brooklyn NY? If so, monies are available from the earnings of the motion picture *Dog Day Afternoon* . . ." John was taken back to Brooklyn to appear before Federal Judge Thomas Platt for his long-awaited appeal hearing. Before the judge that afternoon, he spoke eloquently, at times shedding tears.* He made his plea, and Judge Platt heard it. Specifically citing John's poor treatment in prison and the decision to show *Dog Day Afternoon* to his fellow inmates, Platt cut the sentence from twenty years to fifteen, immediately making John eligible for parole.[36]

Two and a half months later, John was denied parole. He appealed and was granted a new hearing, scheduled for April 1978. While awaiting the hearing, he was given permission to conduct a television interview with CBS journalist Jeanne Parr.

* Sadly, it seems that the text of this statement is now lost.

John hadn't given an interview to anyone since Cliff Jahr and, if he needed any further motivation to agree to the talk, Parr's in-studio guest would be none other than Liz Eden. The two wouldn't interact during the segment, which pasted together a jailhouse interview with John and a live one with Liz. At one point, Parr asked John why he fell in love with Liz. "I don't know," he laughed. "My wife, Carmen, always asks me that question. And I said, I don't know. Because if I knew why I loved him, then maybe I could stop loving him," he said, still refusing the use Liz's preferred pronouns. "But when you don't know why you love somebody . . ."

Later in the interview, John was given the chance to speak directly to Liz. Sitting across the table from Parr in his prison-issued jumpsuit, he grinned at the offer. John looked directly into the camera. "I love you a great deal and I did what I did because I wanted you to be happy." The broadcast transitioned to a split screen, John on the left, Liz on the right. As he went on about how he'd saved her life and how it was all worth it and how much he really truly loved her, Liz looked for a moment as though she might begin to cry. "Are you happy?" Parr asked her.

"Not as happy as I would be if he was out here."

"Do you ever think of him in that prison?"

"There isn't a day that doesn't pass that I don't think of John."

IN LATE MARCH, John was transferred to the federal penitentiary at Danbury, Connecticut, a fulfillment of Carmen and Terry's efforts to have him moved to a facility nearer to home. Less than a month into his stay, John was granted parole. If he behaved himself, he would be released just after Thanksgiving. Once free, John planned to return to Carmen and the children.

"I'm going back to my wife and children," he told the *Daily News*. "She's a beautiful, faithful, loyal wife. Our only problem is that she's a women's libber and I'm an old-fashioned boss type."[37]

Carmen had taken to the idea of women's liberation while John was away. She had even started dating. "Did you know some men are absolutely weird for, y'know, big girls?" she gushed to Jahr. Even with John's return imminent, Carmen had some new footing to fall back on. "He'll always have that urge to see his gay friends," she said. "But I've to take it day by day. Sometimes I joke with him and say, 'If you see your old boy friends, then I'm going to see mine.'"[38]

John wrote to Randy Wicker while in his final months at Danbury. He was subdued about the good news but railed about his lost movie money and the conditions in Connecticut. He was working eight hours a day in the prison power plant, which left too little time for letter-writing and working on his various other legal matters. He was housed in a large dorm that was too crowded and too hot. "We even got to wait in line to take a shit," he wrote. He talked about Liz and her new partner, an eighteen-year-old named Dominic. He liked Dom and hoped to see them both now and again after he got out. John had spoken to George recently. Despite all the work George had done toward his release, John said that he hadn't otherwise talked to him since he'd left Lewisburg. George was due to get out just a few months before John. He encouraged Wicker to get in touch with George after he got out. "I really love him and miss him a lot. Ask him to show you the leather bag I had made for him here in prison." John closed the letter with a cheery smiley face drawn in blue ink and a red heart with the names of Randy and his partner. "Love always / your friend / in struggle / The Gay Bank Robber / Little John (Basso) Wojtowicz."[39]

On November 28, 1978—six years, three months, and six days after his arrest—John Wojtowicz stepped out of a federal holding facility in Manhattan and put shoe leather to pavement as a free man. He had a room waiting for him at a halfway house in Midtown, where he would need to stay until he found a job. Somewhere in a little apartment in Brooklyn, his wife Carmen and their children, now aged eight and twelve, awaited his visit. He'd pledged that he'd make things right with them, that he would find work and return to the family home to make up for lost time. This, he had told everyone, was all he wanted from his post-prison life.

On November 28, 1978, John Wojtowicz was a free man. His first stop was Liz Eden's apartment.[40]

Four

"We Love Love Love You, Sonny!"

—TEXT FROM A HANDMADE SIGN
HELD BY ONE OF SONNY'S SUPPORTERS IN A
NEVER-FILMED SCENE FROM THE ORIGINAL
DOG DAY AFTERNOON SCREENPLAY

It's warm for Lewisburg in October. Nearly seventy degrees by midafternoon with sunshine that bleeds through the ancient curtains of the prison's theater and smudges the pictures on the screen. John knows the film's final act is nearing.

He's read the screenplay a dozen times. He has a good idea of the parts he'll like and the ones that'll set him on edge. He knows he's not going to like what's coming up. It's another scene with that awful woman they got to play Carmen. She's all self-pity and whininess, going on and on about how much Sonny—how much John—had hurt her. That hardheadedness that Carmen admitted to, the tough little core of her personality that both frustrated and impressed John, wasn't there. *Bullshit,* John thinks. Then there's another scene with the mother. Sonny's mother. A teary-eyed dumbbell, standing in the middle of the street, hands out like a beggar. She tells Sonny he should just run away. Just run. She really says that. *Run.* What a dumb idea. *Fuckin' bullshit,* John thinks.

But his mood changes when Sonny begins to dictate his will. The scene itself is a bit of fabrication, of course. John didn't write his will in the bank; he did it a few days later—penning it personally in his crooked and loopy script while in lockup. But the emotion of it all is dead-center accurate. Nearly word-for-word with what John had written, Sonny dictates as Mouth takes shorthand. Everyone is exhausted and raw. By the time Sonny gets to the bit about Leon—about Liz—saying he loves her "as no man has loved another man in all eternity," John can no longer keep it together. Fat tears fall from his face to his prison jumpsuit. "To my mother," Sonny continues, "I ask forgiveness. You don't understand the things I said, and did, but I'm me and I'm different."

Ten minutes later, the caravan makes its way to the airport. There's noise and flashing lights, and the stress shows plainly on everyone's faces. Sonny sits in the front row: nervous, sweaty, exhausted, and clueless. For a moment, John can wonder how long Sonny had been so clueless, so unaware of what was already certain to happen. Had it been since he had come up with the escape plan? Since he'd dickered with Sal over what to do with the hostages? Since he'd walked into the bank in the first damn place? Since sometime far before that? Had he ever had a chance? Ever?

The FBI men on-screen never even bother to take off their suit jackets or loosen their neckties. They look fresh. Everyone else looks damn near dead. The men patter on about food—hamburgers on the plane, they promise—and the code is passed. The driver opens the rigged-up armrest to reveal a pistol. It's all right there, open and plain to the whole world, but Sonny never notices. John can't look away. In a flash of movement, Sal is shot in the head and Sonny is disarmed. The pistol whips around and is pressed to Sonny's temple.

Don't shoot me.

They pull Sonny from the van, gun still at his head. Sal, lifeless and thin, is laid on a gurney and hauled away. They push Sonny against the hood of the vehicle and read him his rights. The hostages—the former hostages—huddle together near the fleet of squad cars. There is no fade to black, no swelling ballad to wrap everything up. It's just the roar of the plane. A few titles flash at the bottom of the screen:

Sonny Wortzik is Serving Twenty Years in Federal Prison
Angela Wortzik Lives With Her Children on Welfare
Leon Shermer is Now a Woman and Living in New York City

Three simple sentences to summarize the three pitiful years that had passed since. Sonny is taken away and the camera settles above the entire scene. The noises and movements are all indistinct. In a minute, the last few feet of the film will rattle through the projector, its gears and levers will fall silent. The room will go quiet, and John will be taken back to his cell somewhere deep in the stink of the federal penitentiary at Leavenworth with nothing waiting for him but seventeen more years. Until then, John can only watch as the camera pulls back and the noise of the jet engines and rescue vehicles peaks. This must be what it feels like to die. This must be what it feels like to be born.

15. the dog

He didn't look much like Al Pacino anymore. He had gained some weight in prison, filling out his sickly early seventies frame to something not at all out of place on a construction site or loading dock. He maintained the little mustache he'd grown on the inside and had coiffed his thick, dark hair into something resembling a Beatles mop top meeting Gillette's "dry look." As John stepped out of the Bryant Hotel as a free man in September 1978, dressed in a windbreaker and bulky blue jeans, the only thing keeping him from once again being among the squarest squares in Manhattan was the brightly colored button pinned to his coat. ANITA BRYANT SUCKS ORANGES, it read.

The gay liberation movement had changed since John had gone away. From the crushing defeat of George McGovern—whose nominating convention had overwhelmingly voted down a gay rights plank in the platform—the movement had gained a handful of champions in places of power. New York City had sent Ed Koch and Bella Abzug, who'd both backed bills to amend the 1964 Civil Rights Act to include "affection or sexual preference" and to bar employment or housing discrimination based on being gay.

Neither bill made it anywhere, but the topics were being pressed. Koch had since been elected mayor and had issued an executive order protecting New Yorkers against anti-gay discrimination.

But these modest gains also brought about the first truly organized political backlash. With similar movements against the Equal Rights Amendment and school desegregation engaging the American Right, anti-gay activists became among the most visible in what was then being called the "Culture Wars." Anita Bryant, the dyspeptically cheerful singer and omnipresent television pitchwoman (her most famed ads were those promoting Florida orange juice), had become the most visible figure in the battle when she took up the cause of opposing an antidiscrimination ordinance in her hometown of Miami in 1976. By 1978, she was among the Right's most vocal culture warriors—and a figure in line with Hitler or Mussolini to the gay community.[1]

John roomed on one of the two floors at the Bryant Hotel leased by the federal government as a community treatment center—government parlance for "halfway house." The fading Beaux Arts building was once one of the gems of Fifty-Fourth Street—within walking distance of Carnegie Hall and Broadway. By the time John arrived it was the type of place where paint chips fluttered from the ceiling if a door was slammed shut. Releasees from federal custody could spend up to ninety days there, depending on the conditions of their parole. With minimal security, they were permitted to sign themselves out each day to look for work or visit family. Two of John's housemates at the Bryant were organized crime figures James "Jimmy the Gent" Burke and Thomas "Tommy D" DeSimone. Burke and DeSimone would eventually get their own version of John's Hollywood treatment, being portrayed respectively by Robert De Niro and Joe Pesci in the 1990 film *Goodfellas*.[2]

But while Burke and DeSimone had the money and connections to bribe the Bryant's guards and secure no-show labor jobs (they were too busy planning the $5 million Lufthansa heist to worry about more trivial matters), John checked himself out each morning at eight to look for work, while occasionally seeing Carmen and the kids or Liz. He carried with him a stack of folders and envelopes, each carefully arranged with plastic-sealed clippings about his crime. Once in a while, he'd be recognized and he'd take time to stop and chat or sign an autograph. He liked to introduce himself as "Dog Day." Eventually, he shortened it to "the Dog."[3]

Newsday, the *Daily News*, and *The Washington Post* all did profile pieces on John during his time at the Bryant. He expressed worry for his tenuous parole situation, saying that employers were all looking for younger men—"They figure a guy my age knows too much"—and shared his plan for an ideal job. "I'd be the world's greatest bank guard," he told the *Post*. "[The] bank could say, 'Hey, Dog Day Afternoon is guarding our bank. Your money is safer than Fort Knox.'" He even proposed giving away a free signed photo of himself to anyone who made a $100 deposit.[4]

After a few weeks on the hunt, however, John finally began to accept the fact that the bank guard idea was pure fantasy. Indeed, with his only professional experience being in banking, it began to dawn on him that any work more glamorous than menial labor was similarly fantastical. At John's request, *Newsday* printed his mother's home phone number and listed his prison work experience as "mowing grass and sweeping floors, mostly." Anyone with a suitable position to fill was asked to call promptly.[5]

But the papers mostly wanted to know about his personal life. To the *Post*, John identified himself as bisexual, albeit with his own twist. Just as he'd previously applied his own unique interpretation of *gay* to mean being attracted to men and women, he now declared that his bisexuality meant he needed "one of each." He said that his plan was to live with Carmen and the kids, to maintain a romantic relationship with George—who was due to be released soon—and to keep a friendship with Liz. Carmen wasn't happy with this arrangement, he admitted, but "she's not the boss . . . I'm the boss." He considered himself married to all three.[6]

Did John have regrets? He did not. He said he wasn't sorry for any of it. He'd saved Liz, he'd saved the hostages, and he'd inspired a smash hit. What was there to be sorry for? He couldn't even be held to account for Sal, he insisted. The cops had been hungry for blood all afternoon, John said. To Bob Kappstatter of the *Daily News*—who'd been on the scene of the robbery and damn well knew John was lying—he claimed that Sal had been held down by two FBI agents while another took his gun and shot him in the chest. "I'm not a repeat offender. I haven't been a criminal all my life. Just one act," John said. He saluted the flag, went to confession, and paid his taxes. "I'm a regular nine-to-five guy," he said. "I'm an average American."[7]

That last one might have been his biggest lie of all.

JOHN WAS JUST a few days away from being sent back to prison when he took a job with Project Return, a private charity that helped recovering addicts, runaways, and former prisoners ease back into society. Project Return president Julio Martinez, a former drug addict himself, caught one of the news stories about John and his search for work and offered him a chance. "He's a very sincere guy," Martinez said. "John is a very, very real person. In the business we're in, I couldn't ask for any more than that."[8]

John would help to keep the books and process government

vouchers but was not permitted to handle money. In late November, John moved out of the Bryant and back into his parents' house in Brooklyn. For $160 a week, John took the train into Manhattan and put in his forty hours. After George's release, he moved in with John and the two lived in coupledom. Terry made the meals and washed the clothes, John Sr. drank beer and said little. In spare moments, John plotted out what he'd do when he finally got his movie money back from that damn victims' board. His grandest dream was the "Dog Day's Inferno" nightclub—a three-level disco with separate tiered dance floors for gay men, lesbians, and straights. Should that not work out, maybe a Dog Day Disco taxi service that would run disco-themed cabs with television screens running *Dog Day Afternoon* on a continuous loop. Failing that, he could probably find himself happy operating something as modest as a restaurant or grocery store.[9]

But outside of his home life and work, John struggled to find himself. For all the tough talk to the newspapers about being "the boss," his relationship with Carmen was damaged beyond repair. Any chance he'd had to right things was scuttled when he chose Liz's Bronx apartment as his first visit after being released over seeing Carmen and the kids. He hadn't even told Liz he was coming. She answered the door in a bathrobe and found John in a "lovey-dovey" mood. She refused to even let him into the apartment. When they did see each other, it was usually out at some bar in the Village. Even when he was with George, John always tried for a kiss and never seemed to grasp the fact that Liz had no interest in going to bed with him. Asked by an interviewer if she still had feelings for him, Liz answered, "I have feelings for a drowning rat."[10]

In February 1979, as the burst of media attention from his release began to fade, John appeared with Liz at a fundraiser at Danny's First Disco in the Village to raise money for bulletproof vests for the officers of the Sixth Precinct. It was an odd concept altogether but made sense for the apolitical Liz and once again self-proclaimed "Goldwater Republican" John. "Our gay brothers and sisters are also police officers," John told a reporter.[11]

A photo of John and Liz on the dance floor ran in dozens of newspapers shortly after, near the back in human interest sections, under headings like "People" or "Today" or "Happenings." They're caught mid-step, Liz looking free and easy with a low-cut top and bare midriff, John with knees bowed in a cheap suit, the angle making him look a good foot and half shorter. The headlines that accompanied the picture brought the breaking news that John was about to be laid off from his job. Project Return had been caught in a budget crunch and John was given his two weeks' notice. There was a comical nature to the articles. Something like "Bank Robber Needs Job to Support Wives" was a typical headline. John was quoted about his old-fashioned ways, how he saved Liz and saved all the hostages, how he considered Carmen, Liz, and George to be his wives. No longer was there furor or fascination, the debates about John—never really settled—simply faded away. He was the subject of a silly photo. The joke in a bad headline.[12]

A month later, a New York appellate court ruled that bank manager Robert Barrett had the grounds to make a claim on the $40,000-plus lingering in an escrow account that had been seized as a result of the so-called Son of Sam law. Other claims would soon follow, chipping away at the pot of money that John hoped might be his refuge. Two weeks after that, Carmen filed suit against John for divorce. She accused him of adultery, both during his prison term and since his release. John denied her claims and promised a countersuit.[13]

Meanwhile, John also faced the possibility of going back to

prison. Employment was a condition of his parole, and he took to running classified ads in gay newspapers begging for work. "John Wojtowicz of Dog Day Afternoon fame is looking for a permanent job. Recent bookkeeping job at Project Return ended by budget crunch. Needs a new job urgently or will have to return to jail." He listed Liz's phone number as his contact. Nothing came from the ads and John returned home full-time without knowing how long he'd remain free.[14]

With the press no longer seeking him out, John went out to generate attention on his own. That summer, he drew notice by appearing at a Greenwich Village protest march aimed at upsetting filming of a new Al Pacino picture titled *Cruising*. The film was based on a real-life series of unsolved murders among patrons of New York City leather bars and was being targeted by picketers at the urging of John's old friend and sometimes nemesis Arthur Bell of *The Village Voice*. Bell saw no way the film could be anything more than a hateful and exploitative vision of gay life and had called for filming in the city to be disrupted. John briefly led the march down Christopher Street that eventually surrounded the lot where the production company was storing its gear. The *New York Post*'s article on the picket even featured a photo of John in action.[15]

He also got a television crew to cover his literal return to the scene of the crime, where John posed for photos and signed autographs outside of the Chase Manhattan branch on Avenue P. While John reveled in another small moment, Santa Strazzella—who was one of his hostages seven years before and just happened to be in the neighborhood—spoke with a reporter who followed along. "It's ridiculous. I mean, young kids of today see that and are gonna wanna rob banks just for the attention they get. It's not fair." Was she still scared of him? "I still get the jitters just remembering that whole night," she said. "It was no laughing matter. I mean he acted crazy, you didn't know which way he was gonna go."[16]

He'd return to the bank several more times, but never again with a media entourage. Sometimes he'd wear a special T-shirt he had made up. Black, with bold white lettering, it read: I ROBBED THIS BANK. Posing, shaking hands, taking verbal abuse, fleeing from threats—it was all the same. It was attention.[17]

IN SEPTEMBER 1979, Liz overdosed again. Too many Tuinals and too much booze and she woke up at Saint Vincent's not even able to remember why she'd done it in the first place. At one point, she flatlined and doctors had to shock her heart back to life. "I guess I'm lucky to be alive," she told a reporter. She said she hadn't seen John in a while (they always asked) and said that she hoped to see him again very soon. Her plans now that she'd come back from the dead? Again? "I hope to get on welfare. After that, who knows?"

A year later, Liz gave an interview to *High Society* magazine and appeared in an accompanying nude photo spread. The interview was conducted by the magazine's publisher Gloria Leonard. Compared to her last major profile, the 1977 *Club* article, Liz gave the impression of someone who was sick of putting up a front. She was single again and out of work. Her sympathies for John were nearly gone, her hopes for herself more muted. "Do you think John robbed the bank to prove his love for you?" Leonard asked.

"I don't think so," she replied. "I don't think John really loves me at all."

"Did he love you then?"

"He may have thought he loved me, but I don't think he did.

He still doesn't consider me a woman. He's got very weird morals and standards."

She had undergone a total of fifteen operations so far in her transition at a cost of more than $66,000. Nearly every procedure since her corrected vaginoplasty had been for cosmetic purposes. She had a perfectionist streak in her that made it hard to stop tinkering. Still, she loved the attention. From the film, from men. She was still picking up men, mostly the ones who looked like they wouldn't have a problem with things as they were. She mostly stuck to the gay scene. The gay bars were safer.

"There is a tendency for the public to have an image of transsexuals . . . as very sad people," Leonard said. "At the time John robbed the bank, you were going through OD's and seeing shrinks. Why were you so unhappy? Was it because you were not a total woman physically?"

"That was part of it," Liz answered. "And I missed my mother all that time. I still miss her."

"Are you happier now?"

"I guess so."

As for John, she felt that prison had pushed him only further away from reality. "He is flipped out and I think that someday he'll do it again, only something worse," she said. Leonard asked her if she still considered herself to be John's wife. "I don't consider myself to be his wife at all."

"Then why does he feel that way?"

"Because he's crazy."[18]

NOT LONG AFTER her issue of *High Society* hit newsstands, John and Liz went on *Let's Talk Dirty*, a zero-budget late-night cable show hosted (quite literally, as it was filmed in his apartment) by adult film star Mark Stevens. They sat one on each side of Stevens on his sofa. Liz wore a billowy blue top and had her red hair permed. John, chubbier since his release, wore a black leather jacket and a messy pompadour. Stevens, lithe and blond, asked Liz about John—whom he called Dog—robbing the bank for her. Stevens said the act was "incredibly amazing." He asked Liz if she felt the same way.

"No, not really," Liz answered. John laughed and shook his head.

"Well, why? I mean, don't you think it's incredible?" Stevens asked.

"Because I don't think John really robbed the bank for me. I never have." Liz looked past Stevens and her eyes met those of John, who was still grinning at the far end of the sofa. "I really honestly believe he was in debt to the mob for an unknown amount of money for my wedding."

For all that is known, all that anyone ever bothered to write down or record, this was the first time Liz ever directly hit John with the accusation. It was as crushing a blow as she could have landed at this point in their history together. It meant that he had never been a political prisoner, had never been one of the last great lovers. It gave Al Pacino's Sonny a morality that John could never muster, an admirable streak of recklessness that had been born in the pages of *Life* magazine, not down in the grimy rooms of Boystown. It meant that John might as well have begged Jim Murphy to put one between his eyes back on the tarmac at JFK. Because it meant he hadn't lived an honest moment since.

Stevens turned back to John. "All . . ." John said, looking directly into the camera, "all you have to remember is that I robbed the bank to get Liz the sex change even though I was against her getting the sex change. And that was the only reason I robbed the bank."

"Didn't you leave anything out?" Liz asked.

Stevens flipped the mic back to John. "Nope."

Back to Liz. "Give me a break." John chortled and Stevens said it felt like he was playing Ping-Pong.

Back to John. "I can't give you a break."

Back to Liz. "Never mind." She waved the microphone away and Stevens flipped back to John.

"Oh, she's getting slick."

John deferred, but Liz wasn't done. She'd never write her book, never find niche stardom like an Andy Warhol girl, never make a movie, never get to play herself. She owed her fame—flickering as it was—as much to the Big Lie as John did. And she liked fame. But the moment felt too honest. Cozied up in a cluttered apartment, recording a segment for broadcast on Channel J—a pay station best known in the straight world for airing nude talk shows and hardcore pornography—she might as well bare all.

Liz sat upright, now almost towering over John. "All right, if you had gotten caught, what was the contingency plan?" she asked. Like a good lawyer, she already knew the answer. She knew that Sal and Robert would have killed themselves. She knew that John would have waited so he could lure Liz to the front door. She knew.

Stevens flipped back to John, putting the microphone right under his chin. He said nothing, but Liz kept going.

"What were you going to do when I came and kissed you at the doorway of the bank?"

Stevens bounced back to Liz, then back to John. John parted his lips, staring into the middle distance, but said nothing.

"The truth, John," Liz said off-mic. "Remember, we don't lie."

John's mouth hung open. "The truth, John," Stevens parroted in an attempt at levity.

The truth, John.

John looked at Liz, half smiling. The little man who lied at will and could never shut up was caught in a moment. Little-john, the old-fashioned Italian, the boss, the gay bank robber, the real fuckin' Al Pacino, the Dog . . . now there was just John. John who'd loved Liz, or at least he thought he did. John who was going to get away with his money and his man or burn it all down trying.

The truth, John.

"Who?" John asked laughing. "Who lies?"

"You do," Liz said. "Go ahead."

John took the microphone from Stevens. "I very rarely lie."

Behind him, Liz sat up on her ankles, her arm resting on the back of the sofa, and half turned toward John. It was the same way that Agent Murphy had sat in the van back at Kennedy, gun out but hidden, ready to end this once and for all.

"Okay," John said, turning toward the camera. "The truth is, if Liz wasn't going on the plane with me"—the camera pulled in tight and John turned away—"to get the sex-change operation, I would have blew her fuckin' ass away."

The camera panned back to Stevens, a stricken look on his face. "You would have blown her away?"

"See, Mark," Liz interrupted. "You didn't know us during that one-year period between the time we met and the time after we got married that he robbed the bank." While John sat silently by, Liz recounted the fights and threats and the series of letters he'd sent counting down the number of days remaining for her to either take him back or take a bullet. "The thing that led me into the mental institution, which everybody talks about, is the fact that I got these threatening notes all the way down to number one and I figured since it was my birthday . . . I said, why don't I just kill myself, it would end all this. And that's just what I did. I tried to kill myself . . . I got the shaft. I might have got the sex change but I got the royal shaft. I can't enjoy it."

BY THE END of 1981, nearly $35,000 of the *Dog Day Afternoon* money in the victim's board escrow account had been allocated to bank manager Robert Barrett, who was dying of complications from diabetes, and Carmen, who had successfully filed a claim as one of John's victims. The fund had continued to grow from repeat showings of the film in theaters and on television, but hostages Maureen Andrews and Santa Strazzella were in the midst of filing their own claims. Carmen also successfully petitioned a court to forbid John from seeing his children. He was a bad influence, Carmen claimed, and he was getting worse. She planned to complete the divorce suit as soon as she received the full amount due to her from the victim's fund.[19]

In July 1983, a team of federal marshals conducted a polite raid at John's parents' house on Flatbush Avenue, leading John off in chains. He had recently visited George, who'd recently been convicted on a robbery charge and sentenced to seven to fifteen years. The act violated two of John's parole conditions: that he not associate with criminals and that he not leave the city. He was still locked up when Carmen was finally able to divorce him. A few months later, with John in the midst of what would be an eight-month stay in jail, Liz celebrated her thirty-seventh birthday with a special screening of *Dog Day Afternoon* to raise funds for gay groups. A notice for the party, held at a Union Square nightclub, ran in *The Connection*, a gay weekly newspaper. It was the last time she'd get to see her name in the papers.[20]

In August 1986, John was arrested again for violating parole.

He had, again, left the city to visit George in prison. "The love affair has been self-destructive," a probation officer told the papers. "Both of them have been told over and over to break it off." John was released about a year later, finally at the end of his amended fifteen-year sentence. In early August, he visited Liz, who had since moved to Rochester. It was a little belated, but John considered it their fifteenth anniversary. Liz was sick, as so many from the old scene in the Village now were. She'd been in an accident a few years before, hit by a car outside of a bar late one evening. Doctors had to set her broken leg with pins and gave her a blood transfusion. It might have been that, it might have been a lot of things. In mid-August Liz checked into Genese Hospital in Rochester. She told everyone who she was.[21]

Liz died two week later. The doctors called it "pneumonia as a complication of AIDS." She had just turned forty-one. The wire service obituary that carried news of her passing across the nation opened with the line, "Elizabeth Debbie Eden, whose desire for an expensive sex-change operation drove her lover to attempt a Brooklyn Bank robbery . . ."[22]

Two months later, Robert Westenberg also succumbed to AIDS. He'd lived quietly since his release from prison, usually staying with family and working here and there—mostly off the books. His drinking became a serious problem, but even as he found solace in the nightlife, he maintained a celibate lifestyle. In April 1987, his grandmother passed away and he moved into her apartment in Queens. Sometime before this, he'd met an older man and begun an affair. The older man had AIDS but never told Robert. Robert died in December, collapsing suddenly and alone in his living room. "To know my brother," Wesley Westenberg said in 2024, "was an experience. Everyone who met him loved his happiness and his sense of humor."

Wesley said that his family still tells stories about Robert to this day. Both he and Liz are remembered fondly and still loved. They were but two of the fifteen thousand AIDS deaths in the United States in 1987.

APPLYING HOLLYWOOD PARLANCE to real life, John was always miscast in his roles. He was too eager and ambitious to be a punch-clock banker, too domineering to be a marital partner. He embraced the sexual freedom of the gay liberation movement and enjoyed its camaraderie, but he was too much a tourist to make a good activist and too full of old-fashioned misogyny to ever allow his queer relationships to flourish. As a bandit, he was too timid; as a revolutionary, he was too conservative. As a post-prison celebrity, he was too dull; as a post-prison political figure, he was too shallow. As the real-life version of an iconic character, he was too much himself; as himself, he was too lost in fantasy.

The Sonny brought to life by Al Pacino came along during an antiestablishment moment in American culture. When he screamed "Attica!" at the cops, it meant something. When he threw cash into the air—a few little drops for the people from a very large bucket—it meant something. Even when it did all fall apart in the end, he'd tried. *Trying* meant something. But John wasn't Sonny. He'd never even really claimed to be. He'd claimed to be Al Pacino, he'd claimed to be the gay bank robber. But when he chose his title, he picked the *Dog*. There is exactly one dog in *Dog Day Afternoon*. It is seen on-screen for only a few seconds during the opening titles, picking through the trash for something to eat.

That cultural moment of the mid-seventies was long past by the late 1980s. Sure, the real-life conflicts that fed the moment hadn't been fixed—they were far worse in most cases—but it just didn't make compelling viewing for the masses anymore. Even within the gay liberation movement, the gravity of debating whether a bank robbery could be a zap seemed frivolous in the era of AIDS. John's moment, the Dog's moment, it had all ended. After he was released from prison for good in 1987, John moved back home and started collecting welfare.[23]

At home, he kept late hours and slept most of the day. He'd still cruise in the Village, picking up trans folks at the West Street piers. Always the sucker for a hard-luck story, John would end up bringing many of them home for a meal cooked by his mother and a warm place to spend a night or two. Terry enjoyed the company and would pose for photos with her son's friends, all smiles in each one.[24]

In 1991, the United States Supreme Court overturned New York's Son of Sam law on constitutional grounds. The victims' board had collected nearly $90,000 that would have otherwise been due to John. In addition to money given to Barrett and Carmen, Maureen Andrews was awarded $15,000 and Santa Strazzella nearly $20,000. About $17,000 remained in escrow, but unpaid judgments against John—including claims by George for legal work—significantly exceeded that total. Faced with this pseudo windfall being used by the state to cut his welfare benefits, John signed away any claim to the remaining funds in 1995.[25]

"I TELL THE FBI to go fuck themselves because I'm not going to betray my partner . . . we're going to get out of that bank, we're going to get on the plane, and do what we have to do without hurting anyone. Because we're the real Americans, not them."

It was 1999 and people were listening to John Wojtowicz again. Pierre Huyghe, a French artist and filmmaker, was interested in how culture melded reality and representation. Huyghe built a soundstage recreation of Sidney Lumet's version of the Avenue P Chase Manhattan branch, hired actors to portray Sal, the hostages, and the police, and brought John in to give his interpretation of what had "really" happened. The layers at work in the piece are remarkable. The viewer observes John's own recollection merging fact and the fiction of the film, while he tries to reassert his own agency over the story. But he also distances himself from responsibility. Two minutes into the ten-minute film, he claims that he wasn't even supposed to be inside the bank. Only when Robert left early was he drawn inside, "to save Sal's life," John says. The piece, titled *The Third Memory*, was exhibited at the Guggenheim in New York City, projected on twin screens. On one, a middle-aged John, gray haired and fat, points a shotgun at his "hostages." On the other, scenes from the 1975 film play out. In a voice-over, John tells his truth—part reality, part Lumet, part pure invention.

By the film's midpoint, John is completely off the rails. On the "sidewalk" in front of Huyghe's bank, he mimics pointing a shotgun at the police and directs a police sergeant to point his own gun back and threaten to shoot. "He tells me, if I make a move, I'll blow your fuckin' brains out," John says. He turns to the actor playing the sergeant. "Okay, say it." And the actor does. John then adds that the sergeant called him a "lousy cocksucker." He motions to the actor, and the actor repeats the line. "Okay, now at this time, I forget about the cops, I forget about everything else, I put the shotgun down on the sidewalk, and I turn around and say to the sergeant—" John sets down his weapon, turns to the actor, and points. "'Who are you calling a lousy cocksucker? I'm a good cocksucker. And if you're a man, you'll put down that shotgun and walk toward me . . .'" John acts out how he challenged the sergeant to a fistfight, how the sergeant shot a hole in the sidewalk at John's feet, how he didn't back down and continued to challenge the cop, and on and on.

The piece was a masterful performance from John. With charming wit, he told a great story and virtually glowed from all the attention and power. He spoke of the history of it all, how each hostage—now all existing in obscurity—would be remembered forever. He attributed the demise of the plan to the actions of Richard Nixon, who'd been furious that coverage of the robbery had interrupted his acceptance speech at the Republican National Convention. He described Sal's death as nothing less than a cold-blooded execution by the FBI. The film closes with a dimly lit real-life John on one screen, a fluorescent light blinking above his head. The other is black. John finishes his fantastical recounting of his arrest. "And that's it."

A few years later, Danish filmmaker Walter Stokman got in touch with John for a more traditional documentary about the real-life story behind the robbery. In lieu of what would have been his star interview, Stokman uses audio of his numerous phone conversations with John. Often pretending to be his own son—whom he had now been estranged from for a decade—John required Stokman to ask, "Can I speak to the Dog?" to speak as himself. John demanded $18,000 for an interview. Stokman offered it, half up front and half after, but John refused. "You don't tell Pacino that he's gotta fuckin' wait for the money," he scolds in one scene. In the end, the film was as much about Stokman's efforts to work around John as it was about John.

Carmen was one of the drama's many players who sat for an interview with Stokman. She kept a tidy apartment in Brooklyn with her boyfriend and cats. She had retired after spending twenty-five years as an educator. She enjoyed traveling and going to the track and maintained a small collection of antique cookie jars. "It took a long time to find love," she said. "I didn't trust anybody after that." Interviews over the next couple of years showed a woman who'd found peace and love but hadn't found them easily. "[John's] the father of my kids and everything," she said in 2006, "but he wasn't a nice person." Dawn Wojtowicz would still see her father occasionally, trying to know the real person and not the character. Sean had broken with him long ago. He wanted nothing to do with his father and changed his last name. Carmen did note, however, that Al Pacino was one of Sean's favorite actors. She felt that meant something.[26]

In 2002, another pair of filmmakers, Allison Berg and Frank Keraudren, met John and would spend the next several years following him and documenting his life and times. John is still witty, his eyes are still wide and engaging. And he still lies. Not as grandly and boldly as he did with Huyghe, but it's still all about him. He's the hero and the victim. At one point, he's back at the bank, which is now home to a medical supply company. He's talking to a passerby when he's asked, "Were you Al Pacino in the movie?"

"I'm the bank robber," he says with his best tough-guy inflection. "Fuck Al Pacino."

Halfway through the film, John appears on-screen looking pale and gaunt. He's down at least thirty pounds from the scene before. It's cancer, he says, skin and breast. He's refused treatment. "I'm waitin' for them to tell me how many days. So I can go party," he says. He smiles, but it's an empty smile.

Near the end, he meets up with his brother Tony, who would visit once a year on leave from the hospital. John explains that he tried to talk to Tony about his condition, but it was all useless. "He doesn't understand about dying, he doesn't understand about cancer," he says. "That's why nuts have more fun."

John sits in a wheelchair as Tony pushes him through the zoo. In mild weather, John is bundled up, a baseball cap that reads BROOKLYN perched on his head. Looking at the hippopotamus exhibit, John tries to get the animals to come back near the rail so Tony can get a better look. "Come on, you asshole, get up here," John calls out. "I'll blow you if you come back." Tony laughs heartily. In a scene earlier in the film, with John still in good health, they visit Coney Island. They eat hot dog lunches and John passes french fries off his plate to Tony when Tony has run out. John tells dirty jokes and swears. "You're so funny, John," Tony tells him. "I'm happy, you know that?" Back at the zoo, the hippo turns around in the pool and swims back toward them. "Look at that, he bent over right in front of me!" John tells Tony. "Don't tell me I don't still got it."

In December 2005, Terry brought John to the hospital. She'd been as devoted to him as ever, caring for him like only a mother could. Even before his decline, she'd done nearly everything for him. He had a bell to call for her. She would even button his clothes. John lingered at the hospital for a few weeks. Near the very end, he became delirious. "He wasn't mean or anything," Terry said afterward. "He was very, very good to me. I feel God just took him . . . I hope he's resting now." John Wojtowicz died on January 2, 2006.[27]

It took months for the newspapers to report that John had died. *The Daily News* mentioned it first in an April 2006 article on a forthcoming anniversary edition of the *Dog Day Afternoon* DVD. By the time Berg and Keraudren's *The Dog* was released in 2014, Carmen and Terry had also passed away.

BACK IN 2002, during John's return to moderate notoriety, he was interviewed by scholar Lisa Photos for an article in the *Journal of Bisexuality*. John tells many of the same lies that he does in *The Third Memory* and *The Dog*. He was not supposed to even be in the bank, it was Sal and Robert who were to blame for any bungling, he did it all to save Liz, he bawled out the judge for not knowing what "love" really was just before his sentencing, he threatened loudmouths in the crowd with a grenade, five thousand supporters from Greenwich Village marched to the scene of the robbery to support him. His stories go largely unchecked, as they did in the films, as they did nearly every day that he decided to tell them. Having been studied in the worlds of high art and academia, John refused to change. He was bawdy and self-centered, but he could sell it with a sense of gravitas and wisdom. Asked once just after his release from prison in 1978 if he'd learned any lessons, he replied, "Yeah, don't rob a bank." But he left behind few traces that he really believed it. He left behind few traces that he'd learned any lessons at all.[28]

Dog Day Afternoon turned fifty in 2025. The milestone came amid severe political and cultural backlash against queer and trans Americans. Retrospectives on the film could not ignore how the struggles of Sonny and Leon to assert their humanity in a hostile world remained so tragically relevant. "I would say it held up because somehow Lumet got to the humanity of it," Al Pacino told *The Guardian* that year. "It plays today even more than it even did then."[29]

Critic Jesse Hassenger, writing for *Polygon*, saw the film's story as surprisingly contemporary. "The period details of *Dog Day Afternoon* may have shifted," he wrote, "but its real subject remains pervasive all across the United States: it's about people who feel like they have no other choice." As part of his "Queer Window" series for *MovieJawn*, Matt Campbell cited the film as a "much more sympathetic and realistic portrayal of transness than you'd likely see in mainstream media in 2025." Like Hassenger, Campbell found parallels in the desperation of Sonny to the present day. "The ending of the film proves that the comradery, the community, that we cultivate may not be able to stand up fully against the power of the State," he wrote. "However, as Leon states in the movie, 'How do they expect you to get uncrazy when you're asleep all the time?' We have to—we must—try. Not only for ourselves, but for each other."[30]

Just as *Dog Day Afternoon* was getting another turn in the cultural spotlight, Luigi Mangione sat in prison, awaiting trial on murder charges. While the same side of the political spectrum that was trying to strip queer Americans of their humanity condemned him as a terrorist, the opposite side had anointed him as a folk hero. His alleged crime—the murder of a health insurance CEO—felt to some like the same kind of desperate stab at oppression that John's bank heist had been. Social media posts of John's mugshot—when he was still a dead ringer for Pacino with a rebellious glint in his eyes—will even draw up the same kind of online lust for which Mangione quickly became famous. Fifty-plus years after the fact, there finally seemed to be a path forward for John to become the queer hero he'd always thought himself to be.

But John was never able to get out of his own way long enough to make this even a possibility. Not with Liz, not with the gay community, not with the press. Certainly not in his documentary appearances near the end of his life, where he gave no introspection or apology for the worst of his behaviors. It's a futile exercise to imagine John Wojtowicz as anything but exactly who he was. A different man might have changed, a different man might have learned. But a different man wouldn't have stuck a shotgun right between the eyes of 1972's America, shouted, 'Yeah I'm gay, so what?' and demanded what he needed to make himself whole. That part could have made him a modern-day hero. That's the part that still makes Sonny so admirable. But eventually the camera pulled back on Sonny, leaving him lost among the lights and noise at the end of his long day. John Wojtowicz—Littlejohn, the Great Gay Bank Robber, the Dog—needed to make his day last for the rest of his life.

BACK IN 2002, in the middle of a marathon phone interview with Photos, the tape in her recorder ran out. She paused the conversation and flipped the cassette. John wanted to check to make sure it was still recording properly. He'd had trouble with this before, he said, the audio turned out lousy and he was misquoted. Photos told him he could do a soundcheck to make sure everything was in order. Say whatever you like, she told him. Without pause, John spoke up. "This is the Dog and the Last Real Man. That's my slogan. That's why when all the girls ask me, 'Hey, Dog, where can I find a real man?' I says, 'I'm him.' They go, 'What do you mean you're him?' I says, 'I'm the last real man. There ain't any more after me.'"[31]

acknowledgments

First off, I'd like to give a nod to some people whom I've never met and who had nothing at all to do with this project, but nonetheless provided badly needed distraction, laughter, and entertainment during the process: Tim Robinson; Queen Kwong; the Chapo boys; Rifftrax; Doja Cat; Tropical Fuck Storm; Robert Mitchum; Patti Harrison; Tom Waits; John Waters; my tcdb.com trading partners; Matt Baume; Bryan and Chris (Queeber and the Gris); the Guys Discord; Techmoan; Stavros Halkias; Tim Heidecker and Gregg Turkington; Jon Bois; Brace, Liz, and YC; Craig Finn; Robert Stack; Jackson Chourio; and Pam Grier.

Closer to home, I want to thank everyone at the New York Public Library and its Billy Rose Theater Division; the Lesbian, Gay, Bisexual, and Transgender Community Center in the West Village; and the ONE Archives at the University of Southern California. The archival holdings at these libraries made this work possible, as did all the contributors and donors to the Internet Archive. Although many of them are now gone, I also want to acknowledge the daring and deeply essential work done by the many members of the queer press I have referenced throughout this book. In particular, I'd like to thank Morty Manford, Cliff Jahr, and Arthur Bell for maintaining such incredible archives of their notes and work. And special thanks is due to Randolfe

Wicker and his personal archivist Devlyn Camp. The Wicker Papers—freely available online—were nothing short of a godsend for this project in its early stages. In addition, I'd like to thank Lou McCarthy, Wesley Westenberg, Walter Stokman, and Malcolm Stokes for their great assistance with this story.

Many of my Marquette University colleagues are due thanks as well. Particularly the LGBTQ+ Research Community, including Jason Farr, Alison Efford, Ben Pladek, Emily Horner, Maxwell Gray, Liz Kaune, and Em Fossell, who helped me through one of the earliest drafts of this story. A special nod is also due to the faculty and staff of the Raynor Memorial Libraries and all the members of United Campus Workers of Wisconsin.

Deep gratitude is also due to my agent, Sandy Lu, who did so much in making this into the book it became. And also to Dan López, Dan Smetanka, Jake Lovell, Laura Berry, Olenka Burgess, Wah-Ming Chang, Amina Washington, and Victoria Maxfield at Counterpoint Press, who took this from a humble Word document to a real damn book.

And with all the love I can muster, I want to thank my wife, Erika, who makes all of this worthwhile. Also our little ones—Pearl, Pierogi, and Loretta. I want to thank my mom, who first took me to the movies, and remember my dad, who started my great research and writing journey by always insisting that I "look it up." Love also to Angie and Rik, Frida and TJ, Jim Bauhs, and Emma Schnieder. And last, to the children in my life—Cecilia and Josey Yamashita—stay curious, kids.

notes

1. Brooklyn and Queens

1. "Killing Is Common in Lewisburg Federal Prison, Freed Inmate Says," *New York Times*, June 3, 1976.
2. Untitled Eden interview, undated, Liz Eden Papers, Lesbian, Gay, Bisexual, and Transgender Community Center Archives, New York, 49, 56.
3. Eden interview, 41–42, 49.
4. Eden interview, 41–43.
5. Eden interview, 42–43.
6. *The Dog*, directed by Allison Berg and Frank Keraudren, Unleashed Films, 2013.
7. Randy Wicker, "The Little Bank Robber and the Big Lie," *Gay*, October 30, 1972; *The Dog*, dirs. Berg and Keraudren; P. F. Kluge and Thomas Moore, "The Boys in the Bank," *Life*, September 1972; Randy Wicker, "The Many Loves of Littlejohn," book proposal, undated, Randy Wicker Archive.
8. Clifford Jahr, Dog Day Afternoon Notes, undated, Clifford Jahr Research Files, New York Public Library.
9. Wicker, "The Many Loves of Littlejohn."
10. Jahr, Dog Day Afternoon Notes; Wicker, "Little Bank Robber."
11. Wicker, "Little Bank Robber"; *The Dog*, dirs. Berg and Keraudren.
12. Eden interview, 47–49.
13. Eden interview, 47–49.
14. Eden interview, 47–49.
15. Eden interview, 51.

16. Eden interview, 51, 56–57; Barbara Trecker, "The Gay Robber's 'Wife' Waits for Sex Change," *New York Post*, September 5, 1972.
17. Trecker, "The Gay Robber's 'Wife'"; Eden interview, 53, 63.
18. Eden interview, 52–53.
19. Eden interview, 52–53.
20. Eden interview, 63; Trecker, "The Gay Robber's 'Wife.'"
21. Eden interview, 34.
22. Trecker, "The Gay Robber's 'Wife.'"
23. Eden interview, 55; *The Dog*, dirs. Berg and Keraudren.

2. War

1. *Based on a True Story*, directed by Walter Stokman, Kasander Film, 2004; Wicker, "Little Bank Robber."
2. *Based on a True Story*, dir. Stokman.
3. Cliff Jahr, "Dog Day Aftermath," *Playboy*, August 1976; *Based on a True Story*, dir. Stokman; Jahr, Dog Day Afternoon Notes.
4. Jahr, "Dog Day Aftermath"; *Based on a True Story*, dir. Stokman; Jahr, Dog Day Afternoon Notes.
5. *The Dog*, dirs. Berg and Keraudren; Jahr, "Dog Day Aftermath."
6. Cliff Jahr, "The 'Dog Day' Bank Robber Learns Moviemaking, Like Crime, Does Not Pay," *Village Voice*, September 29, 1975; Jahr, "Dog Day Aftermath"; *The Dog*, dirs. Berg and Keraudren.
7. Jahr, "Dog Day Aftermath"; *The Dog*, dirs. Berg and Keraudren.
8. Lisa Photos, "The Dog and the Last Real Man: An Interview with John S. Wojtowicz," *Journal of Bisexuality* 3, no. 2 (2003).
9. Photos, "The Dog and the Last Real Man."
10. Photos, "The Dog and the Last Real Man"; Randy Shilts, *Conduct Unbecoming: Lesbians and Gays in the U.S. Military* (New York: St. Martin's, 1993), 65, 69–71.
11. Wicker, "Little Bank Robber"; *The Dog*, dirs. Berg and Keraudren.
12. Jahr, Dog Day Afternoon Notes.
13. Jahr, Dog Day Afternoon Notes; Jahr, "Dog Day Aftermath."
14. Jahr, "Dog Day Aftermath"; Jahr, Dog Day Afternoon Notes; *Based on a True Story*, dir. Stokman.
15. Jahr, Dog Day Afternoon Notes.

16. Randy Wicker, "8/31/72 Notes," Randy Wicker Archive; Jahr, Dog Day Afternoon Notes; Kluge and Moore, "The Boys in the Bank."
17. *The Dog*, dirs. Berg and Keraudren; Wicker, "Little Bank Robber."
18. Jerry Lisker, "Homo Nest Raided, Queen Bees Are Stinging Mad," *New York Daily News*, July 6, 1969.
19. Emily S. Rueb, "A Wife Recalls Her Estranged Husband's 1972 Failed Bank Robbery," *New York Times*, City Room Blog, August 22, 2012, archive.nytimes.com/cityroom.blogs.nytimes.com/2012/08/22/a-wife-recalls-her-estranged-husbands-1972-failed-bank-robbery/.

3. All Welcome, Dress Optional

1. David Carter, *Stonewall: The Riots That Sparked the Gay Revolution* (New York: St. Martin's, 2004), 102–103, 215.
2. Carter, *Stonewall*, 80–81, 88; Phillip Crawford Jr., *The Mafia and the Gays* (2015), 31, 77.
3. Carter, *Stonewall*, 102–103, 183, 262–63.
4. Carter, *Stonewall*, 102–103, 183, 262–63.
5. Carter, *Stonewall*, 219–20, 227.
6. Carter, *Stonewall*, 44; Arthur Bell, *Dancing the Gay Lib Blues: A Year in the Homosexual Liberation Movement* (New York: Simon & Schuster, 1971), 15, 17, 35–37, 57, 130.
7. Bell, *Dancing the Gay Lib Blues*, 58, 138–39, 141.
8. *Based on a True Story*, dir. Stokman.
9. Susan Stryker, *Transgender History: The Roots of Today's Revolution*, rev. ed. (New York: Seal Press, 2017), 109; Photos, "The Dog and the Last Real Man."
10. Wicker, "Little Bank Robber"; Eden interview, 62.
11. Dan Hertzberg, "Bank Gunman: A Troubled Paradox," *Newsday*, August 27, 1972; Jahr, Dog Day Afternoon Notes.
12. Eden interview, 36, 40–41.
13. Eden interview, 66, 64–65.
14. Eden interview, 64–65.
15. Carter, *Stonewall*, 242; Bell, *Dancing the Gay Lib Blues*, 42;

"The Snake Pit," NYC LGBT Historic Sites Project, www.nyclgbtsites.org/site/the-snake-pit/, accessed January 18, 2024.

16. Carter, *Stonewall*, 253; Bell, *Dancing the Gay Lib Blues*, 97, 100–101; Hugh Ryan, "The Stonewall Riots Weren't New York City's Only Queer Uprising," *Daily Beast*, April 8, 2019, www.thedailybeast.com/stonewall-wasnt-new-york-citys-only-queer-uprising-remembering-the-haven-riot.
17. NYC Landmarks Preservation Commission, "GAA Firehouse Designation Report," June 19, 2019; Wallace Hamilton, *Christopher and Gay: A Partisan's View of the Greenwich Village Homosexual Scene* (New York: Saturday Review, 1973), 44–45.
18. Arthur Bell, "Littlejohn & the Mob: Saga of a Heist," *Village Voice*, August 31, 1972; Jahr, Dog Day Afternoon Notes.
19. *The Dog*, dirs. Berg and Keraudren; Jahr, Dog Day Afternoon Notes; Bell, "Littlejohn & the Mob."
20. Martin Gottlieb, "He Wants to Change 'Dog Day' to 'Love Story,'" *New York Daily News*, September 7, 1977; Cy Egan, Judith Michaelson, and Barbara Trecker, "Did Bank Bandit Pull Earlier Jobs?" *New York Post*, August 24, 1972.
21. Bell, "Littlejohn & the Mob."
22. Jahr, Dog Day Afternoon Notes.
23. "The Dog and The Last Real Man."
24. Jahr, Dog Day Afternoon Notes.
25. Pete Fisher, "Gay Couples Celebrate Engagement at Marriage License Bureau," *Gay*, July 5, 1971; "Gay Activists Alliance Zap at the New York City Marriage Bureau," NYC LGBT History Sites Project, www.nyclgbtsites.org/site/gay-activists-alliance-zap-at-the-nyc-marriage-bureau/, accessed January 23, 2024.
26. *The Dog*, dirs. Berg and Keraudren.
27. *The Dog*, dirs. Berg and Keraudren; Fisher, "Gay Couples Celebrate."
28. Fisher, "Gay Couples Celebrate."

4. Boystown

1. Liz Eden and Richard Barraclough, "TS (and It Doesn't Mean Tough Shit, Either!)," Liz Eden papers, 2–3; Eden interview, 1.
2. Eden and Barraclough, "TS," 2–3.

3. Eden and Barraclough, "TS," 3; Eden interview, 1.
4. Eden interview, 1; Eden and Barraclough, "TS," 3, 4.
5. Eden interview, 3.
6. Eden interview, 6; Eden and Barraclough, "TS," 4; Murray Schumach, "A Blighted 'Affair' Led to Bank Holdup," *New York Times,* August 24, 1972.
7. Eden interview, 7.
8. Eden and Barraclough, "TS," 4; Randy Wicker, "Aron Interview," September 13, 1972, Randy Wicker Archive.
9. Eden interview, 7.
10. "Little John Wojtowicz: Gay Wasn't Good," *The Advocate,* September 27, 1972; Eden interview, 32; Wicker, "Little Bank Robber."
11. Crawford, *The Mafia and the Gays,* 87.
12. Arthur Bell, "Christopher's Emperor," *Village Voice,* July 22, 1971; Crawford, *The Mafia and the Gays,* 90.
13. Crawford, *The Mafia and the Gays,* 88, 92; Bell, "Christopher's Emperor."
14. Crawford, *The Mafia and the Gays,* 88, 91, 92; Bell, "Christopher's Emperor."
15. Bell, "Littlejohn & the Mob."
16. Egan, Michaelson, and Trecker, "Did Bank Bandit Pull Earlier Jobs?"; Eden interview, 2.

5. Run Like Hell

1. Photos, "The Dog and the Last Real Man"; *The Dog,* dirs. Berg and Keraudren.
2. Jahr, "Dog Day Aftermath"; Eden interview, 18.
3. Wicker, "Little Bank Robber"; Randy Wicker, "Notes," August 31, 1972, Randy Wicker Archive.
4. "N. Y.'s First Drag Wedding," *New York Mattachine Newsletter,* October/November 1971; Egan, Michaelson, and Trecker, "Did Bank Bandit Pull Earlier Jobs?"
5. Ernest Aron letter to the editor, Arthur Bell Papers, New York Public Library; Randy Wicker email to Ryan Wolowsky, "Posting on Facebook About New York Post Interview About the Dog," July 25, 2014, Randy Wicker Archive.

6. "Clerk Wants Tighter Law Against Gay Marriage," *The Advocate*, June 24, 1970; Michael Waters, "A Bureaucratic Prologue to Same-Sex Marriage," *Lapham's Quarterly*, June 24, 2019.
7. "Liz Eden and Dog Day Afternoon: Part 1," A Gender Variance Who's Who, August 22, 2020, zagria.blogspot.com/2020/08/liz-eden-and-dog-day-afternoon-part-i.html.
8. Ernest Aron letter to the editor; Eden and Barraclough, "TS," 5; Wicker, "Little Bank Robber."
9. Paul Meskil, "Seek Insider in Bank Holdup," *New York Daily News*, August 24, 1972; "Little John Wojtowicz: Gay Wasn't Good"; Randy Wicker, "On the Day of His Castration," *Gay*, March 26, 1973.
10. Wicker, "Little Bank Robber"; Meskil, "Seek Insider in Bank Holdup."
11. Meskil, "Seek Insider in Bank Holdup."
12. Eden and Barraclough, "TS," 5; Egan, Michaelson, and Trecker, "Did Bank Bandit Pull Earlier Jobs?"; Eden interview, 2.
13. Egan, Michaelson, and Trecker, "Did Bank Bandit Pull Earlier Jobs?"; Wicker, "Little Bank Robber."
14. Eden interview, 4; Egan, Michaelson, and Trecker, "Did Bank Bandit Pull Earlier Jobs?"
15. Eden interview, 3–4.
16. *The Dog*, dirs. Berg and Keraudren; Wicker, "Little Bank Robber."
17. Eden and Barraclough, "TS," 5.
18. Eden and Barraclough, "TS," 6.
19. Wicker, "Little Bank Robber."
20. Wicker, "Little Bank Robber."
21. Eden interview, 5; Wicker, "Notes."
22. Eden interview, 5, 7.
23. Randy Wicker, "Bye John," *The Advocate*, March 14, 1973; Eden and Barraclough, "TS," 7; *The Dog*, dirs. Berg and Keraudren.
24. Eden interview, 5.
25. "Here Comes the Bride," *Drag*, vol. 2, no. 6, 1972.
26. John Hunter, "The Gay Insider," *Gay*, March, 1972; Bell, "Littlejohn & the Mob"; "Little John Wojtowicz: Gay Wasn't Good."
27. "Little John Wojtowicz: Gay Wasn't Good."

28. Eden interview, 7; Wicker, "Notes."
29. Eden interview, 8.
30. Eden interview, 8.
31. Eden interview, 8; Wicker, "Little Bank Robber."

6. No Such Luck

1. Schumach, "A Blighted 'Affair'"; Kluge and Moore, "The Boys in the Bank."
2. Robert Hanley, "Bank Bandit Slain," *New York Times,* August 24, 1972; Stephen Brockelman, "Summer, 1972: A Bank Robbery, Some Penny Candy, the FBI, and My Dog Day Afternoon," Brockelpress, September 13, 2014, brockelpress.com/2014/09/13/a-bank-robbery-penny-candy-the-fbi-and-a-dog-day-afternoon-in-nyc/.
3. Hamilton, *Christopher and Gay,* [80].
4. "Little John Wojtowicz: Gay Wasn't Good."
5. Hamilton, *Christopher and Gay,* [80].
6. John Wojtowicz and Sal Natuarale, Federal Bureau of Investigation (FBI) file, March 28, 2017, archive.org/details/JohnWojtowiczAndSalvatoreNatuarale, 147; Hamilton, *Christopher and Gay,* 81; Brockelman, "Summer, 1972."
7. Egan, Michaelson, and Trecker, "Did Bank Bandit Pull Earlier Jobs?"
8. "Westenberg, 'The Forgotten Man,' Defers Plea," *The Advocate,* March 14, 1973.
9. "Gay Boy Goes 'Straight,'" *Gay,* January 1974; Murray Schumach, "3rd Suspect Seized in Bizarre Holdup," *New York Times,* August 25, 1972; "Dog Day Afternoon: The Reality of It All," Warner Bros. Records, 1975.
10. Wicker, "Little Bank Robber"; *Based on a True Story,* dir. Stokman; Hertzberg, "Bank Gunman"; "Little John Wojtowicz: Gay Wasn't Good."
11. Little John Basso, "Sadism," *Gay Alliance of Brooklyn Newsletter,* June 17–25, 1972.
12. "Bella at the Baths," *Gay,* July 10, 1972; "Gay Teachers OK'd by Washington DC School Board," *Gay,* July 10, 1972.

13. "Wojtowicz Sane, New Out Sought," *The Advocate*, November 22, 1972; Wicker, "Little Bank Robber."
14. "Little John Wojtowicz: Gay Wasn't Good"; Wicker, "Little Bank Robber."
15. Eden and Barraclough, "TS," 8.
16. Eden interview, 11.
17. Eden interview, 11.
18. Trecker, "The Gay Robber's 'Wife'"; Eden interview, 36.
19. Trecker, "The Gay Robber's 'Wife'"; Penney Lewis, "The Lawfulness of Gender Reassignment Surgery," *American Journal of Legal History* 58, no. 1 (2018): 56–86.
20. Eden interview, 27; Eden and Barraclough, "TS," 8.
21. Wicker, "Aron Interview"; Eden interview, 43–44.
22. Eden and Barraclough, "TS," 9; Eden interview, 12.
23. Eden interview, 12.
24. Eden interview, 12.
25. Eden interview, 14, 44.
26. Eden interview, 14; Eden and Barraclough, "TS," 9.
27. Eden interview, 14–15.
28. Eden interview, 14–16.
29. Eden interview, 16; Wicker, "Little Bank Robber"; Eden and Barraclough, "TS," 9.

7. He's Crazy

1. Arthur Bell, Notes from GAA Meeting, August 25, 1972, Arthur Bell Papers, New York Public Library.
2. Untitled Robert Westenberg article, undated, Randy Wicker Archive.
3. Jerry Parker, "Going Through a Dog Day Again," *San Francisco Examiner*, December 22, 1974; "Gay Boy Goes 'Straight'"; Untitled Robert Westenberg article.
4. Wicker, "Little Bank Robber"; Hamilton, *Christopher and Gay*, 82.
5. Hamilton, *Christopher and Gay*, 82.
6. Schumach, "A Blighted 'Affair'"; "Wojtowicz Gets 20 Year Sentence," *The Advocate*, May 23, 1973.
7. Eden interview, 19.

8. Eden interview, 19.
9. Kluge and Moore, "The Boys in the Bank"; Jahr, Dog Day Afternoon Notes; Randy Wicker, "Village Voice Sued by Mike Umbers," *Gay*, December 11, 1972.
10. "Little John Wojtowicz: Gay Wasn't Good"; FBI file, 184–85.
11. Wicker, "Little Bank Robber"; Untitled Robert Westenberg article.
12. "Westenberg, 'The Forgotten Man'"; John Wojtowicz to Cliff Jahr, October 29, 1975, Clifford Jahr Research Files, New York Public Library; FBI file, 89, 123, 332; Egan, Michaelson, and Trecker, "Did Bank Bandit Pull Earlier Jobs?"
13. Hertzberg, "Bank Gunman"; "Westenberg, 'The Forgotten Man.'"
14. FBI file, 98.
15. Eden interview, 19.
16. Eden interview, 19.
17. Robert Rosberg, *Game of Thieves* (New York: Arno, 1980), 205.
18. FBI file, 98.
19. Jahr, "The 'Dog Day' Bank Robber"; "Westenberg, 'The Forgotten Man'"; FBI file, 122.
20. "Dog Day Afternoon: The Reality of It All"; FBI file, 125; Barbara Trecker, "The Gay Bank Robbery: Two Years After," *New York Post*, November 7, 1974.
21. "Dog Day Afternoon: The Reality of It All"; FBI file, 125; Trecker, "The Gay Bank Robbery."
22. "Dog Day Afternoon: The Reality of It All"; FBI file, 125; Trecker, "The Gay Bank Robbery"; Untitled Robert Westenberg article.
23. FBI file, 122; Rosberg, *Game of Thieves*, 205; Jahr, "The 'Dog Day' Bank Robber."
24. *Based on a True Story*, dir. Stokman.
25. Untitled Robert Westenberg article.
26. FBI file, 106; "Dog Day Afternoon: The Reality of It All"; "Westenberg, 'The Forgotten Man'"; Trecker, "The Gay Bank Robbery."
27. FBI file, 106; "Dog Day Afternoon: The Reality of It All"; "Westenberg, 'The Forgotten Man'"; Trecker, "The Gay Bank Robbery."
28. *The Dog*, dirs. Berg and Keraudren.

29. Jahr, Dog Day Afternoon Notes.
30. Untitled Robert Westenberg article.
31. FBI file, 122.
32. Rosberg, *Game of Thieves*, 205; "Dog Day Afternoon: The Reality of It All."
33. Schumach, "3rd Suspect Seized."
34. Rosberg, *Game of Thieves*, 205.
35. FBI file, 86, 101.
36. Rosberg, *Game of Thieves*, 208; "Dog Day Afternoon: The Reality of It All."
37. Rosberg, *Game of Thieves*, 208.
38. FBI file, 84, 92.
39. FBI file, 84, 92.
40. FBI file, 90; Rosberg, *Game of Thieves*, 208.
41. Rosberg, *Game of Thieves*, 209.
42. Rosberg, *Game of Thieves*, 203–204.
43. "It's So Easy to Rob a Bank," *Business Week*, February 10, 1973; Kluge and Moore, "The Boys in the Bank"; Daniel Edward Rosen, "The Deacon and the Dog," *City Journal*, Summer 2022, www.city-journal.org/article/the-deacon-and-the-dog.
44. Rosberg, *Game of Thieves*, 209, 211; *Based on a True Story*, dir. Stokman.
45. Untitled Robert Westenberg article.
46. Rosberg, *Game of Thieves*, 209, 211.
47. "Dog Day Afternoon: The Reality of It All."

8. Enough to Send You Back in Time

1. Andrew Tulley, *Inside the FBI: From the Files of the Federal Bureau of Investigation and Independent Sources* (New York: Dell Publishing, 1987), 230–31.
2. Rosberg, *Game of Thieves*, 210.
3. Tulley, *Inside the FBI*, 230–31.
4. "Dog Day Afternoon: The Reality of It All."
5. Eden interview, 30; Untitled Robert Westenberg article.
6. Rosberg, *Game of Thieves*, 211.

7. Tulley, *Inside the FBI*, 230–31.
8. Nicholas Gage, "A 25-Year FBI Agent Foiled Robbers' Attempt to Flee by Jet," *New York Times*, August 24, 1972; Rosberg, *Game of Thieves*, 203–204.
9. Frank J. Prial, "2 Hold 8 Hostages in a Bank in Brooklyn," *New York Daily News*, August 23, 1972; Rosberg, *Game of Thieves*, 212.
10. Tulley, *Inside the FBI*, 231; Aaron Edwards, "Recalling the Real 'Dog Day Afternoon' 40 Years On," *New York Times*, August 22, 2012; Hanley, "Bank Bandit Slain."
11. Tulley, *Inside the FBI*, 231.
12. Tulley, *Inside the FBI*, 231.
13. Bell, Notes from GAA Meeting; Joseph P. Fried, "Thousands of Residents Keep an All-Night Vigil," *New York Times*, August 24, 1972.
14. Brockelman, "Summer, 1972."
15. Brockelman, "Summer, 1972."
16. Prial, "2 Hold 8 Hostages."
17. Tulley, *Inside the FBI*, 231–32.
18. "WCBS - Brooklyn Bank Heist," SoundCloud, Stephen Brockelman, soundcloud.com/stephen-brockelman/wcbs-brooklyn-bank-heist, accessed August 28, 2024.
19. Rueb, "Wife Recalls Her Estranged Husband"; Wicker, "Little Bank Robber."
20. Brockelman, "Summer, 1972."
21. Gary J. Badger Statement, Arthur Bell Papers, New York Public Library.
22. Michael Knight, "3,000 Residents Watch, Cheer as 2 Gunmen Hold Police at Bay," *New York Times*, August 23, 1972.
23. Prial, "2 Hold 8 Hostages."
24. Jahr, Dog Day Afternoon Notes.
25. Meskil, "Seek Insider in Bank Holdup"; Don Douglas, "Gay Bank Robbery," *Gay Scene*, September 4, 1972; FBI file, 125; Bell, Notes from GAA Meeting.
26. Prial, "2 Hold 8 Hostages."
27. Eden interview, 20.

28. Eden interview, 20–22.
29. Eden interview, 21–22.
30. Eden interview, 21–22.
31. Eden interview, 21–22.
32. Eden interview, 21–22.
33. Tulley, *Inside the FBI*, 232; Wicker, "Little Bank Robber"; Eden interview, 22.

9. Gunshot

1. Rosberg, *Game of Thieves*, 214.
2. Rosberg, *Game of Thieves*, 214; Frank Taggert and Marc Schogol, "They Came for Some Action," *Newsday*, August 23, 1972.
3. Taggert and Schogol, "They Came for Some Action"; Knight, "3,000 Residents Watch, Cheer."
4. Richard Schwartz, "An On-Looker Speaks from Experience," *New York Post*, August 23, 1972.
5. Eden interview, 22.
6. Kluge and Moore, "The Boys in the Bank"; Eden interview, 22; Jahr, "Dog Day Aftermath."
7. Jahr, "The 'Dog Day' Bank Robber."
8. John Wojtowicz to Liz Eden, September 9, 1972, Randy Wicker Archive; Rosberg, *Game of Thieves*, 217.
9. Untitled Robert Westenberg article.
10. Eden interview, 24; Wicker, "Little Bank Robber."
11. Eden interview, 24; *The Dog*, dirs. Berg and Keraudren.
12. Kluge and Moore, "The Boys in the Bank."
13. Kluge and Moore, "The Boys in the Bank."
14. Kluge and Moore, "The Boys in the Bank."
15. Kluge and Moore, "The Boys in the Bank."
16. Kluge and Moore, "The Boys in the Bank."
17. Kluge and Moore, "The Boys in the Bank."
18. "Little John Wojtowicz: Gay Wasn't Good"; *Based on a True Story*, dir. Stokman.
19. Kluge and Moore, "The Boys in the Bank"; FBI file, 224.
20. Rosberg, *Game of Thieves*, 217.
21. Rosberg, *Game of Thieves*, 217.

22. Rosberg, *Game of Thieves*, 217–18.
23. Rosberg, *Game of Thieves*, 217–18.
24. Rosberg, *Game of Thieves*, 220.
25. Hannah Ritchie, "Airline Hijackings Were Once Common but Are Very Rare Today," OurWorldInData.org, www.ourworldindata.org/airline-hijackings-were-once-common-but-are-very-rare-today, accessed August 28, 2024.
26. Rosberg, *Game of Thieves*, 220.
27. Rosberg, *Game of Thieves*, 220.
28. Rosberg, *Game of Thieves*, 220.
29. Rueb, "Wife Recalls Her Estranged Husband"; *The Dog*, dirs. Berg and Keraudren.
30. "Dog Day Afternoon: The Reality of It All"; Rueb, "Wife Recalls Her Estranged Husband"; *Based on a True Story*, dir. Stokman; Wicker, "Little Bank Robber."
31. Taggert and Schogol, "They Came for Some Action"; Prial, "2 Hold 8 Hostages."
32. Hertzberg, "Bank Gunman"; Eden interview, 22; John J. Goldman, "FBI Shots Save 7 Held by Robber, Gay Partner," *Los Angeles Times*, August 24, 1972; Jahr, Dog Day Afternoon Notes; "Bank Saga's End," *New York Post*, August 23, 1972.
33. Kluge and Moore, "The Boys in the Bank."

10. The Black Rose of Death

1. Jahr, "The 'Dog Day' Bank Robber."
2. *Based on a True Story*, dir. Stokman.
3. Rosen, "The Deacon and the Dog."
4. Prial, "2 Hold 8 Hostages."
5. "Bandit in Trap Bares Strange Life," *New York Daily News*, August 23, 1972.
6. Bell, "Littlejohn & the Mob."
7. Bell, "Littlejohn & the Mob."
8. Ellen Fleysher, "To Crooks, It's All Pie in Sky," *New York Daily News*, August 24, 1972; Prial, "2 Hold 8 Hostages."
9. Bell, "Littlejohn & the Mob."
10. Bell, "Littlejohn & the Mob"; Wicker, "Little Bank Robber."

11. Kluge and Moore, "The Boys in the Bank."
12. "Incongruities of Ordeal Recounted by Hostages," *New York Times*, August 24, 1972; FBI file, 47, 324–25.
13. "Incongruities of Ordeal"; FBI file, 47.
14. Kluge and Moore, "The Boys in the Bank"; Bob Kappstatter, "Some Bitter Memories of Dog Day Afternoon," *New York Daily News*, November 26, 1978.
15. Kluge and Moore, "The Boys in the Bank."
16. Rosberg, *Game of Thieves*, 222; Hanley, "Bank Bandit Slain."
17. FBI file, 224–25.
18. *Based on a True Story*, dir. Stokman.
19. Rosen, "The Deacon and the Dog."
20. Rosen, "The Deacon and the Dog."
21. Bell, "Littlejohn & the Mob"; Kluge and Moore, "The Boys in the Bank."
22. Rosen, "The Deacon and the Dog."
23. Rosberg, *Game of Thieves*, 223; Kluge and Moore, "The Boys in the Bank"; *Based on a True Story*, dir. Stokman.
24. Rosberg, *Game of Thieves*, 223.
25. Kluge and Moore, "The Boys in the Bank."
26. Bell, "Littlejohn & the Mob"; Fried, "Thousands of Residents"; Wicker, "Little Bank Robber"; Eden interview, 23.
27. Rosen, "The Deacon and the Dog"; Rosberg, *Game of Thieves*, 224.
28. *Based on a True Story*, dir. Stokman.
29. FBI file, 87; Kluge and Moore, "The Boys in the Bank"; Frank Taggert, George DeWan, and James W. Sullivan, "(1) Bank Robbery, (2) Skyjack Try and (3) an FBI Marksman Ends It All," *Newsday*, August 23, 1972.
30. FBI file, 226.
31. "Losing a Lover, He Robs a Bank," *The Advocate*, September 13, 1972; Rosberg, *Game of Thieves*, 225.
32. Rosen, "The Deacon and the Dog."
33. Rosberg, *Game of Thieves*, 226.
34. Rosberg, *Game of Thieves*, 226.
35. Edwards, "Recalling the Real 'Dog Day Afternoon'"; "Incongruities

of Ordeal"; Rosberg, *Game of Thieves*, 226; Rosen, "The Deacon and the Dog."

36. Edwards, "Recalling the Real 'Dog Day Afternoon.'"

11. You Never Smile

1. Eden interview, 23.
2. Eden interview, 23.
3. Eden interview, 24.
4. FBI file, 288–90.
5. Randy Wicker, "The Boys in the Bank," ERA, April 1974; Bell, Notes from GAA Meeting; FBI file, 360.
6. FBI file, 258.
7. FBI file, 122–25.
8. "1973 Westenberg Interview," Randy Wicker Archive.
9. "1973 Westenberg Interview"; "Westenberg, 'The Forgotten Man.'"
10. "1973 Westenberg Interview."
11. Edward Alwood, *Straight News: Gays, Lesbians, and the News Media* (New York: Columbia University Press, 1996), 48, 81.
12. Alwood, *Straight News*, 88–90, 94.
13. Alwood, *Straight News*, 54, 102–103.
14. Alwood, *Straight News*, 121.
15. Prial, "2 Hold 8 Hostages"; Jahr, Dog Day Afternoon Notes.
16. Hertzberg, "Bank Gunman"; Prial, "2 Hold 8 Hostages"; George Frazier, "A Gay Trip to the Bank," *Boston Globe*, September 1, 1972.
17. Alwood, *Straight News*, 92.
18. Thane Hampton, "A Very Queer Bank Robbery," *Gay*, October 2, 1972.
19. Hampton, "A Very Queer Bank Robbery."
20. C. (Mac) McConnohie, "The Great (?) Gay (?) Bank Robbery (?)," *Gay Liberator*, October 1972.
21. "FBI Slays Gay Bandit," *Gay Revolution Networker*, undated.
22. Arthur Bell, "Gay Lib Appraises a Gay Desperado," *Village Voice*, September 21, 1972.
23. Bell, "Gay Lib Appraises a Gay Desperado"; Bell, "Littlejohn & the Mob."

24. Eden interview, 25.
25. Eden interview, 25.
26. Wicker, "Little Bank Robber."
27. Wicker, "Little Bank Robber."
28. Randy Wicker to John Wojtowicz, September 20, 1972, Randy Wicker Archive.
29. Wicker, "Little Bank Robber."
30. Eden interview, 26; John Wojtowicz to Liz Eden, August 25, 1972, Randy Wicker Archive; Anni Arbour, "The Herstory of Liz Eden: Part 2," *Trans Ascending,* anniarbour.substack.com /p/the-herstory-of-liz-eden-part-2, accessed February 19, 2026.
31. Bell, "Gay Lib Appraises a Gay Desperado."
32. Barbara Trecker, "Gays Fear Bias in Bank Case," *New York Post,* August 25, 1972.
33. Trecker, "Gays Fear Bias."
34. Trecker, "Gays Fear Bias"; McConnohie, "The Great (?) Gay (?) Bank Robbery (?)."
35. Hampton, "A Very Queer Bank Robbery."
36. Bell, Notes from GAA Meeting.
37. Bell, "Littlejohn & the Mob."
38. "GAA Statement on Brooklyn Bank Robbery," Gay Activist Alliance Press Release, August 26, 1972.
39. Parker, "Going Through a Dog Day Again."
40. FBI file, 20.
41. Frank Taggert, "A Former Hostage Seeks Safer Work," *Newsday,* August 27, 1972.
42. Wicker to Wojtowicz, September 20, 1972.
43. Wicker, "Little Bank Robber"; Hanley, "Bank Bandit Slain"; John Wojtowicz to Carmen Wojtowicz, August 24, 1972, Clifford Jahr Research Files, New York Public Library.
44. Trecker, "The Gay Robber's 'Wife.'"
45. Randy Wicker to John Wojtowicz, October 2, 1972, Randy Wicker Archive; Wicker to Wojtowicz, September 20, 1972; John Wojtowicz to Randy Wicker, October 2, 1972, Randy Wicker Archive.

12. Love Is a Very Strange Thing

1. Jahr, Dog Day Afternoon Notes; Jahr, "Dog Day Aftermath."
2. Wicker, "Little Bank Robber."
3. Press release, undated, Arthur Bell Papers, New York Public Library; Wicker, "Little Bank Robber."
4. FBI file, 324–25.
5. John Wojtowicz, Last Will and Testament, September 12, 1972, Randy Wicker Archive.
6. Wojtowicz to Wicker, October 2, 1972.
7. Wicker, "Little Bank Robber."
8. Wicker to Wojtowicz, September 20, 1972; Wojtowicz to Wicker, October 2, 1972.
9. Wicker to Wojtowicz, September 20, 1972.
10. "Wojtowicz Sane, New Out Sought."
11. Eden interview, 26; Wicker to Wojtowicz, October 2, 1972.
12. Parker, "Going Through a Dog Day Again"; Andrew Yule, *Life on the Wire: The Life and Art of Al Pacino* (New York: SPI Books, 1993), 114.
13. Randy Wicker to John Wojtowicz, November 8, 1972, Randy Wicker Archive.
14. Jahr, "Dog Day Aftermath"; Eden interview, 28; Wicker to Wojtowicz, November 8, 1972; Wicker to Wojtowicz, September 20, 1972.
15. Eden interview, 27–28.
16. Martin Efland to Mark Landsman, November 29, 1972, Cliff Jahr Papers; John Wojtowicz Boys in the Bank release, November 30, 1972, Cliff Jahr Papers; Press release, undated, Arthur Bell Papers; Jahr, "The 'Dog Day' Bank Robber"; Parker, "Going Through a Dog Day Again."
17. Wicker, "On the Day of His Castration."
18. Wicker, "On the Day of His Castration"; "Sex Change for Ernie," *Gay News*, March 21, 1973.
19. Lewis, "Lawfulness of Gender Reassignment Surgery," 56–86; Anna Zurada et al., "The Evolution of Transgender Surgery," *Clinical Anatomy* 36, no. 1 (2018): 878–886.

20. Wicker, "On the Day of His Castration"; "Sex Change for Ernie"; Lewis, "Lawfulness of Gender Reassignment Surgery," 56–86; Zurada et al., "Evolution of Transgender Surgery."
21. Wicker, "On the Day of His Castration."
22. Wicker, "On the Day of His Castration"; "Sex Change for Ernie."
23. Wicker, "On the Day of His Castration."
24. Wicker, "On the Day of His Castration."
25. Wicker, "On the Day of His Castration."
26. Wicker, "On the Day of His Castration."
27. Wicker, "On the Day of His Castration."
28. Wicker, "On the Day of His Castration."
29. Press release, undated, Arthur Bell Papers.
30. Press release, undated, Arthur Bell Papers.
31. Wicker, "Bye John."
32. Wicker, "Bye John."
33. Eden and Barraclough, "TS," 10; Eden interview, 44–45.
34. Wicker, "Boys in the Bank."
35. Press release, undated, Arthur Bell Papers; Wicker, "Boys in the Bank"; "Sex Change for Ernie."
36. Wicker, "Boys in the Bank."
37. "Wojtowicz Gets 20 Year Sentence."
38. Wicker, "Boys in the Bank."
39. Wicker, "Boys in the Bank."
40. Wicker, "Boys in the Bank."
41. Wicker, "Boys in the Bank."
42. Wicker, "Boys in the Bank."
43. Wicker, "Boys in the Bank."
44. Eden interview, 29; Wicker, "Boys in the Bank."
45. Wicker, "Boys in the Bank."

13. Seasons in the Sun

1. *Based on a True Story*, dir. Stokman.
2. Eden and Barraclough, "TS," 11; "NYU Continues 'Homosexuality' Course," *Gay*, January 1973; Randy Wicker, "Gays Pour Through New York," *The Advocate*, July 18, 1973.
3. Eden and Barraclough, "TS," 11.

4. Jahr, "Dog Day Aftermath"; Eden and Barraclough, "TS," 11.
5. Eden interview, 61.
6. Nan Robertson, "Hoffa Makes Plea on Prison Reform," *New York Times*, June 14, 1972.
7. "Killing Is Common in Lewisburg"; "Tells of Effort to Adjust," *Washington Post*, April 2, 1972.
8. John Wojtowicz to Frank Pierson, September 29, 1973, Clifford Jahr Research Files, New York Public Library.
9. John Wojtowicz to Liz Eden, January 13, 1974, Liz Eden Papers, Lesbian, Gay, Bisexual and Transgender Community Center Archive; John Wojtowicz to Liz Eden, December 4, 1973, Liz Eden Papers, Lesbian, Gay, Bisexual and Transgender Community Center Archive.
10. Wojtowicz to Eden, January 13, 1974; Lewis Grossberger, "The 'Dog' Is Out of the Joint," *Washington Post*, October 2, 1978.
11. John Wojtowicz to Liz Eden, January 20, 1974, Liz Eden Papers, Lesbian, Gay, Bisexual and Transgender Community Center Archive.
12. "Gay Boy Goes 'Straight'"; Untitled Robert Westenberg article.
13. "Gay Boy Goes 'Straight'"; Untitled Robert Westenberg article.
14. "Gay Boy Goes 'Straight'"; Untitled Robert Westenberg article.
15. Trecker, "The Gay Bank Robbery."
16. Parker, "Going Through a Dog Day Again."
17. John Wojtowicz to Liz Eden, February 3, 1974, Liz Eden Papers, Lesbian, Gay, Bisexual and Transgender Community Center Archive; John Wojtowicz to Liz Eden, February 10, 1974, Liz Eden Papers, Lesbian, Gay, Bisexual and Transgender Community Center Archive; John Wojtowicz to Liz Eden, February 17, 1974, Liz Eden Papers, Lesbian, Gay, Bisexual and Transgender Community Center Archive.
18. John Wojtowicz to Liz Eden, February 25, 1974, Liz Eden Papers, Lesbian, Gay, Bisexual and Transgender Community Center Archive; John Wojtowicz to Liz Eden, March 3, 1974, Liz Eden Papers, Lesbian, Gay, Bisexual and Transgender Community Center Archive; John Wojtowicz to Liz Eden, March 25, 1974, Liz Eden Papers, Lesbian, Gay, Bisexual and

Transgender Community Center Archive; John Wojtowicz to Liz Eden, April 4, 1974, Liz Eden Papers, Lesbian, Gay, Bisexual and Transgender Community Center Archive.

19. John Wojtowicz to Liz Eden, April 6, 1974, Liz Eden Papers, Lesbian, Gay, Bisexual and Transgender Community Center Archive; John Wojtowicz to Liz Eden, April 10, 1974, Liz Eden Papers, Lesbian, Gay, Bisexual and Transgender Community Center Archive; John Wojtowicz to Liz Eden, April 14, 1974, Liz Eden Papers, Lesbian, Gay, Bisexual and Transgender Community Center Archive; John Wojtowicz to Liz Eden, April 15, 1974, Liz Eden Papers, Lesbian, Gay, Bisexual and Transgender Community Center Archive.
20. *The Dog,* dirs. Berg and Keraudren.
21. Jahr, "Dog Day Aftermath."
22. Jahr, "Dog Day Aftermath."
23. Yule, *Life on the Wire,* 114–15; *The Making of Dog Day Afternoon,* directed by Laurent Bouzereau, 2006; Maura Spiegel, *Sidney Lumet: A Life* (New York: St. Martin's Press, 2018), 260.
24. Yule, *Life on the Wire,* 114–15; *The Making of Dog Day Afternoon,* Bouzereau; Spiegel, *Sidney Lumet,* 260.
25. *The Making of Dog Day Afternoon,* Bouzereau; "Dog Day Screenwriter Responds," Clifford Jahr Archive.
26. *The Making of Dog Day Afternoon,* Bouzereau.
27. Randy Wicker, "Dog Day Afternoon," unpublished, undated, Randy Wicker Archive; *The Making of Dog Day Afternoon,* Bouzereau; Sidney Lumet, *Dog Day Afternoon,* DVD audio commentary, 2006.
28. *The Making of Dog Day Afternoon,* Bouzereau; Lumet, *Dog Day Afternoon,* DVD audio commentary; Susan King, "Chris Sarandon Reflects on 'Dog Day,'" *Los Angeles Times,* September 25, 2015.

14. **Hollywood**

1. Trecker, "The Gay Bank Robbery"; Wojtowicz to Jahr, October 29, 1975.
2. Parker, "Going Through a Dog Day Again."

3. Jahr, "The 'Dog Day' Bank Robber."
4. Jahr, "The 'Dog Day' Bank Robber."
5. Jahr, "The 'Dog Day' Bank Robber"; Manny Neuhaus, "The Great Transexual Rip-Off," *Fifty-One Newsmagazine*, September 22, 1975.
6. Neuhaus, "Great Transexual Rip-Off."
7. Neuhaus, "Great Transexual Rip-Off."
8. "Dog Day Afternoon," *Gay News*, October 23, 1975.
9. Trecker, "The Gay Bank Robbery"; Jahr, "Dog Day Aftermath"; Neuhaus, "Great Transexual Rip-Off."
10. Jahr, "Dog Day Aftermath"; Neuhaus, "Great Transexual Rip-Off"; Jahr, "The 'Dog Day' Bank Robber."
11. Jahr, "The 'Dog Day' Bank Robber."
12. Jahr, "The 'Dog Day' Bank Robber."
13. Rosen, "The Deacon and the Dog."
14. Wicker, "Dog Day Afternoon."
15. John Wojtowicz, "Real Dog Day Hero Tells His Story," *Jump Cut*, no. 15, 1977.
16. Jahr, "The 'Dog Day' Bank Robber."
17. Jahr, "The 'Dog Day' Bank Robber."
18. Wojtowicz, "Real Dog Day Hero"; Jahr, Dog Day Afternoon Notes.
19. Jahr, Dog Day Afternoon Notes; Grossberger, "'Dog' Is Out of the Joint."
20. John Wojtowicz to Carmen Wojtowicz, November 2, 1975, Clifford Jahr Research Files, New York Public Library.
21. "Harassment by Others Lands 'Little John' in Solitary," *Philadelphia Gay News*, May 1976; Jahr, Dog Day Afternoon Notes; John Wojtowicz to Carmen Wojtowicz, November 30, 1975, Clifford Jahr Research Files, New York Public Library; John Wojtowicz to Carmen Wojtowicz, January 29, 1976, Clifford Jahr Research Files, New York Public Library; John Wojtowicz to Carmen Wojtowicz, February 4, 1976, Clifford Jahr Research Files, New York Public Library; John Wojtowicz to Carmen Wojtowicz, February 11, 1976, Clifford Jahr Research Files, New York Public Library; John Wojtowicz to Carmen Wojtowicz,

February 21, 1976, Clifford Jahr Research Files, New York Public Library.

22. John Wojtowicz to Carmen Wojtowicz, January 21, 1976, Clifford Jahr Research Files, New York Public Library.
23. John Wojtowicz to Clifford Jahr, February 23, 1976, Clifford Jahr Research Files, New York Public Library.
24. Clifford Jahr to John Wojtowicz, February 15, 1976, Clifford Jahr Research Files, New York Public Library.
25. Jahr, Dog Day Afternoon Notes; Jahr, "The 'Dog Day' Bank Robber."
26. "Dog Day Night—from Join Hands," *After Stonewall*, no. 2, 1977; "Gay Bank Robber Transferred," *Philadelphia Gay News*, October, 1976.
27. Wojtowicz, "Real Dog Day Hero."
28. "The End of a Love Story," *Newsday*, May 6, 1977.
29. Eden and Barraclough, "TS," 13.
30. Randy Wicker to John Wojtowicz, January 18, 1976, Randy Wicker Archive.
31. Randy Wicker to John Wojtowicz, May 24, 1978, Randy Wicker Archive.
32. William O'Donnell to John Wojtowicz, October 28, 1976, Randy Wicker Archive; John S. Wojtowicz to William G. O'Donnell, January 2, 1977, Randy Wicker Archive.
33. "Gay Bank Robber Transferred"; *John Stanley Wojtowicz v. United States of America*, United States Appeals Court for the Second Circuit, Docket 76-2106.
34. "Criminals' Revenues from Stories Curbed," *New York Times*, August 13, 1977.
35. Stephen Klain, "It's Payoff Time for Victims in Crime Titled 'Dog Day Afternoon,'" *Variety*, November 23, 1977; Steven P. Vargas, "New York's Son of Sam Law: Alive and Well," *Touro Law Review* 11, no. 3 (1995).
36. George James and Martin Gottlieb, "He Could Howl for Joy," *New York Daily News*, September 6, 1977; Gottlieb, "He Wants to Change."
37. James and Gottlieb, "He Could Howl for Joy."

38. James and Gottlieb, "He Could Howl for Joy."
39. John Wojtowicz to Randy Wicker, June 30, 1978, Randy Wicker Archive.
40. *The Dog*, dirs. Berg and Keraudren.

15. The Dog

1. Alice Michaud; Louis-Georges Tin; Marek Redburn; Kyle Mathers, *The Dictionary of Homophobia: A Global History of Gay and Lesbian Experience* (Vancouver: Arsenal Pulp Press, 2008), 84.
2. Doug Feiden, *The 10,000,000 Dollar Getaway: The Inside Story of the Lufthansa Heist* (New York: Diversion, 1979).
3. "Afternoons Drag for Dog Day," *Newsday*, September 25, 1978.
4. "Afternoons Drag for Dog Day"; Grossberger, "'Dog' Is Out of the Joint."
5. "Afternoons Drag for Dog Day"; Grossberger, "'Dog' Is Out of the Joint."
6. Grossberger, "'Dog' Is Out of the Joint."
7. Kappstatter, "Some Bitter Memories"; Grossberger, "'Dog' Is Out of the Joint."
8. Kappstatter, "Some Bitter Memories."
9. "Dog Days Looking Up," *Newsday*, November 11, 1978; Kappstatter, "Some Bitter Memories"; Harry J. Stathos, "His Dog Days Inspired a Movie," *The News World*, December 5, 1978; *The Dog*, dirs. Berg and Keraudren.
10. Gloria Leonard, "The Garden of Liz Eden," *High Society*, November 1980.
11. "Dog Day Thief Needs Job to Support Wives," *Journal News* (White Plains, NY), February 28, 1979.
12. "Dog Day Thief Needs Job."
13. "Wojtowicz Faces Prison Again," *Report Dispatch* (White Plains, NY), March 13, 1979; "Wojtowicz Faces Suit," *Daily Advertiser* (Lafayette, LA), March 29, 1979.
14. Classified ads, *Gaysweek*, April 16, 1979.
15. Nathan Lee, "Gay Old Time," *Village Voice*, August 28, 2007; Chris Oliver, "Cruising for a Bruising," *New York Post*, July 27, 1979.

16. *The Dog*, dirs. Berg and Keraudren.
17. *The Dog*, dirs. Berg and Keraudren.
18. Leonard, "Garden of Liz Eden."
19. "Dog Day Victim Gets $20,000 in Film Profit," *Newsday*, November 12, 1981; "Dog Day Robber Barred from Seeing Kids," *New York Daily News*, May 8, 1981.
20. Thomas Hanrahan, "Dog Day Con Back in Kennel," *New York Daily News*, July 6, 1983; "Liz Eden's Birthday Party," *The Connection*, August 3–16, 1983.
21. "Elizabeth Eden, Transexual Who Figured in 1975 Movie," *New York Times*, October 1, 1987; "AIDS Kills Woman Behind 'Dog Day,'" *Los Angeles Times*, September 30, 1987.
22. "Elizabeth Eden, Transexual"; "AIDS Kills Woman Behind."
23. Bill Hughes, "Dog Day Afternoon Wins Its Day in Court," *Journal News* (White Plains, NY), January 18, 2003.
24. *The Dog*, dirs. Berg and Keraudren.
25. Salvatore Arena, "A Ruling Is Due on 75G Earned by Celeb Nasties," *New York Daily News*, February 5, 1993; Hughes, "Dog Day Afternoon Win"; Dennis Hevesi, "Cases Under 'Sam' Law: Notorious but Few," *New York Times*, February 20, 1991.
26. Celeste Katz, "Dog Day's Journey," *New York Daily News*, April 23, 2006.
27. Katz, "Dog Day's Journey."
28. Kappstatter, "Some Bitter Memories."
29. David Smith, "Al Pacino on Dog Day Afternoon at 50," *Guardian*, September 21, 2025, www.theguardian.com/film/2025/sep/21/al-pacino-dog-day-afternoon-50th-anniversary.
30. Jesse Hassenger, "50 Years Ago, Al Pacino Made a Perfect Crime Thriller That Was Ahead of Its Time," *Polygon*, September 21, 2025, www.polygon.com/dog-day-afternoon-at-50-al-pacino-sidney-lumet/; Matt Campbell, "Dog Day Afternoon Still Shows the Power of Community Over Authority," *MovieJawn*, September 16, 2025, www.moviejawn.com/home/2025/9/15/queer-window-dog-day-afternoon-feature.
31. Photos, "The Dog and the Last Real Man."

© Randy Pralle II

matthew j. prigge is an author and librarian from Milwaukee, Wisconsin. He has written six books, including a work on film censorship that was made into a feature-length documentary, *Outlaws, Rebels, & Vixens*. He is a faculty librarian at Marquette University in Milwaukee and lives with his wife, Erika, and a rescued cat named Loretta.